LANGUAGE AND LITERACY SERIES
Dorothy S. Strickland and Celia Genishi, SERIES EDITORS

ADVISORY BOARD: RICHARD ALLINGTON, DONNA ALVERMANN, KATHRYN AU,
EDWARD CHITTENDON, BERNICE CULLINAN, COLETTE DAIUTE,
ANNE HAAS DYSON, CAROLE EDELSKY, JANET EMIG,
SHIRLEY BRICE HEATH, CONNIE JUEL, SUSAN LYTLE

(Continued)

Life at the Margins

LITERACY, LANGUAGE, AND TECHNOLOGY IN EVERYDAY LIFE

Juliet Merrifield
Mary Beth Bingman
David Hemphill
Kathleen P. Bennett deMarrais

Teachers College, Columbia University
New York and London

Published by Teachers College Press, 1234 Amsterdam Avenue, New York, NY 10027

Copyright © 1997 by Teachers College, Columbia University

All rights reserved. No part of this publication may be reproduced or transmitted in any form or by any means, electronic or mechanical, including photocopy, or any information storage and retrieval system, without permission from the publisher.

Library of Congress Cataloging-in-Publication Data

Life at the margins : literacy, language, and technology in everyday
  life / Juliet Merrifield . . . [et al.].
      p.   cm. — (Language and literacy series)
    Includes bibliographical references (p.   ) and index.
    ISBN 0-8077-3665-1 (cloth : alk. paper). — ISBN 0-8077-3664-3
  (pbk. : alk. paper)
      1. Literacy—Social aspects—Appalachian Region.   2. Literacy—
  Social aspects—California.   3. Socially handicapped—Appalachian
  Region—Interviews.   4. Socially handicapped—California—
  Interviews.   5. Technological literacy—Appalachian Region.
  6. Technological literacy—California.   7. Educational anthropology—
  Appalachian Region.   8. Educational anthropology—California.
  I. Merrifield, Juliet.   II. Series: Language and literacy series
  (New York, N.Y.)
  LC152.A66L54   1997
  302.2'244'0974—dc21   97-30137

ISBN 0-8077-3664-3 (paper)
ISBN 0-8077-3665-1 (cloth)

Printed on acid-free paper
Manufactured in the United States of America

04 03 02 01 00 99 98 97   8 7 6 5 4 3 2 1

Contents

Acknowledgments

THIS BOOK HAS HAD an overlong gestation period and many midwives. The original research was conducted under a contract from the U.S. Congress, Office of Technology Assessment (OTA). First thanks are due to program officer Dr. Linda Roberts. Not only was she prepared to give a research contract to a team unknown to her, but her conception of the questions to ask and her insights about the findings made the relationship an exceptionally fruitful one. But the contract could not have been undertaken without the support of Sheadrick Tillman, then assistant vice chancellor for research at the University of Tennessee, who believed that good work could be done with little funding.

In both Tennessee and California, the researchers worked as teams, and the authors wish to have on record the contributions of those teams, which went beyond their work on individual profiles. Several Center for Literacy Studies staff members went beyond the call of duty in getting the report together, particularly Linda Fleming and Connie White.

The decision to rework the original report to OTA as a book, in order to reach a wider audience among adult educators, was encouraged by reviewers, including Hanna Fingeret, Hal Beder, Elsa Auerbach, and Shirley Brice Heath. Their comments on the text provided new insights and encouraged us all. Hanna Fingeret in particular was an unfailing source of guidance and wisdom.

While the four authors were involved in editing and reworking parts of the text for the book manuscript, Beth Bingman and Juliet Merrifield did the lion's share of the work of final editing and production. Our original editor at Teachers College Press, Sarah Biondello, was a helpful and unpressuring guide. Brian Ellerbeck was patient with a contract and a manuscript that disappeared without trace for long periods. Kenneth Walker, current associate vice chancellor, Office of Research, shepherded us through the University of Tennessee bureaucracy.

At the heart of it all, are the 12 individuals who agreed to tell the researchers about their lives, their families, their literacy, and their learning. The purpose of the research was for their voices to be heard by the rest of the world. Their words make this book. We thank them.

Life at the Margins

LITERACY, LANGUAGE, AND TECHNOLOGY IN EVERYDAY LIFE

❧ 1 ☙

Overview

THE WORLD OF ADULTS with limited literacy skills is largely unknown territory. The research base is slim indeed. We know little enough about what most adults read, how they use literacy in the various domains of their everyday lives, and how they interact with technology. We know still less about how adults with limited ability to read and write lead their lives in this print-based society, especially the great majority who are not enrolled in literacy programs.

Indeed, conventional concepts of literacy get in the way of developing such an understanding. We often make simplistic assumptions: that there is a dichotomy between literacy and illiteracy (you either have it or you don't); that people who do not read and write well do not engage in literacy tasks and activities; that literacy is an essential "basic" skill enabling us to learn other skills and perform other tasks; and that adults who are not "literate" lead impoverished lives, socially and culturally as well as in terms of literacy. These assumptions suggest that there is little worth investigating in the world of adults with limited literacy skills.

All of these easy assumptions are challenged in new concepts about literacy derived partly from cognitive psychology as well as in ethnographic studies of literacy uses in everyday life. After many years of unsuccessful attempts to define literacy and assign it exact measures, we have come to recognize literacy as constantly changing because it is inherently connected to a particular context. As Kazemek (1988) argues, there is a body of research that

> shows that literacy is a relative phenomenon, one that is both personal and social: it occurs in different contexts, situational as well as cultural; it depends upon the reader's and writer's purposes and aims for engaging in literacy acts; and it varies according to the nature of the text. (p. 467)

The social construction of literacy has been a particular concern of cognitive psychology and sociolinguistics in the last few years, reflecting a new interest in those disciplines in examining cognitive activities in their contexts (Cook-Gumperz, 1986; Rogoff & Lave, 1984; Sternberg and Wagner, 1986). In the contextual view of literacy individuals may vary in how, where, and when they use literacy. Different demands and uses of literacy may exist for the same individuals in different settings or contexts. Work-related literacy differs both in content and in style and purpose from reading for pleasure or in school. Particular individuals may change over time in their uses of literacy; literacy cycles exist, including periods of a-literacy, or nonreading (Szwed, 1984).

However, this new conceptualization of literacy presents us with problems of language. We have no simple words for literacy as many-faceted skills, as social and cultural practices embedded in particular contexts, constantly being redefined by individuals and social groups. If we no longer accept literacy as a single set of skills, it no longer makes any sense to speak of "illiterates"—for where would we place the cutoff point along the continuum? Neither can we speak accurately of people with low literacy or high literacy: If literacy is contextual, a person may be low in one kind of literacy and high in another (low on the literacy of tax and insurance forms, for example, high on the literacy of novels). We have faced this dilemma in our own research. We wanted to explore literacy in the everyday lives of people whose literacy is limited, yet our language to describe just what we meant by limited literacy was, and remains, inadequate. Until we can create new descriptive language to accompany our new concepts of literacy, we will use the term "limited literacy skills" to describe people whose English-language literacy *skills* would likely be below high school level if they were tested with conventional literacy assessments. Their ability to perform literacy *tasks* and their engagement in literacy *practices* are another story, one that is described in the profiles of each person. We describe here the lives of people who have found many ways to deal with literacy tasks in a print-based society, who engage in a variety of literacy practices, who are intelligent and resourceful, caring parents and hard workers. They do not read and write very well.

This study was originally commissioned and funded by the U.S. Congress, Office of Technology Assessment, and carried out in 1991 and 1992 by research teams at the Center for Literacy Studies, the University of Tennessee, and at San Francisco State University. The ethnographic profiles of 12 diverse adults with limited literacy skills in two geographic areas of the United States have three main purposes:

- To examine individuals' lives as wholes, to focus not only on their literacy limitations—what they *cannot* do—but also on their strengths—what they *can* do

- To understand people's lives within the context of region and culture as well as within the various personal domains of their lives—work, community, home, and family
- To understand the strategies that people use to meet the literacy and technology demands they encounter in their daily lives

The qualitative research methods of participant observation, ethnographic interviews, and archival data collection were used to capture rich descriptions of individual lives. Methodologists such as Erickson (1986), Goetz and LeCompte (1984), Marshall and Rossman (1989), McCracken (1988), Spradley (1979, 1980), and Yin (1989) guided our research, which also builds upon several areas of research in adult education and cognitive psychology.

Lytle and Wolfe (1989) distinguish four broad views or approaches to the concept of literacy: literacy as discrete skills, literacy as discrete tasks, literacy as social and cultural practices, and literacy as critical reflection and action. These views are progressively more complex and more interconnected with context. Each has its own associated theory and educational practices.

Literacy as skills views literacy as a set of discrete skills that exist regardless of context. It is assumed that these skills (primarily encoding and decoding words) must be mastered first, before other content or skills can be learned. This view has permeated "academic," or school-like, approaches to literacy education for many years.

Literacy as tasks views literacy in relation to accomplishing specific tasks, usually life or work tasks. At its broadest, this approach to literacy concentrates on the *use* of literacy in any aspect of life, but it has flourished recently especially in the context of job-related literacy. The expressed goal of job-related functional literacy programs is to improve workers' performance on the job. To do so, some functional literacy adherents, such as Sticht and McDonald (1989), argue that process and knowledge cannot be separated: that improved job performance results by working on both literacy skills and job-content knowledge together in the same program.

Literacy as practices places literacy tasks squarely in their social and cultural settings. Proponents of this view recognize that literacy tasks change in different settings. Literacy tasks that are essential in one context may be insignificant in another: Reading bus schedules, for example, may be important to residents of the inner city but of no importance to rural residents who live 60 miles from the nearest bus route. Hanna Fingeret (1992) gives some practical examples of literacy in context: "Many literacy students find that literacy tasks change in different situations; for example, using their cultural knowledge they fill in the form for the welfare system somewhat differently than the form applying for credit to buy a new couch" (p. 6).

Literacy as critical reflection and action is a view quite widespread in literacy campaigns of the Third World "South" but less common in the United States. This approach views literacy as the route to personal empowerment and social change. Paulo Freire, the most influential proponent of this approach, summed up its essence when he suggested that people need to be able to read their world and write their own history (Freire & Macedo, 1987).

These four ways of understanding literacy have been developed primarily as regards native English literacy rather than second-language acquisition. Although adult literacy instruction and adult instruction in English for speakers of other languages (ESOL) have much in common, in practice there is little connection either at the level of theoretical framework or at the level of instructional methodology and practice. Current ESOL issues center around *language* acquisition among adults, rather than *literacy* acquisition. It is not clear whether the process of acquiring literacy in a second language is closer to oral-language acquisition or closer to literacy acquisition by native language speakers. Nor is it clear whether those who are in the process of acquiring literacy in a second language use it in the same ways as first-language literacy. These unknowns are particularly pressing with the influx of immigrants who are not literate in their native language or whose native language may not exist in written form.

The research base on literacy practices in general, whether of native or non-native English speakers, is rather limited. Nevertheless, three broad areas of research offer intriguing insights and often rich descriptive data about literacy: a series of ethnographic studies of literacy uses in everyday life, including a few studies of immigrant families and literacy; another series of research studies on workplace uses of literacy; and several ethnographic studies of "practical problem solving" in everyday settings.

ETHNOGRAPHIC STUDIES OF EVERYDAY LITERACY

Ethnography provides rich, descriptive data about "the contexts, activities, and beliefs of participants" (Goetz & LeCompte, 1984, p. 17). Several studies provide insights into literacy uses in diverse communities. Shirley Brice Heath spent nearly a decade in two working-class rural communities of North or South Carolina—Roadville, a white millworkers' community and Trackton, a community of African American working families—and with the teachers she identified as "townspeople." In *Ways with Words*, Heath (1983) examines how adults and children in two communities learn and use language and literacy. Denny Taylor and Catherine Dorsey-Gaines (1988) described families on Shay Avenue, an inner-city neighborhood in New Jersey. The researchers spent time with both adults and children, talking to them about their lives, observing their use of literacy, collecting samples of what they read and wrote. Hubbards, Nova Scotia, a rural suburb of Halifax, was the site for Lorri Neilsen's work (1989). A new resident in the community, she visited widely, was involved in her children's school, and conducted long interviews with three adults.

These ethnographic studies help us appreciate the multiple uses of literacy. They also highlight the extent to which the uses of literacy vary in different contexts, defined by culture, economics, geography, and gender as well as by years of schooling or job situation. One of the strongest impressions from the review of existing ethnographic studies is the critical importance of context to how literacy is defined and used.

The studies show reading and writing being used for many purposes. The people from Heath's working-class communities of Trackton and Roadville used literacy in a more limited number of ways than the middle-class townspeople or the Hubbards suburbanites. But the families of Trackton, Roadville, and Shay Avenue had a variety of literacy practices.

Clearly, literacy demands in everyday life are many and varied. How do people with limited literacy skills cope in these situations? Are they isolated, unable to participate? Are they left out economically? Are they unable to provide proper parenting for their children? Two ethnographic studies focus on the literacy uses and strategies of adults whose literacy skills are limited.

Fingeret (1982, 1983) focused on how people function in a literate society. She interviewed 43 adults who were students in literacy programs or had limited literacy skills. She discovered that rather than the isolated, incompetent individuals of the stereotypical "illiterate," most of the people she talked to led full, active lives as members of social networks, and, despite their lack of reading skills, functioned rather well. Some were active in neighborhood networks and some on a more cosmopolitan level that involved them in a wide variety of activities and contexts.

Their networks of friends and family shared and exchanged: one might do some plumbing, another take care of children, another read. While the person who could not read and write may have been hindered to some extent in dealing with literate society, they were helped by other members of their social network. In most instances, Fingeret found that this was a relationship of exchange rather than of dependency.

Zeigahn (1990) interviewed 27 adults with limited literacy skills, both Native Americans and Anglos, who lived on the Flathead reservation in northwestern Montana, focusing on the individuals' relationships to literacy. Zeigahn found that literacy was a tool that some valued and others did not, and that could be circumvented in many situations. Like Fingeret, she found reciprocal relationships or social networks. One woman who was a poor reader was able to give advice on marriage and raising children to younger women. Husbands and wives helped each other.

The ethnographic literature suggests we all have strategies to deal with unfamiliar or difficult situations. When pipes freeze, our strategy may be to get out a blowtorch or call a plumber. Both work; both enable us to "function."

Literacy Among Language-Minority Families

Ethnographic research on everyday literacy among non-native English speakers is very limited. A small number of studies of families give some insights into how literacy is used and how much it is valued. Delgado-Gaitan's (1987) study of literacy among four Mexican immigrant families found that each used a variety of types of literacy texts in their everyday lives. These included both Spanish and English newspapers, letters from family members, and children's schoolbooks. The parents in the Delgado-Gaitan study did not regard themselves as readers and had little formal education. But these immigrant families valued education highly, seeing it as the key to upward mobility for their children.

Auerbach (1989) found that the experiences of families associated with the University of Massachusetts at Boston English Family Literacy Program were at odds with the assumptions of conventional "transmission of school practices" models of family literacy. The common assumptions of family literacy are that (1) language-minority students come from literacy-impoverished homes where literacy is not valued or supported; (2) family literacy involves a one-way transfer *from* parents *to* children; (3) success in school is determined by parents' ability to support and extend school-like activities in the home; (4) school practices are adequate and it is the home factors that determine who will succeed; and (5) parents' own problems get in the way of creating positive family literacy contexts.

The reality, Auerbach argues, is very different. First, parents in the UMass/Boston program consistently valued literacy and education, rewarded their children, and provided emotional and physical support. Secondly, Auerbach (1989) found that the direction of literacy interactions was not only from parents to children. Children were often "brokers" between their non-English-speaking parents and the outside world: "Instead of the parents assisting children with literacy tasks, the children help their parents with homework, act as interpreters for them, and deal with the outside world for them" (p. 171).

Auerbach points out a wide variety of contextual factors that may contribute to literacy development, beyond the amount of specific school-like activities that parents do with their children. School-related factors may be as important as the home context, and parents in the UMass/Boston program suggested ways that parents could offer "critical support" to their children's teachers, in order to have some input into schooling. Finally, Auerbach argues that the problems and issues that parents must deal with in their own lives can become pathways for increasing their own uses of literacy, rather than becoming "barriers" to increasing literacy, if these issues become part of the curriculum.

These limited studies from non-native English-speaking families support the findings from studies of low-income native speakers: that we must put away the stereotypes of illiteracy, including impoverishment in the home, a low value placed on education, and little involvement in literacy-related activities.

Another series of studies, starting from a different base of philosophy and research methods, describe literacy practices in the domain of work. Concern about the lack of fit between adult workers' literacy skills and the changing demands of work is a driving force behind today's "literacy crisis." Research on work-related literacy indicates that literacy demands and uses in the workplace are very different from school-related ones. Two main bodies of research illuminate how workers deal with the literacy demands of their jobs. One consists of a series of assessments of on-the-job reading and writing demands by Sticht, Mikulecky, Diehl, and others. The other consists of ethnographic research on "practical problem solving" in work settings carried out by psychologist Scribner and associates.

READING AND WRITING ON THE JOB

Sticht's research in the military (1975) and later research by Mikulecky, Diehl, and others in various civilian work settings have several consistent findings (Diehl, 1980; Mikulecky, 1982, 1984; Mikulecky & Ehlinger, 1987; Spencer, 1987; Sticht & Mikulecky, 1984). These studies find that workers in most types of employment do considerable job-related reading, from 30 minutes to 2 hours per day. Most of the studies agree that the reading done by lower-level workers is neither less in amount nor easier than that done by higher-level workers. Job-related reading is primarily "reading-to-do" (as opposed to "reading-to-learn," which is the primary purpose of school-based reading). "Workers read and write to accomplish tasks, solve problems, and make evaluations about the usefulness of material. . . . Students in secondary schools read primarily to obtain information needed to answer teacher questions" (Mikulecky & Ehlinger, 1987, p. 4).

Work-related literacy demands are strongly repetitive and contextualized—that is, related to knowledge that the worker already has. Workers have repeated opportunities for reading and rereading the material, and their job experience provides them with knowledge that they can use in comprehending the written material. This helps explain why workers commonly comprehend job-related material at least two grade levels higher than the general reading material they can comprehend.

The studies also suggest that general literacy skill is only one small factor in job performance. Mikulecky has carried out several studies assessing job performance and comparing it with literacy skills: He found that different literacy skills did not account for differences among performance groups (Mikulecky, 1985). Mikulecky and Ehlinger (1987) suggest that "metacognitive" skills are more important than literacy skills per se: "Superior job performers differ from their less able counterparts in their ability to think through what is needed on the job and then to apply reading and writing abilities to complete these job tasks efficiently" (p. 11).

Workers with more limited reading abilities do not necessarily adopt other strategies to get their work done. Diehl, Sticht, and others have looked for evidence of use of strategies such as "auding" (listening to others explain) by lower-level readers. Their research has not shown any higher use of these alternative strategies by lower-level readers. Instead, "use of the context, and the repetitive nature of job tasks, probably enables many workers to read material on the job that they would not be able to read in isolation" (Diehl, 1980, p. 264).

Literacy Demands of Work for Non-Native English Speakers

As with the ethnographic studies of literacy uses in everyday life, the primary research on literacy practices at work has been with native English speakers. The lack of similar studies of literacy demands and practices on the job among non-native speakers of English is particularly troubling in view of the demographic changes taking place in the U.S. work force, in which non-native speakers of English are becoming an increasingly important force.

Understanding of workplace literacy demands and uses for non-native speakers of English is still in its infancy. Clearly, one of the most basic distinctions that needs to be drawn between the literacy needs of native speakers and non-native speakers of English has to do with the added burden of developing oral/aural proficiency as well as cultural understanding.

One of the best sources on investigating workplace language functions for non-native English speakers and developing workplace-based ESOL programs remains the work of British researchers Jupp and Hodlin (1975). Their work, which was of considerable merit and rigor, was nonetheless done more than 20 years ago in British factories, and it focused primarily on the language needs of South Indian workers. It is likely that the workplace language demands placed by contemporary U. S. industry on immigrant workers from a wide variety of cultures may be somewhat different.

Subsequently, a series of isolated studies have investigated issues of language and culture among workers with limited English proficiency in the United States. One study investigated the kinds of entry-level jobs taken by non-native speakers of English (Cangampang & Tsang, 1988). Another inquired into the opinions employers hold of refugee employees (Latkiewicz, 1982). Still another investigated promising patterns of job-related training design for non-native speakers of English (Hemphill, 1985).

In a survey of 52 employers in the Chicago area, Mrowicki (1984) found that six primary language-related factors were perceived as "problems" among workers with limited English proficiency:

1. Failure to ask when something is not understood
2. Ability to understand company policy
3. Ability to report problems on the job
4. Failure to follow directions
5. Failure to obey safety regulations
6. Relations with other employees

Unfortunately, however, none of these studies have been integrated with one another, and there has been no consistent research agenda either articulated or pursued in this critical area. Rather, there have been scattered articles and monographs that advocate various approaches, but little research evidence as to their success.

Practical Problem Solving on the Job

Insights into often-impressive cognitive skills brought to bear in commonplace situations emerge from the research on "practical intelligence" that some cognitive psychologists have been conducting over the last ten or more years. Wagner and Sternberg (1986) summarize this work:

> We believe that much of the learning that matters to success in real-world pursuits happens in the absence of formal instruction. Furthermore, we view traditional IQ tests as measures of only a subset of the competencies required for maximal learning from and performance in everyday situations. (p. 51)

Scribner (1986) describes the concept of "practical thinking" as

> thinking that is embedded in the larger purposive activities of daily life and that functions to achieve the goals of these activities . . . practical thinking

stands in contrast to the type of thinking involved in performance of isolated
mental tasks undertaken as ends in themselves. (p. 15)

Ethnographic research relating to cognitive and literacy activities on
the job has been carried out by Scribner and her associates in a milk-
processing plant (reported in Scribner, 1984, 1986). The researchers carried
out systematic observations and experiments to reveal how workers develop strategies for solving familiar problems on the job. The workers use
literacy texts in formulating the problems (order sheets, price tickets) and
in devising solutions (price lists, box labels). But their restatement of the
problem and their own solution to that problem go far beyond the con-
straints of the texts themselves.

In one example, researchers recorded observations of product assemblers filling mixed case and unit orders. Assemblers often did not follow
the written order literally. An order for 10 quarts could be formulated as
one case less 6 quarts, and it could be assembled in a variety of ways from
partially filled cases, depending on what was available. On all occasions,
the mode in which the order was filled "was exactly that procedure that
satisfied the order in the fewest possible moves—that is, of all alternatives,
the solution the assembler selected required the transfer of a minimum
number of units from one case to another" (Scribner, 1984, p. 17).

The "least-effort" solution was arrived at even though it often required
the assembler to switch from one base number system to another. Errors
were virtually nonexistent among experienced assemblers. In contrast,
novices and students made more mistakes and more often followed literal
solutions that involved many more transfers. However, in paper-and-pencil
arithmetic tests administered to the same workers who were so accurate
and sophisticated in their mathematical skills in practical problem solving, they made many errors on problems similar in format to those they
solved so well on the job.

The researchers found that experienced workers had creative and sophisticated solutions to commonplace problems. They found that components lying outside the formal problem (objects and information—including texts—in the work environment, goals and interests of the problem
solver) were incorporated by workers into the problem formulation and
solution. Workers continuously found new ways to solve old problems.

PROBLEM SOLVING IN EVERYDAY ACTIVITIES

Other studies of problem solving in everyday situations also show how
selectively and creatively people use literacy in these activities. Lave,

Murtaugh, and de la Rocha (1984) studied problem-solving activities in the prosaic setting of grocery shopping. "Expert" shoppers (who ranged in formal education level from the eighth grade upwards) used a variety of complex and fairly sophisticated mathematical calculations to aid in their decision making in grocery stores. Of particular interest here is how they used literacy.

Lave and colleagues (1984) argue that, "in general, over time, the expert shopper transforms an information-rich arena into an information-specific setting" (p. 76). That is, although grocery stores are "print-rich"—full of signs, labels, packaging texts—people are very selective in what they read. Mostly, the researchers found that expert shoppers look at the signs showing where different items are shelved only in an unfamiliar setting or when they are shopping for a nonroutine item. For the most part, shoppers establish routine routes through grocery stores that take them past the shelves where they buy items and avoid excessive walking along aisles that are not used. Shoppers also usually consult packaging, price labels, and so on only when they are establishing a new choice or updating an old result. Most purchases are routine, based on old assessments of relative value.

The findings of the ethnographic research stand in sharp contrast to the same shoppers' performance on standard paper-and-pencil arithmetic tests. Twenty-five shoppers were tested with a paper-and-pencil math test on the same operations they used in grocery shopping. Average scores were 59% on the arithmetic test, "compared with a startling 98 percent—virtually error free—arithmetic in the supermarket" (Lave et al., 1984, p. 82).

Studies of practical problem solving suggest that our methods for assessing people's literacy are inadequate. Expert problem solvers routinely devised complex, least-effort solutions requiring quite sophisticated mathematical operations, but they performed rather poorly in tests designed to assess proficiency in the same operations. Workers commonly read and comprehend work-related literacy materials that are more difficult than those they can read in a general reading test. This research suggests that many people who perform below targeted levels for "functional literacy" may nevertheless be functioning adequately, or to their own satisfaction, in their everyday lives. Although not extensive, ethnographic research on adults with low literacy skills seems to confirm this possibility.

RESEARCH: ANSWERS AND QUESTIONS

Research on everyday uses of literacy may be limited, but it is full of insights for how literacy should be conceived and how literacy education programs should be conducted. Ethnographic and other studies challenge the assumptions of the "deficit" concept adults with low incomes and low levels of literacy. They underscore the importance of context in literacy use and the concept of reading and writing as a process for negotiating meaning between person and text. They reveal "many literacies" in everyday life and many strategies by which adults with limited literacy skills deal with literacy tasks.

In addition, the research reveals the vital role that context plays in relation to literacy. Recent developments in cognitive science indicate that knowledge and processes are intertwined, and the research on everyday uses of literacy confirms that when the process (literacy as skill) is separated from the knowledge (literacy practices), everyone looks much less skilled than they really are.

Just as there are different literacies in different aspects of people's lives (work, home, shopping, school), so there are different ways that people have found to relate and adjust to literacy tasks. These may include using members of social networks as "readers" (Fingeret, 1982) or using technology to take the place of literacy skills (using tape recorders, for example, instead of writing memos, or telephoning instead of writing letters). These may also include spouses and children serving in intermediary roles in relation to certain aspects of the outside world (Auerbach, 1989).

The research on everyday literacy raises many questions about how adults with low literacy skills live their lives in a print-based society. We know less than we should about how people in different kinds of communities and cultures actually use literacy. We know little about the kinds of demands that changing technology places on adults with low literacy skills. We do not know enough about how they use technologies for literacy. We know little about their expectations for their own and their children's literacy, about their attitudes toward literacy and toward technology. We know less than we should about factors affecting their decisions about further education. These questions focused our research on a series of ethnographic profiles of 12 adults from a wide variety of social, economic, cultural, and geographic backgrounds.

Research Methodology

Qualitative research values and explores the meaning people place on their life experiences. Qualitative researchers try to understand these by observing and talking to people in their everyday settings with as little disruption to those settings as possible. In this study we wanted to uncover the meaning people make of their everyday literacy experiences.

We began the project in 1991 by building our research teams—one in San Francisco and one in Knoxville. Most team members had formal training, and all had experience in qualitative research methods. All the Appalachian profilers had taken at least two graduate courses in qualitative research methods and ethnographic field methods under Professor Kathleen Bennett deMarrais and other methodologists at the University of Tennessee. Most of the Californian researchers were graduates of or graduate students in the adult education program at San Francisco State University and had taken qualitative research courses taught by Professor David Hemphill and others. Researchers on both teams were very familiar with the community contexts in which we asked them to work. This collective expertise enabled us to determine the types of individuals we wanted to profile and to use the researchers' community contacts to locate these participants.

Each of the research teams planned to profile six adults and sought diversity in age, gender, social and ethnic backgrounds, and literacy skill. Researchers used their community contacts to identify adults who had the particular characteristics we were looking for. The Appalachian team profiled two white Appalachian men (one rural and one urban), two African American women (currently urban), one rural white Appalachian woman, and a rural Mexican American woman migrant worker. The ages of these individuals ranged from 26 to 41, and their literacy skills varied from very limited to close to high school proficiency.

The California team profiled a young Latino man originally from Nicaragua, an older woman from Mexico, a female refugee from northeastern Africa, two Asian men, and a female emigré from Byelorussia (in what was then the Soviet Union). Their ages ranged from 17 to 53, their proficiency in English ranged from minimal to fairly fluent, and their prior educational backgrounds ranged from only nonformal education to a master's degree.

In early meetings, the research teams discussed ways of gaining access to participants, research strategies, interview techniques, and specific ethnographic interview questions. The teams at each site met regularly throughout the course of the research to review research questions, data-collection progress, and analyses of the data.

A pilot profile conducted by Beth Bingman in the summer of 1991 enabled us to see whether our planned methods could provide a holistic picture of our participants. The methods worked well, and the pilot helped us refine our research questions, strategies, and interview schedules. We found that a series of informal conversation-like interviews and formal audiotaped interviews with each participant elicited a wealth of information about educational histories, work histories, family relationships, and uses of literacy and technology.

Each participant was interviewed at length several times over the course of the three-month research period (fall 1991). Most of the interviews were conducted in English; however, Nura Tola's were conducted in Oromo, David Wong's in Cantonese, and those of Alicia Lopez and María Reyes in Spanish. In each case, this was also the first language of the researcher or the researcher was very fluent in that language. The place for the interviews also varied. Some people were interviewed entirely in their homes, others in their places of work (or education programs), others in several places. For example, Kathleen Bennett deMarrais talked with Les Willard informally for hours at a time over the course of three months. She still continues to talk with him regularly. However, since he was uncomfortable with more formal taped interviews, this strategy was kept to a minimum. He participated in only one two-hour taped interview. Similarly, David Wong did not wish to be tape-recorded; instead, the interviewer took extensive notes.

Researchers used participant observation in different ways, according to the unique situations of the people profiled. Some researchers were able to observe in work situations, others in home settings. In some cases, participant observation was considered to be too intrusive for the respondents. In addition to the interviews with our participants, several researchers also interviewed others who could give them relevant background information. One researcher interviewed a restaurant manager about the literacy demands on waitresses; another interviewed a local agricultural extension agent concerning literacy and farming; another contacted local agencies for background information on electricians' licensing requirements.

The database for each person we profiled consists of (1) a set of fieldnotes taken by researchers throughout the data-collection process, (2) transcriptions of audiotaped interviews, and (3) archival data related to literacy uses. Researchers also used a checklist of everyday literacy activities developed by the research teams. The archival data include restaurant tickets, a high school diploma, church bulletins, and other reading material. The fieldnotes include notes about conversations with the people profiled that were not audiotaped, about the participant observations, and about the researchers' reactions to interviews and observations. The researchers noted questions they needed to explore further or concerns they had as they progressed through the data-collection phase.

The research teams met again as data collection was being completed to compare and analyze their findings. We began to define and discuss common themes and differences among participants, and to look for missing data in the profiles. Based on a series of such discussions, individual researchers finalized their data collection. They analyzed their individual findings using methods of constant comparison and analytic induction (see

Goetz & LeCompte, 1984) and wrote drafts of their profiles. These drafts were read and commented on by other members of each research team before final revisions.

Based on the discussions of each research team and more detailed analysis of the individual profiles, a small group of authors wrote an overview section for each group of profiles as well as a synthesis of findings and conclusions from the two groups of profiles. After the final report to the U.S. Congress, Office of Technology Assessment had been submitted (Center for Literacy Studies, 1992) and used in its report to Congress on literacy issues (U.S. Congress, Office of Technology Assessment, 1993), the principal authors began to think about getting the profiles out to a wider audience than would read the technical report; they revised the manuscript extensively, shortening it and combining the literature review with the Introduction.

The value of these qualitative profiles is as case studies. Although we attempted to profile a variety of participants according to their ethnicity, social class, age, and gender, we do not intend for these profiles to be representative of any particular population. As in most qualitative research, the case studies here can be used to both generate theory and test theory. Yin (1989) argues that case studies

> are generalizable to theoretical propositions and not to populations or universes. In this sense, the case study, like the experiment, does not represent a "sample," and the investigator's goal is to expand and generalize theories (analytic generalization) and not to enumerate frequencies (statistical generalization). (p. 21)

We believe that the profiles presented here can be compared to the current literature and theories on adult literacy and can be used to challenge some of the theories from that literature as well as raise new questions for researchers to explore through both qualitative and quantitative methods of scholarly inquiry.

As a research team, we tried to establish a high degree of internal reliability (the degree to which other researchers, given a set of previously generated constructs, would match data in the same way as we did) by using multiple researchers, low-inference descriptors, verbatim quotes, mechanical recording, and peer examination of our data, as suggested by Goetz & LeCompte (1984). These measures have also enabled us to achieve validity in the study. We believe that through our in-depth interviewing, careful recordkeeping, data triangulation, multiple researchers, and heavy reliance on our participants' voices, we have captured authentic representations or reconstructions of their lives.

The Research Teams

The principal investigator for the project was Kathleen P. Bennett deMarrais, who was at the time an assistant professor at the College of Education, the University of Tennessee, Knoxville. Bennett deMarrais was trained as an anthropologist of education at the University of Cincinnati. She brought both knowledge and considerable experience of qualitative methodologies (particularly ethnography) to the research project. The project director was Juliet Merrifield, director of the Center for Literacy Studies and adjunct faculty in the College of Education, the University of Tennessee, Knoxville. Merrifield was trained as an anthropologist at the University of London and has a D.Phil. in politics from Oxford University, England. She has more than 20 years of research experience in both Britain and the Appalachian region of the United States.

The California coordinator was David Hemphill of San Francisco State University. Hemphill is associate professor and co-director of the Center for Adult Education. He is the author of texts on training immigrant populations in job-related skills. For 15 years he was program coordinator in a community-based program in which immigrants could study English and find jobs. He teaches courses and conducts research in qualitative methods.

The Appalachian profilers were Mary Beth Bingman, Kathleen Bennett deMarrais, Faye Hicks-Townes, Loida Velazquez, and Connie White. The California profilers were Mari Gasiorowicz, Lensa Gudina, David Hemphill, Sally Ianiro, Tom Nesbit, and Chui Lim Tsang. Principal authors of Chapter 3 were Juliet Merrifield and Mary Beth Bingman; the principal author of Chapter 5 was David Hemphill. Juliet Merrifield was principal author of Chapters 1 and 6, with major contributions of ideas and analysis from David Hemphill, Mary Beth Bingman, and Kathleen Bennett deMarrais.

The book has three main sections. The first section reports on the group of six profiles from the Appalachian region, with an introduction to the region and the people, the series of profiles, and an overview of the findings from this group. The second section reports on the six profiles from the California Bay Area, again with an introduction to the region and the people, the series of profiles, and an overview of findings from this group. The final section is a synthesis of findings relating to literacy, technology, and learning across all the profiles.

ఙ 2 ఙ

Appalachian Profiles

APPALACHIA IS A REGION of contrasts: poverty amidst a wealth of natural resources; environmental destruction amidst spectacular natural beauty; chronically low education levels in a population skilled in survival and with a strong cultural heritage. To the superficial eye, it can seem a region in which time has stood still. Yet appearances mask dramatic changes over the last 100 years, and especially in the last 40 years.

In the 1950s, when some of those we profiled were born, a massive population exodus from rural Appalachia took place as coal mines were mechanized; thousands of families left for factory jobs in the cities of the North. In the 1970s, when a short-lived boom hit the area, many migrants returned to the communities that had never ceased to be "home." By the 1980s the boom was over and jobs were again in short supply, but the northern cities, too, were in decline. With no place to go, many families have stayed, living in trailers or in old frame houses, getting by as best they can.

While the urban Appalachian areas have always had a broader economic base than the rural areas, they, too, have undergone significant change in recent years. Their manufacturing base in textile and furniture has eroded. Cities such as Chattanooga, Tennessee, and Charleston, West Virginia, which were dependent on a single large industry, have seen that industry decline. In place of manufacturing, the service sector has grown, and cities such as Knoxville, Tennessee, have become retail sales and distribution centers.

Two of our profiles are set in southwestern Virginia, a mountainous area with an economy based on coal mining, forestry, farming, and factories. In a remote corner of the state, far from interstate highways and the state capital, it is an area easily overlooked. While the families of the area have traditionally farmed, nowadays few can survive entirely by farming. Many drive great distances to work in coal mines or factories. The area is poor, incomes are low, lives are often hard, yet people choose to remain. They stay because of the natural beauty of the land, the kinship support

17

networks, the opportunity to raise gardens and to trade goods and labor, and their strong ties to the land and community. The two people we profile here are Tom Addington, a 27-year-old landless farm laborer, and Marcy Osborne, a quiet woman of 40.

Three of our profiles are set in the city of Knoxville, Tennessee. Lying in the broad Tennessee Valley, between two mountain chains, Knoxville is an Appalachian city. It is far more white than most southern cities (with a non-white population in the city of 16%). Many of its white inhabitants have ties with the mountain areas. Knoxville's history and economy have been bound up with Appalachia through trade and as the headquarters and finance center for coal companies. Despite the presence of the main campus of the University of Tennessee, the headquarters of the Tennessee Valley Authority, and the nearby massive weapons installations at Oak Ridge, Knoxville still often seems like an overgrown small town. Here we profiled Yuvette Evans, a 26-year-old African American woman; Les Willard, a 36-year-old white man; and Lisa Bogan, a 37-year-old African American woman.

Even though Appalachia is conventionally regarded as primarily white, all areas, both rural and urban, have small African American populations. Increasingly, too, the region is becoming temporary, sometimes permanent, home to other minorities. In particular, the Appalachian areas that still have significant agriculture see regular movement of migrant farmworkers. Mainly Mexican American, with some African American, Haitian, and other groups at times, the migrant farmworkers move in largely invisible streams through the region. East Tennessee, southwest Virginia, and western North Carolina all are home at times to migrant farmworkers. María Reyes is a 41-year-old Latina of Mexican origin, born in Texas, who at the time of interview was trying to establish a more settled life in a small town in North Carolina.

These profiles give us some insights into the lives of adults who have varying levels of difficulty with reading, writing, and math. The people interviewed took the time to share with us their joys and sorrows, the difficulties they have overcome, their hopes for their children. They talked about the place of literacy in their everyday and work lives, about their use of technology, and about what they can and cannot handle. These are voices seldom heard. We are privileged to hear them.

TOM ADDINGTON

By Mary Beth Bingman

Tom Addington is a 27-year-old farmer, or more accurately, farmworker, since he doesn't own land and is paid wages to work for other people. He lives with his wife and three young children in a four-room frame house on a farm in Scott County, Virginia. He left high school without graduating and reads with difficulty. A family man, Tom thinks about his life and what he hopes to do. His plans are centered around meeting the needs of his children, aged 5, 3, and 2. While he is not entirely satisfied with his own situation, he believes he can "move on." During these interviews his children were always around, and Tom told of taking them fishing and on walks through the woods. His children seem to be a motivating force in his life:

> I like being called Dad and stuff like that. I love my kids, very much. I'm glad I've got them and they're healthy and stuff. And I guess the biggest majority is taking care of them. I don't mind that too bad 'cause if a man's gonna amount to anything he's got to get out here and work for it. If he ain't got no kids at all, he's got to. It ain't gonna be reached down to him, I don't think.
>
> It's about hard, well, it's kindly hard on me every day 'cause, you know, I never know where I'm gonna get ahold of the next penny at. And I know they need something all the time. I've just got to get out there and look and see where it's at.

Scott County, Virginia

Tom was born in Scott County and has lived there most of his life. Scott County is in the far southwestern corner of Virginia, bordering Tennessee, a rural county with fewer than 50 people per square mile. The 1990 population (23,204) is down nearly 2,000 from 1980. Gate City, the largest town and county seat, has a population of 2,200. The five other towns are much smaller. Most people live on the 445 miles of secondary roads that crisscross the county, 345 miles of which are unpaved.

Many people leave the county each day to work in Kingsport, Tennessee, or the mines of other Virginia counties. At the same time, there are 4,000 farms in Scott county. Many of these are small, under 100 acres, and most farmers work at another "public" job. Many of the poorest people in the county work as farm laborers, either for wages, for rent, or "on shares" (sharecropping).

In 1990 in Scott County, 49% of adults over age 25 had not graduated from high school; 30% had completed less than the ninth grade. The county has many of the problems typical of the Appalachian region: There is no hospital, housing is often substandard, and many families live below the poverty level.

The county is beautiful, bordered by Stone Mountain and High Knob on the north and by the Clinch Mountain on the south, with ridges and valleys between. Both the Clinch and Holston Rivers flow through the county.

Life and Work

In order to understand the context of Tom's life and his uses of literacy and technology, one must understand something about the cultivation of tobacco. Tobacco has been the primary cash crop in this county for many years. The amount sold from any farm is controlled by the government, and tobacco is often grown "on shares" with the owner of the land.

Tobacco is a labor-intensive crop. It is also second only to cotton in the amount of pesticides used in its production. Although much of the way tobacco is grown has changed little over the years, the pesticide use in particular makes it a very "modern" crop that takes work nearly year round. In this area it is grown in small fields, often on hillsides. Growers use tractors to prepare the ground and to pull the setting machine, but most of the work is done by hand. In the fall or winter, beds are prepared for raising the plants. A bed usually measures 100 feet by 9 feet. The ground is carefully prepared by plowing and disking, then raked smooth and sterilized by covering the bed with plastic sheeting and releasing canisters of gas under the plastic. This gas, methyl bromide, kills both insects and weed seeds. In the early spring, the bed is fertilized and sown with tobacco seed nearly as fine as dust. The young plants grow in the bed for about six weeks until they are about a foot high.

In the meantime, the fields are prepared with a tractor, by plowing, disking, fertilizing, and disking again. When the fields are ready, the plants are big enough, and danger of frost is past (usually in May), the fields are set or planted. After the fields are set, they are cultivated three times by tractor and twice by hand when the plants become too tall to plow. Tobacco plants can grow as high as 6 feet and have leaves up to 2 feet long. When the tobacco gets "head high," it is sprayed to prevent the growth of suckers, new shoots from the sides. These suckers used to be removed several times by hand, but now the suckering is done chemically with MH30, a growth regulator.

In the summer the tobacco is "topped": The top leaves and flowers are cut out. When the leaves begin to turn yellow, in the late summer, the tobacco is ready to cut. The tool for this is a tobacco knife, a short square blade on the end of a handle, or a machete. The stalk is cut at the base and then speared onto a stick. Each stick will hold about six to eight stalks. These sticks of tobacco are left in the field for three to five days to lose some of their moisture and weight.

Once field-cured, the sticks of tobacco are loaded onto a wagon and hauled by tractor to the barns. Burley tobacco barns are fairly open buildings with rows of rafters, 4 feet apart and about 6 feet over each other. Farmers, working in groups, hang the sticks across the rafters, starting at the top of the barn and working downward until the barn is filled. Tobacco in this county is air-cured and hangs for about two months until it dries and turns from greenish yellow to reddish brown. It is then ready to strip.

When the tobacco is cured, the sticks are taken down. This has to be done when it is "in case," damp enough not to crumble. The stalks are removed from the sticks, and individual leaves are stripped from the stalks; the leaves are graded by size and color. The tobacco is then baled, packed into a box, and tied with string into 100-pound bales. The bales are loaded onto trucks and taken to the tobacco warehouses in town where they are sold, usually in time to have money for Christmas and to pay property taxes on the land.

The House. Tom lives in "the second white house you see after you don't turn at the forks of the road, down in a sinkhole with tobacco and cattle around the house, a mile or mile and a half off the Far Hollow road." The white frame house is set down off the road. The driveway isn't paved, but the road is. Tobacco is growing around the place, but the yard is of a good size and mowed. Two or three riding toys sit in the yard. The mailbox on the road, handmade of plywood and tin, has no name or number.

The kitchen is furnished with a sink, stove, and refrigerator. Cereal boxes are lined up on the counter. In the front room are a couch and armchair, a bookshelf, a low table, and a television (black-and-white) on a stand. The news is on. On the walls are a calendar from a local business, a paper heart with the word *Todd*, and a large framed print of a painting of Jesus kneeling in the garden. On another print, Tom had cut out places in the paper and put in arrowheads to form a design. The table is decorated with plastic flowers.

We talked the first time in the front room, or living room, and later on the porch. The covered porch is the full width of the house, and an old living room suite (couch and two chairs) provides plenty of seating. The porch faces down the valley and has a good view.

Tom's parents, twin brother, and five older sisters all still live in the county. His father has worked at various things—logging, mining, construction. When Tom was 7, the family moved to Toledo, Ohio, where his father worked in a Campbell Soup factory. But the family returned to Virginia after three or four years, because of the tornados, Tom recalls.

Work. Most of Tom's life is taken up with work. Tom's activities outside his family and work are limited by lack of transportation. He sees his wife's family often because they just live "down the road," and he gets together with his own family for an occasional cookout. He watches a little television, a baseball or football game when he gets the time. "I guess when I go ahunting, that's the biggest fun I've had. Biggest majority of the time I'm always doing something or other, piddling around the farm, maybe building a fence or something."

Although he was aware of a local election, Tom doesn't vote. He no longer attends church:

> I used to go to church. And the preachers wasn't right, so I quit going to church. I enjoyed it now, I enjoyed church and stuff. I believe in it. But the churches I went to, they'd always come back and try to pull me up by the arm, try to pull me up there [to the altar], and that's not right. And if God wants you to be saved, He'll let you know when the time's ready.

Tobacco farming is the work Tom is most involved in. He helps his landlord and also works for a friend on a crew that hires out to other farmers to help with the most intensive tobacco work. In addition to work in tobacco, he helps put up hay and may "dig a little herb" (ginseng) to sell to local dealers. At present he is paid by the hour or in exchange for rent, but he hopes to be able to raise a crop of tobacco on shares next year:

> Right now I just work in other people's, but next year, if nothing don't happen, I'll be araising on the halfs. Round here it's hard to make a living. And most people around here lean on tobacco and stuff to make it. And I believe I'll try next year to try to get myself started on it, some 'baccer, and go from there, you know, maybe build myself up. 'Cause I don't, well, I worked on a couple of public jobs. It didn't last long, so I'd rather just do farm work.

The "public jobs" he has done include trimming trees and spraying right-of-ways for a tree company and loading trucks at a local tobacco warehouse.

Educational History. Tom dropped out of high school when he was 17 and "taking ninth-, tenth-grade subjects." He started school in a Scott County elementary school, went to school in Toledo for a few years, and came back to Scott County. He dropped out of one of the rural high schools, where he was in a special education class.

We talked quite a bit about his school experiences and about why he did not learn to read. He puts a lot of the blame on the schools:

> I wasn't learning nothing, they just passed me to get rid of me. They'd send me down on the ball field, rake the ball field off, or tell

me to go to sleep or something or other. They never would try to learn me how to read or nothing like that. Seemed like they didn't have enough patience, so I just quit going. I wasn't learning nothing. They wouldn't try to learn me nothing, so I just quit going, I just quit going. They ought to took their time, 'cause I was willing to learn. They ought to took their time to learn me, but they didn't seem like they cared that much.

At the same time, he also questions his own abilities. Although he feels he is good at math and remembers getting an A in math in school, he describes himself as "slow about learning" and doesn't seem sure about why he can't read:

You know I was willing to learn. I was willing to learn how to read, grow up to be, you know, maybe something better than what I am now besides doing farm work, maybe you know be on a public job making good money, something like that, doing carpenter work or something. But it just seems like it wasn't for me to learn how to read or something or other. You know it bugs me every now and then, and then I don't know what went wrong. I'm slow, I'm slow about wanting to learn how to read or something. I ain't got the patience for it now but back then when I was going to school, you know I was wanting to learn. I don't know. It just went downhill.

I could blame the teacher for some of it, and I could blame some of it on myself. Sometimes I'd go up and ask the teacher how to do this and sometimes I wouldn't. So I guess it works both ways there. If I had it done over, I guess I'd probably made them learn me. I don't know if I could've made them or not but I'd have tried.

Tom has had some positive school experiences. I asked him if there was a difference in the schools in Ohio and Virginia, and he replied,

They's a lot of difference. Up there they seem like, you know, they care. They would try to learn you if it took them all day to learn you one word. They seemed like they, you know, want you to learn.

He also spoke about taking guitar lessons in school in Ohio, saying that he thought if he had stayed in Ohio, "I'd be a'playing just about anything."

Tom had some schooling as an adult when he spent seven months in Richmond in a correctional institution after he was "in a little bit of trouble." There he had classes in math, English, science, and spelling:

They'd sit there, they'd have six or seven of us in a class, and they'd learn us how to read. But when I left from there, I just had a third-grade average. You know before I went there I thought I had maybe a little bit bigger average, but come to find out I just had a third-grade average. But I was alearning, I was learning real good. You know I took spelling. They tried to learn me how to spell words. They was really wanting to learn me how to read.

But when he came back from Richmond he "had a wife and child by then and it was time to start doing a little bit of something and I forgot all about it, reading, something like that."

Since his time in Richmond, Tom has not been involved in any adult education, although he was approached by a friend about literacy tutoring. But he hasn't felt he has the time:

I'm kinda bashful, you know, 'cause I just won't let anybody come in and try to learn me to read, something like that, 'cause I know it makes them angry and I get angry and just don't want to do nothing.

At the same time, although he recognizes that "there's more out there than just me that can't read, so I shouldn't be ashamed of that," he would like to read better:

I'd like to read. I'd like to know more, like to pick something up and just go ahead and read it. But I just pick something up and look at it and lay it back down. I can read a little bit, but far as a big old long word or something or other, I don't know what that is. They's a lot of words I know. Take these little old kid books or something or other like that, I can pick them up and about read them. But you take a newspaper or something or other, I pick it up, they'll be words I don't know how to read. It wouldn't take much that I could learn how to read 'cause I know quite a few words. I could learn how to read, I think, pretty easy if I had the time and patience and somebody who could teach me.

Everyday Literacy and Technology

Tom is not a nonreader, but he reads poorly. He says the only writing he does is when he signs his name:

There's a few signs I could read. If I see pop in the store, I know what name of every kind of pop and stuff like that. Maybe candy bars, all the candy bars. But as far as picking up a paper that's got writing on it, they may be a few words I can read on it. My wife writes me a letter, you know, I can read that pretty good. They's a few things I can read. Big words mostly what I got problems with 'cause I don't try to sound them out or try to piece them together. And when I come to a big word, I just pass it up and go to the next word. If I know it I'll say it and if I don't, I just keep going on.

While Tom does not read much himself, literacy has a place in his family. His wife, Betty, went through the eighth grade and does read. She reads books to the children easily and fluently. She does word-find puzzles from a puzzle book. She reads the occasional piece of mail other than the expected light or hospital bills:

Well, like if I go to the post office and I see a bill, I about know where my bills are going to come from. But if I see something in there different, that bugs me 'cause I don't know where it's from or like that. I always just bring it here and let the old lady read it, and if she says something she says it and if she don't I don't pay it no mind.

The reading material in the home includes a few children's books and coloring books, Betty's puzzle books, and a large Bible. "I used to pick it up every now and then and read. I don't pick it up now. I should. I guess if I'd sit down you know, I'd probably learn it quick."

Getting a Good Deal. Math ability helps Tom when he shops. He usually goes to the grocery store twice a month. He goes because he thinks he can get more for their money than his wife.

I look at the prices and stuff on it. You know they got, say in the meat aisle or something or other like that, they'll have the prices on one thing. And the same meat'll be down right below it or above it have a different price on it, and I just go by, you know from there. But most of the time, you know, if I want it bad enough, I just go ahead and get it. I don't care for her going shopping and stuff, but it seems like she don't get as much. For the same amount of money.

To a large extent, Tom operates in a cash economy. He has never had a bank account and doesn't file a tax return except to get earned income credit if he's been paid by someone who withholds. The family does receive food stamps and help from the Women, Infants and Children (WIC) program for food for the children. He used to buy on credit at local stores that will carry an account for customers but has stopped:

> I ain't got no credit, at no stores. I used to have, but I stopped 'cause, you know I stopped it 'cause these little old stores now, they'll run it more up on you than what you're really getting. And I just quit . . . fooling with it.

Lack of transportation is probably the most immediate problem resulting from Tom's lack of literacy. While he has owned vehicles, he traded them because he was never able to get a driver's license:

> You know I ain't got no transportation. I guess that makes it harder on me than anything 'cause there ain't no transportation. I ain't never had a driver's license. I went tried it once, failed it, and ain't never been back. The woman read me the questions, but I ain't never read the book and I just went down there and tried to get them and I never got them, so you know that embarrassed me and I just ain't never been back to try for them. Maybe one of these days I'll get them.

In an area where the only public transportation is school buses and the shopping town is 20 miles away, not being able to pass the driver's license test is a serious problem. To shop or go to the doctor or visit their child's school, Tom and Betty must catch a ride with a family member.

Technology. The technology Tom encounters in his personal life is limited not because he lives and works in a rural area but primarily because he is poor. When asked what equipment in addition to the television and stereo he has in his home, he answered, "a stove, refrigerator, a washing machine, . . . clock." The washer is a wringer washer that can be filled by hand, since there is no water and no bathroom in the house. The television antenna is a coat hanger. The house is heated by a wood stove. Other family members have VCRs; none have cable television.

In his work Tom operates various machines—tractors, tobacco setters, front-end loaders, chain saws. He is involved with the technology of agricultural chemicals to some extent, mixing and spraying. But he seems to have had little or no encounter with computerized technology beyond, perhaps, his sisters' VCRs. Local banks don't have cash machines, and in any case he doesn't have an account. He does not use credit cards. He doesn't have a telephone. The farm equipment he uses is relatively small and unsophisticated. They don't own a microwave. In many ways Tom is involved with the technologies of earlier times. These are perhaps technologies that do not require much in the way of literacy, but it is probably not lack of literacy that has limited Tom's involvement with more contemporary technology, but lack of income.

The work Tom does involves skills such as how to drive a tractor or spear tobacco. It also involves technical knowledge. He knows what needs to be done to grow tobacco and in what sequence these steps are taken. He uses agricultural chemicals and determines how much of what he needs. He has skills as a mechanic. He gardens and knows his environment as a hunter and an herb digger. In none of these areas did his knowledge come from literacy and schooling. He does identify situations when more reading ability would benefit his work, but he has been able to work at farming for 16 years.

Tom talked about how he learned about farming and how he deals with situations in which reading would be helpful:

> Well, what I've learned, I've learned off of other people. 'Cause I don't read nothing like that, can't read, so what I've pretty well learned I learned off other people. I've helped a lot of people, and people showed me how to do stuff like that.
>
> Well, in a way you know if I had to do it myself I guess I'd be a'hurting. But I always have somebody there to read. I guess at a lot of stuff 'cause that's the way I go about doing it. I guess, you know, about how much you should need and all this 'cause I've done it for a while. I usually come out being about right. . . .
>
> My daddy taught me a lot about mechanics and I can work on just about anything. Well, that's another good thing I like to do besides farm work, I like to work on vehicles and stuff.

He expects help from the friend he works for if he grows his own crop next year:

> We were raised up [together] and we get along pretty good. He helps me and I help him and I learn a lot from him, you know. He reads, stuff like that. Next year I'm gonna put some [tobacco] out, maybe swap work or something with him.

The local agricultural extension agent, Russell Martin, affirmed some of what Tom said about how less literate farmers learn to do their work. "Many of the people that don't read, they listen and put it up in their brain." When a new procedure is introduced, the agents hold demonstrations around the county. Often the less literate farmers stand at the back of the crowd and watch without saying anything or asking questions. But after the demonstration, they may be the only ones who can really explain the procedure. Martin seemed quite impressed with the ability of these farmers to remember. "They've got it upstairs, using human computers." He commented on how skillfully many nonliterate farmers could handle numbers. "They can beat a pocket calculator." He also noted that while these less literate farmers adopt new practices, "a number [of them] will be one, two, three seasons late," and some suffer economically because of this. This might be particularly the case when conditions change quickly, as in blue mold infestations.

When asked about safety in the use of chemicals when people can't read the labels, Martin answered, "What I have found so far is that the people who can't read are more careful." He thought that they could recognize a word like *Ridomil* the way "we might recognize a Chinese character" and know what is in a container. Later he restated, "People who don't read and write are more careful than those who do."

Tom seems to have the ability with math that Martin noted. He believes he learned from his father:

> I picked it up I guess off my dad 'cause he'd sit around and the kids come in from school, they'd ask him math questions. I'd be sitting over there and I'd listen and just caught it off him. I just took right off on that.

For example, he explained how he determines the number of sticks to charge a farmer for after he has cut a field:

> Well, you count one row, we always count one row, and if you got, say, 100 sticks in a row and you got 20 stick-rows, that'd be 2,000 sticks. And we always go like that.

But while Tom seems able to use mathematics, he is vague about time. He doesn't remember the months to plant, and he seemed unsure about how long ago, even in terms of months, something had happened.

Family Literacy. Tom and Betty are concerned about their children's education. Betty reads to them, and Tom tells them stories. They have taught the oldest child, who is in kindergarten, to write his name. He also counts to 10 and recognizes letters. Tom says the children watch "Sesame Street" "all the time." Before one interview, the family was sitting on the porch, after Tom had worked all day in tobacco, as the oldest child showed them the papers he had brought home from kindergarten. These were worksheets that included connecting dots to form a picture and circling all of a particular shape. On the top of one sheet, the teacher had put "-1" where the child had failed to circle a square. Tom reminded him gently, "You gotta start looking there, son, you missed one." They see a better education as important to their children's future and do what they can to encourage them:

> I look forward to moving on now. I got a family of my own I gotta try and take care of them, maybe satisfy them. If I don't end up with a lot myself, I'd just like to see them be happy and get what they want.

MARCY OSBORNE

By Mary Beth Bingman

Marcy Osborne is a 40-year-old white Appalachian woman with a rural background who now lives in the small town of Gate City, Virginia, working there as a companion and housekeeper for an older woman. She is divorced and has three children, the youngest in his senior year of high school. Although Marcy dropped out of school in the seventh grade, she is able to read most of what she wants and has taken GED and nurse's aide classes.

Every weekday morning Marcy walks the four blocks between the apartment she shares with her mother and the apartment where she works. She works for Sue, an elderly woman who lives in a new apartment complex for older and disabled people. She describes her job as: "I guess it would be housekeeping 'cause that's what I do, do things for her you know." Marcy arrives at 6:30 A.M., prepares Sue's breakfast, and helps her dress for the day. She stays all day, cleaning the two-room apartment, preparing the meals, making sure Sue takes her medicine, and being her friend and companion. "I don't believe Sue would accept anybody else like she has me. She depends on me for more than she does her own kids." At 6:30 in the evening Marcy walks back home.

Marcy is a quiet woman. At first she seems shy, but this may just be an initial reserve. She is cheerful and laughs easily. She seems self-contained and determined. She dresses in jeans and sweaters chosen because they suit what she describes as "my own style." She has raised three children mostly by herself, having been on her own for 12 years. Her youngest son is now 19, and while Marcy plans to stay with her mother as long as she needs to, she also has a sense of independence and adventure. We talked some about how her life has changed over the years and what she would like to do:

[I'm] more independent. If a man asked me to marry him right now, I'd say forget it, no way. I don't believe I'd ever get married again. I like being free. That way if I want to go somewhere I go, if I don't I won't. If you've got a man, they're always there ready to tell you when you can go, when you can't go.

I'd like to travel. I was telling Sue the other day I'd like to go somewhere, just take off and keep going. I would. I'd like to go to Wyoming. I don't know why, I've always wanted to go there. I just want to go.

The Community

Gate City is the county seat of Scott County (see "Tom Addington"). It is a small town, the 1990 population of 2,200 down several hundred from 1980. It has been the main shopping town for this agricultural county and still has two farm supply stores, three supermarkets, a dry goods store, several small restaurants, four franchised fast-food restaurants, and two small discount stores. The old courthouse holds county offices, and the jail is next door. Several lawyers' offices are nearby, as are offices of the county's service agencies. The school board office and the county's only library are on the main street. There are only two small manufacturing enterprises. Jackson Street is old enough and unchanged enough that the Hollywood producers of *The River* used it as the set for a 1950s small town, giving county residents temporary employment as extras.

Yet in many ways Gate City has become a suburb of Kingsport, Tennessee—a bedroom community, as the town manager calls it. The majority of city residents work in Kingsport's industries, and most do their shopping in the malls and major discount stores of the larger city. So Gate City, which has been important since settlers on the road to Kentucky came through the pass, or "gate," where Moccasin Creek cuts through Clinch Mountain, has become a place to do your county business if you live in the rural part of the county and a place to live, but not work, for most residents of the town.

Marcy lives with her mother and son in a building on the main street in Gate City. There are two apartments, one on the main level and one in the basement. Marcy lives on the main floor. There is a tiny bit of yard next to the sidewalk, and Marcy has planted flowers. The living room is large, with two couches, a bed with a homemade quilt, and several chairs and tables. A large television with "rabbit ears" sits in front of the fireplace at the end near the door. A hall and a dining room open off the room. The floors are wood, and the walls have a light paneling. There is a large window at one end of the light and airy room. The walls are decorated with a large poster of Jesus with a tulle frame, a picture of a cross made with match sticks, a pencil drawing of two kittens made by a niece, several family photographs, other religious pictures, a calendar. In the dining room are a table and chairs as well as a small freezer.

Life and Work

Although Marcy has lived in Gate City for two years, she grew up in rural Scott County. Her father died when she was 10, and her mother raised four daughters by doing farm work:

> I've got three sisters. Ain't got nary brother. Well, we lived back in the sticks. I guess we just went wild back there. Well, it's called Tom's Branch, we lived back in there till I was about 14, I guess. Then we moved to where the swinging bridge is at Smith's Ferry, that's where we lived. I've come in many a evening, not even eat nothing, working tobacco. Get in about dark.

Marcy talked about the differences between the ways she and her children grew up, even though they all lived in rural sections of the county. Her own childhood memories sound like those of a much earlier age than the 1950s:

> Well, they have it a lot easier now than what I did. And I guess I had it easier than my mother did. There's more money now, easier to get a job. Well they had more clothes than I did, 'cause I remember when I went to school I had about three dresses to wear. They had a lot more clothes than I did. I had to walk about two mile out of that holler. They didn't have that far to walk. Well we didn't have no TV when I was growing up, well not till I got about 14. We had an old battery radio. Didn't have nothing like a stereo, nothing like that. We didn't have an electric stove, we had a wood stove. We had to carry water from a spring. We had a wringer washing machine. Well when I was growing up we didn't have a wringer all the time. We didn't get one till later on. Had to use a washboard. If we got a toy, it was at Christmas time. A doll, that was about it. Or a coloring book, something like that. We didn't get very much. [My kids] got dolls, coloring books, and it didn't have to be Christmas for them to get it.

Marcy married in her early 20s and had three children, two girls and a boy. Her husband worked in sawmills in Scott County, and they lived first near where she grew up and then at Sweetwater in southern Scott County. Marcy began to work as a janitor in the school while she lived in Sweetwater. Marcy's husband had a problem with alcohol, and she left him to raise her children alone:

> The trouble with him was when he was drinking. He was really mean, you know. That's really the thing that come between me and him I guess was his drinking. I just couldn't cope with it.
>
> [It was scary] trying to raise the kids on my own. It wasn't really that much problem, though. They enjoyed, you know, being with me, and when me and their father was together, why when he was drunk, it kept them scared to death all the time. A many a night they went to bed with their shoes on because they knowed if he started raising cane, I was gonna get up and leave with them. And they kept their shoes on.
>
> Well really I made it better after I left my husband 'cause he drunk all the time. If he had money, he went and spent it on something to drink. A lot of times we had to come to Mommy's to get something to eat. So I really made it better, you know, after I got on my own. 'Cause he wasn't there you know to waste what money I did get.

The family lived on money from the Aid to Families with Dependent Children (AFDC) program:

> Well, when I had all three of the kids home, it was $327, $327 [a month] or something like that. Then when the oldest got married, it was $265. Then when the other one got married, it was $207. Well see we got food stamps. That bought the food. What I had left I paid the electricity bill and bought the kids clothes. It wasn't easy, but when you have to, you have to I guess.

While Marcy has been separated from her husband for 12 years, it took her several years to afford a divorce:

> We was separated for about, I guess, seven year before we got a divorce. It took me a long time to come up with the money to pay for it, you know. And I had to pay so much and then wait and pay so much again, and it cost me a lot more doing that, too. It cost me $644. My sister got her divorce and it only cost her $350 'cause her husband paid it straight out. That way it didn't cost as much.

Educational History. Marcy left school when she was 17 and in the seventh grade. She had been sick a lot and had not been able to go to school regularly. She and her sisters rode the school bus to a three-room school, but they had to walk to the bus stop:

> We had to walk out of that holler, about two miles and in the winter time it got rough. There for a while I couldn't go. I had that rheumatic fever, I was so weak I couldn't do nothing. I was 6 when I started. I was 8 when I had that rheumatic fever. I had to stay out for about two year. It took me a long time to get straightened out.
>
> I had this one teacher, Miss H____, and she was really mean, everybody else thought she was mean, but I liked her. I learned more under her than I did any of them. I'm the only one didn't get a paddling when I was in her room. The rest of them got a paddling. I didn't. They all accused me of being her pet, but I just done what she wanted me to do, you know. I guess I was scared of her.

None of Marcy's sisters finished school. "My mother didn't go. I think she might have went through the third grade. He [Dad] didn't go very far either." Her husband went through the fifth grade. Her children, however, have done well in school. "The two girls, they done good. The oldest one didn't graduate 'cause she quit and got married, but the middle-sized one graduated. My son graduates this year." Her son has had some trouble with reading and was in a special education class for learning disabilities for a time. Marcy worked with her children when they were in school, helping them as much as she could:

> I'd sit down and help them with their math and what I could, you know. There's a lot of things I couldn't help them with, I didn't know nothing about. When you don't go far in school, you don't learn much.
>
> There was some of that math I couldn't understand. Math I'm pretty good, but algebra. History I never did like. They used to say "writing." Now they say "writing in cursive," and when my daughters first come home talking about it, I said "What are you all talking about!?" You know I hadn't heard nothing like that. I didn't know what they were talking about.

As an adult, Marcy has continued her education. She took a 10-week nurse's aide course at the community college in the next county. She would have liked to continue, but she rode with her sister and when her sister decided not to go on, Marcy couldn't either:

It was 10 weeks. Well, they really wasn't nothing hard about it. They had a book we had to read and then we done the tests from that, you know. A lot of times we just sat around and talked, you know. We didn't have to do that much. We'd have to take a test, I think, about every week, a written test. And most of the time we just took blood pressure and stuff like that. How to take a temperature, how to take a pulse, stuff like that. We didn't have to give no shots or nothing like that. I wanted to take the rest of them. You're supposed to take more than that, you know, more than I did. Well, you're supposed to take biology class and all that. I was aiming to take them, but she backed out of taking any more so I didn't fool with it.

Marcy was also involved in a GED program that operated in Gate City for a year. That class has since been discontinued. She would like to continue both these programs if the classes met at night and in her local community.

Everyday Literacy and Technology

"I read pretty good. But now there's some words I get confused on, you know, like big long words and stuff." Marcy is a reader. In addition to the Bible, she reads and writes in her work and to accomplish things in her everyday life. She also reads for fun, "newspapers, *True Story* books, about anything I can find to read." She reads the daily *Kingsport Times-News* and the weekly Scott County paper. "Well, I read the deaths, the horoscopes, and like where people's in court and stuff like that. I like to read that. I don't read the sports. I don't care nothing about sports." She also reads tabloids, like *The Weekly World News*, that have "crazy stuff in it, things you wouldn't believe, but I like to read it." She reads *Reader's Digest* but not novels. "I don't like long stories. If they ain't short, I ain't gonna read it." She also enjoys doing word-find puzzles. While she doesn't use recipes regularly, she does for candy or cakes.

Writing is not something Marcy likes to do, but she uses writing when she needs to, writing grocery lists, birthday cards, and an occasional letter to her sister. She relies on her memory rather than a written calendar:

I'm pretty good at . . . if I have to do something, I remember the date. And phone numbers, I can remember them, if they're important, I can remember. I got so many in my head one of these days they're all gonna get mixed up and it's hard telling who I'm gonna call. I just remember, I don't know. Seems like once I dial it, that's it, I remember it.

Financial reading and writing is one area where Marcy has some difficulty. She doesn't have a checking account or credit cards. She pays bills by money order. Many bills are paid in cash—rent, electricity, telephone, water—at local offices. Her sister often does this for her and her mother because Marcy works during the hours these offices are open. When Marcy has unfamiliar forms to fill out, she gets her sister's help. "Something I have to fill out . . . I always get my sister to help me. She went to the same grade I did, but she learnt more than I did. She's good at filling papers out."

While she was married, Marcy handled all the bills. Tax forms she always took "to somebody that knowed what they was doing." When she first had to fill out school-lunch forms, she took them to the school and got help, but after that she did them herself.

Transportation. Marcy doesn't drive. She started to learn but she "run into a toilet" and didn't try any more. She says she may try to learn again. Her daughters drive and her sister has offered to teach her. Now she either walks or her daughters take her where she needs to go. She has traveled very little outside the immediate area: a weekend trip to North Carolina with a friend; a few visits to her sister's in Rogersville, about 40 miles away; and trips to the children's rehabilitation center in Charlottesville with her daughter, who had a back problem. The trips to Charlottesville were in a cab; they traveled there and back, 250 miles each way, in a day. Her children have not traveled much either.

Marcy gave me directions to several places we were discussing, but she doesn't have much confidence in her ability to find her way around:

> I doubt it [that she could find her way around Kingsport]. I get lost in the hospital when I go down there. I always like to take somebody with me 'cause I don't know my way around that much. One day we went to Big Stone Gap, and my youngest daughter—she's easy to get confused—she said, "Are we in Kingsport?" She thought we was in Kingsport. She's in Big Stone.

Getting information about health issues is an important use of reading for Marcy. When her daughter was being followed by the rehabilitation clinic because of scoliosis, Marcy read the booklet that explained the exercises her daughter needed to do. She reads food ingredient labels because her mother is diabetic and must limit her sugar intake. She read in the nurse's aide course and maintains an interest in health matters. "Well, I used to go down to the health department and get them pamphlets and if they're anything in the doctor's office when I go, I read that."

In her everyday activities, Marcy encounters little computerized technology. She doesn't use a bank machine or credit cards. She rarely goes to the library and hasn't used the computerized card catalogue. She doesn't have a microwave because she is concerned about her mother's pacemaker. She does use a tape recorder and television. Sue has cable television. Her daughters have a VCR. When the family lived at Sweetwater, they had a satellite dish for a time:

Well at [Sweetwater] we had one of them disk. I like to never learned how to work it. I get it all mixed up, you know. We'd have to turn the disk with one button and the station with the other. I like to never learned how to use that thing. My daughters could work it good, but now I couldn't. They just looked on it and found out what buttons to push and that's how they learned. I finally learnt there at the last how to work it, then lightning struck it and we never did get it fixed.

At work Marcy has encountered some technology. When she began work as a school janitor, she had a run-in with a floor buffer:

Well, they had this buffer. And I tried to use it one day and it tried to take me through the side of the building. And they never would ask me to try to use it no more. It did, it had me going every which a way.

In her current job as housekeeper, there is little use of technology except for normal home appliances. The apartment building is equipped with an intercom at the front entrance as well as doorbells at each apartment. Neither are common in this area. Most people just ignore the doorbell and knock. And while Marcy knows how to operate the intercom, she says she usually knows who is coming and just buzzes them in:

Well you can push it down and ask who it is and talk to them if you want to. I never do, though. Most time I know who's coming you know.

Well, I've always cleaned house and stuff like that, so when they told me what to do, well, I just go on and do it. They told me what I have to do before I come out here. I cook for her, and clean house, and make sure she has her medicine, stuff like that.

Taking care of Sue's needs is not complicated, but it does involve several tasks involving literacy or numeracy. Every month Sue's children come and grocery shop for her. Marcy writes a list of what she will need. She plans a month ahead:

> When I first come here, they had already bought groceries you know. I just go by that and if Sue wants anything extra, I tell them. That's the way I work it. Sometimes for bread I go down to the Quickstop. For two, it don't take that much.

Marcy must also manage Sue's medication. I asked Marcy to show me how she organizes the medicine. Sue takes several pills twice a day. Once a week, Marcy sorts the medicine into little plastic boxes designed for organizing medication:

> She don't know what kind she takes. I have to put it in a box. I fix her medicine on Wednesday. It's like on Monday of a morning and of a night, two boxes, that's the way we do it. She has to take six of a morning and four of a evening.

One box is blue and marked P.M. and EVENING and the other is pink and marked A.M. and MORNING. Each box is divided into seven separately lidded compartments, one for each day of the week and marked SMTWTFS. Marcy said the daughter-in-law used to sort the medication, but that she told her, "If you want me to do it, I will. I've watched you so much, I could close my eyes and do it." So now Marcy does it. She reads on the prescription bottle whether the medication is to be taken once or twice a day. The ones that are only taken once go into the morning box; the ones for twice go into the morning and evening boxes. Sue also takes a vitamin, which Marcy doesn't put in a box.

Family Literacy: Changes over Generations. While this profile is of Marcy, her mother is an important part both of Marcy's everyday life and of understanding the roles of literacy and technology in the lives of people in Scott County over the past 70 years. Granny looks like Marcy, short and solid, but is of course much older. In this section, Granny tells the story of her life:

> Well, if I live to see the 24th day of March come I'll be 78 years old! My mother she died when I was 5 years old and my Grandpa and Grandma raised me. I had to learn to cook for they was sick a lot, my Grandma and Grandpa both was. I had to learn to cook when I was 10 years old. And never got to go to school much on account of

I had to milk and feed everything, I had it hard. [At one point a tear runs down her face, but her voice is firm and strong]. I went to school a little. . . . I didn't get no education at all. Never did learn to read and write good, but everything that, every lesson that we had in school, they'd write it, make us read it writing [script], so that's why I learned to read writing and couldn't read print. They had books, but they'd write the lessons down and make you read them on writing. They was about forty in the schools that I went to. Teachers was rough, one teacher to each school. And they didn't know what a principal nor nothing like that was in school when I went to school. They didn't.

In many ways, in the past 30 years Marcy and her mother have gone from a nineteenth-century to a twentieth-century life. They grew up in a similar fashion, in an isolated part of a rural county without many conveniences and in "hard times." But there were differences. When Marcy was 14 her mother sent to town and got a television, expanding their connections to the rest of the world. And today her son plans to join the Marines at least in part to travel. His girlfriend is a Norwegian exchange student, and the hobby he shares with a friend is collecting exotic snakes and spiders.

But both Marcy and her mother are ambivalent about the changes in their lives. Granny lives in town and seems to love it; Marcy misses the quiet of the country. They both talk of people today having it "too easy" and making it too easy for their children.

> MARCY: I think now, people has it too easy. Too much modern stuff! Yeah, like water in the house. When I was growing up we didn't [have it]. Why, I know Mommy and them didn't. And electric stoves. We had to use wood stoves to cook on. Most people uses microwaves now.
>
> GRANNY: I'd rather have a wooden cook stove any time, and I'd rather have just a coal stove. I don't like electricity too much. You have a time getting warm by these electric heaters. Your cooking's a lot better tasting that you cook with wood than you do with electricity, I think.

Summary

How does limited literacy affect Marcy's life? In situations where lack of education and literacy get in her way, Marcy has ways of coping. Her sisters have been and continue to be a support to her, both with her family and with tasks involving reading and writing. Usually Marcy can read what she needs, but in many situations she gets the information she needs in other ways. She observes or asks and then remembers how to perform various tasks. She gets information from television and friends, although she also uses the newspaper and telephone book.

Use of everyday technology does not seem to be an issue in Marcy's life, except possibly learning to drive. And it may well be that when she has the need to drive and the money for a car, she will learn to drive. Except for the floor buffer, Marcy does not seem to have had problems with technology. She is not enthusiastic about new things, but, as with the intercom in Sue's apartment, she can use them when she needs to.

Marcy didn't finish school and she hasn't gotten her GED. There are things she has trouble reading and writing. But it doesn't seem that her life is limited greatly by any lack of literacy. It probably has been limited to some extent by poverty. But Marcy lives a full life: She does work she and other people value, has raised her children, supports and receives support from her family. She seemingly enjoys life, though she is aware of its darker sides and ponders these issues. She has plans she hasn't fulfilled yet, plans for more education and travel, but these are not dreams that are out of her reach.

YUVETTE EVANS

By Connie White

Yuvette Evans is a 26-year-old African American woman, a waitress and mother of two children. With her 9-year-old daughter, Jessica, and her 5-year-old son, Arliss, she lives in public housing in the Lonsdale neighborhood in inner-city Knoxville, Tennessee. Yuvette finished part of the twelfth grade. Although she has been unable to complete any of the three adult education programs in which she has enrolled and still does not have a GED, Yuvette reads fairly well.

Yuvette's life revolves around concerns of raising her children and making a living. She is proud of being able to work and earn money for the things the family needs, to "pay out of [my] pocket instead of somebody else doing it." Her AFDC payment is small, and Yuvette is working hard to try to lift her family out of poverty.

Yuvette's personal values, the way she spends her time and how she lives her life, are a source of pride. "I don't hang out. I don't go out in public and drink. I don't do drugs. I stay home. I might go with my girlfriend shopping, watch her shop. I mostly stay in the house."

Yuvette's dreams reflect her daily struggles with hard economic realities and the gap between what everything in our culture points to as "the good life" and the life that she and her children lead. Even in her dreams, Yuvette does not imagine the good life will come easy. She expects and wants to work, but at a job of some skill and dignity.

> One time I was thinking about rich people, maybe they need a bookkeeper or accountant, or maybe at a big business. Atlanta's a big city, try to get a job down there. Or maybe Nashville. Get that money . . . just having a good job, living good . . . have no worries when bill time come wondering how you gonna get by. I'd go shopping and get the kids stuff.

Lonsdale

Lonsdale is a neighborhood in the midst of change. Older residents remember an almost rural community, neighbors who knew one another, and small businesses that served the area. Historically, there was a "black section" and a "white section," a division that even now remains noticeable. As Knoxville grew, Lonsdale added homes and public housing. It was a working-class community with a strong neighborhood identity. For many residents, Lonsdale retained the warmth and familiarity of a small town. In the 1960s and 1970s, Knoxville, like most of the rest of urban America, experienced "white flight" out of the center city into the surrounding area. Economic conditions deteriorated as money for services and schools followed the affluent white migration. Inner-city neighborhoods like Lonsdale were hardest hit and suffered further from economic restructuring that caused many residents to lose jobs in manufacturing and textiles. The jobs available in the area are mostly low-paying and without benefits such as health insurance.

Yuvette lives deep in the heart of the "projects." Her home is one of 12 apartments in a red brick building that looks just like every other red brick building for blocks. The front room is bare except for a couch and matching chair, a couple of tables, and an assortment of photographs of Yuvette's son and daughter. There are no books, magazines, or other printed material in sight, except for a Bible.

Yuvette does not want to live in Lonsdale. She does not want to be a part of community life. At times she seems almost a prisoner, only going outside to leave the community, apparently almost never to visit or perform activities within the community:

I moved to Lonsdale two years ago. I just don't like to be out here. If I could I'd have a house. I wanted a house before I came here. But they didn't have a house. They just had this. You have to take it or maybe there won't be another chance. Nothing against the people out here, I just don't want to get in contact. You know people . . . it's hard to trust anybody. I just as well stay in the house. They probably figure that I think I'm better than anybody. That's not it. I just want to stay out of trouble.

In her life in the community, Yuvette practices a self-imposed isolation, seeing only Anna and Janie from the neighborhood. Both Anna and Janie are very important to Yuvette; Anna is someone Yuvette can tell her problems to, and both provide guidance and stability in her life. Their opinions and ideas are of great interest: Yuvette listens to them. Anna and Janie seem to fill some void in Yuvette's life, to replace the family and community interaction that she does not have.

Yuvette seems very concerned for her children's safety. The harshest reprimand I saw her administer happened when Arliss left the front yard and went out of sight around the corner of the building. At least a part of Yuvette's dissatisfaction seems to come from living in public housing.

The manager came here to inspect. I was cleaning the oven, had the cleaner in there letting it soak. She told me to pick up the paper in the yard. I went to do that. She said [pointing at the oven] "You're going to clean that . . . up too, ain't you?" Janie told me to write it down, put the date and everything, and make a complaint about her. It don't do no good, she's like that with everybody. People treat you like that when you don't have nothing. They act like they're high up over you, people do, when you're low-income.

Yuvette's alienation from the community is reflected in her thinking about her relationship to the community and civic responsibility. Yuvette doesn't see herself as having any power to affect what happens in the "outside" world. Although she reported that she occasionally watches the news on TV, Yuvette does not read books, magazines, or newspapers. She doesn't mention current happenings or appear interested in news-making events, even as they relate to her own life. "No, I don't have a card, don't vote. Janie say you need to vote. You know, have a say so. But I figured one vote . . . if I don't vote it won't matter." This doesn't prevent her, however, from recognizing power/political issues, such as labor/management questions and her treatment by the housing inspector.

Life and Work

Yuvette was born in rural central Georgia. Before she was a year old, her father found work in Knoxville and the family moved here. Times were better economically for the family, Yuvette reports, once they came to Tennessee. Yuvette describes her mother as a strong woman, the primary person who shaped her life and continues to have a (sometimes unwelcome) influence on her:

> In some people's families, the mama say "Just wait till your Daddy get home!" It wasn't like that at my house. My mama pop us if we didn't do right. She didn't wait on Daddy.

Yuvette struggles to reconcile her difficult time growing up, and the continuing differences she has with her parents, by reminding herself what life has been like for them:

> Mama went to sixth or seventh grade, Daddy didn't get that far. They had it hard, back in Georgia. They had to quit school to work and help their people. When I was coming up, Mama worked at night. She had different factory jobs—Levi's, Standard Knitting Mill [apparel plants]. Daddy took care of us when Mama was working. He worked, too, at Lays and JFG [food processing plants].

Yuvette has a difficult time talking about her growing-up years. Because both parents worked and had to be away from home at different hours, Yuvette says she doesn't have much of a feeling of "family." Although there was enough money to get by, Yuvette remembers a great deal of unhappiness as a child because of her parents' absence and her mother's overprotection:

> You probably think this is being mean. When I was little, I used to say I wish I had other parents. My mom was kind of strict. She mostly kept me in the house. I guess she didn't want me to mess with no boy. I guess I can't complain. You know, we made it, as grown-ups. I didn't have too many friends. I guess I wasn't the talking type. Anna's the only good friend I had.

Yuvette resents having been treated differently from her brother by her parents:

> You know my brother, he's a boy, he can go. I had to stay at home and stuff. It's always, I can't wait till I can get grown. People used

to come by and [say to my parents] "Look your son's a'coming out."
They'll say no, I couldn't even go anywhere.

Work. Yuvette is a part-time waitress at Shackney's, a national chain with
several restaurants in Knoxville. She is eager to talk about her work. Yuvette
works about 20 to 30 hours a week, from 5 P.M. until 9 P.M., or sometimes
until midnight:

> People say, "What you do at Shackney's?" They don't think it's
> nothing. But it's a hard job. There's a lot to it. When I first started,
> I was doing salad bar and they wanted me to train and do wait-
> ress. And you know sometimes I got nervous. You have to call in
> on a microphone and say "ordering please" and tell them what
> you need. You have to be a salesman; you have to say, "Would
> you like to try this today?" I get nervous sometimes. But I like
> waitressing, because of the tips. On a good night, I can bring in
> maybe $30, $40.

This is the third job Yuvette has held; she worked for a while at
Wendy's and at a daycare center. She is proud of her work record. "I've
never got fired off a job, never walked out. I hope I'll be here a while. We
really need the money, Christmas coming up and all."
Despite her good record and the tips, Yuvette's pride is often on the
line at work. "I'm independent," Yuvette says, making it clear that her
dignity is worth something, too:

> They don't care about us up there at that job. You can tell that by
> the way they treat us. No insurance, no benefits. And the managers,
> they're always showing out in front of the customers. It's like the
> waitresses don't matter. If they want you to respect them, they got
> to respect you, too.

Yuvette interprets these insults as an issue of unequal power between
management and workers, not in a racial sense. Even though the restaurant is located in an area that has a large African American population,
few African Americans work there. But Yuvette is willing to give her employers the benefit of the doubt:

> You know I'm the only black in the evening, but there's a cook and
> a busboy in the morning. My friend was saying I should complain
> 'cause they don't have many black people there. But I figure if
> they were prejudiced they wouldn't have hired me or the other
> two.

Yuvette especially likes the teamwork of waitressing. She likes to help out the other waitresses and feels that she is part of a cooperative effort:

> You know we have a buddy system, we help each other out. One waitress might go get a drink order, give it to another to ring up 'cause she has so much to do. Or the cook might ask, "Will you make me a Mello Yello" because they're not allowed out of the kitchen and we can't go in there.

Yuvette also enjoys the pride her children have in her job. She says that her children "tell everybody" that she is a Shackney's waitress. "His teacher was telling me [Arliss said] 'my mom work at Shackney's.' He say, 'She a cook. She cook chicken.' It made us laugh, it was so funny."

The manager of another Knoxville Shackney's gave his viewpoint on the literacy demands of a waitress's job:

> A waitress needs to be able to read the menu, the ticket, and the computer (preregister) keyboard. Sometimes she may need to help a customer with the menu. Not all of the customers can read or understand it. She takes a customer's order and circles it on the ticket here. She goes to the preregister and puts in her number. Then she rings in the order. The computer automatically puts the date and time. The waitress has to write in the table, whether it's the smoking or nonsmoking section, and what time she calls in the order. Then she writes the time it comes out of the kitchen right here. For breakfast it's a little harder, because the entrees aren't written out in the same way on the ticket.
>
> It's very important that the waitress gets the order put down and rung up on the computer just right. If a waitress makes a mistake and she or the customer catches it, you have to have a manager to come and fix it. Nobody else can remove any charge from the computer.
>
> There really isn't a screening process for literacy skills when we hire. If I'm interviewing, I look at how she fills out the application, whether her writing is neat. I also have her write her address. That way I get a pretty good idea. We generally don't have any problems with waitresses not being able to read and write. They do pretty well learning the preregister.
>
> The salary is $2.13 an hour. You can make good money with the tips. A good-looking girl with a good personality can bring in $100 a day in tips.
>
> Almost all of our people are full-time. I believe they get a week's vacation after a year. No sick leave; that's only for manag-

ers. Waitresses would probably abuse that real bad. If they had it, they'd take it.

Despite the manager's comments, Yuvette and other waitresses say the norm for tips is generally less than half the hundred-dollar mark. His statement also hints at the paternalism and mistrust that Yuvette says is typical of managers' attitudes toward waitresses. Although technology has become a part of the job in recent years with the addition of the preregister, literacy requirements remain somewhat minimal.

Educational History. Yuvette reports an educational history characterized, like other parts of her childhood, by social isolation and disconnectedness. She has nothing particularly positive or negative to say about her teachers:

> I always did like to work with numbers, liked to count. I used to count the colors in my clothes, count everything. In elementary, I used to make good grades. As I got older, something just really dropped. And you know I didn't have too many friends there. I didn't like school. I'm not gonna lie. Sometimes I didn't go. Most times I didn't go. I never really participated, you know went to parties like other high school kids, they go to their prom and stuff. My mom, you know, she really didn't let me go anywhere. I didn't do anything really. I just go and do my work, half the time when I did go. I got to twelfth grade at Fulton High School. I did all right. My grades were OK, not honor roll but mostly not bad. I did pretty well considering I was hardly ever there.

Yuvette got pregnant when she was 16. She has little to say about that part of her life, which must have been very difficult, given her upbringing. But she refuses to blame her pregnancy for not finishing school. "No, after the baby came, it wasn't much difference with school. Mama kept her, while I went to school. When I went. Wasn't often." Yuvette was in the twelfth grade when her mother moved to Atlanta:

> I wish I would have stayed up here. They said my diploma was already ready, just was lacking English and taking summer school. I should have used my head and stayed. I really didn't drop out, you know, I went down there to Atlanta and took classes.

In the past eight years, Yuvette has enrolled in three separate adult education programs but has not gotten her GED. When she first moved to Atlanta as a teenager, Yuvette attended a high school for adults at night. "We had accounting and I liked it; I thought it was so easy. He gave us something to do and I always got it right. But I didn't get to stay in it because we moved to Florida." Yuvette tried to keep up with her class while she was away or reenroll when she came back:

> We kept moving back and forth. I liked the accounting class, but the other classes were hard. I was going at night and the school was on a street, it was bad, all kind of people hanging out. And I used to have to catch the bus and the subway. I came back here and stayed with my pa.

Back in Knoxville, a social worker asked Yuvette if she was interested in working toward her GED. Yuvette began attending GED classes run by the Job Training Partnership Act (JTPA) program. Even though she made several attempts in the JTPA program, Yuvette was not able to stay with the classes. She seemed unable to feel a part of the program, unable to connect with either the teacher or the other students. Yuvette described classes in which there was little interaction among students, with a disengaged, authoritarian teacher who "used to talk about church and stuff, which is fine. But she would explain a little bit, and then we have to do the work. Maybe if I had another teacher . . . "

Fortunately, Yuvette's experience of isolation was not repeated in the Knox County School's Even Start Family Literacy Program, which she joined later. This federal program was open to parents who have children under age 7 and included the provision of child care and transportation.

Yuvette's Even Start class emphasized group work and cooperation. Her teacher designed activities that promoted interaction among the students:

> You know when we do the work, we help each other, it being like a group thing. The teacher, she help you, she be right there helping you. You're all put together and when we first start out, we do a newspaper thing. We all read it together and we're asked the questions. She'd say, "Who want to do the first one?" We'd all compare, we're reading it and we'll say to each other. We'll see if we got the same answer, and check it and we all go through it again. At the JTPA, it wasn't like that. I like Even Start best.

Family obligations and the need to support herself and her children worked against Yuvette's continued participation in Even Start. The Even Start program began at 9:00 A.M. and continued until 12:30 P.M., the time that Arliss went to Head Start. When her children returned home from school, Yuvette had time only to get ready for work and get them to the babysitter's. When Yuvette got off from work, the children were generally already asleep and often spent the night with the babysitter. Yuvette was spending very little time with her children. She also didn't feel that she could quit work:

> I tried to do both of them [work and go to school]. If it was just me, I'd do both. But I've got Arliss and Jessica. If I do both, I'm not gonna be having time for them. See there was no money coming in. You know paying rent . . . I'm the only one paying the bills.

Since she stopped going to Even Start, Yuvette can spend mornings with Arliss. But she hopes to find a way to go back to Even Start:

> If I can get all my bills paid up, then I'll probably go back to school. I really do need goals . . . I need my GED. I'm going to start back going to Even Start, I really am. But [for now] it be too late.

Working for Something Nice. Yuvette's economic struggle is the focus of much of her energy and concern. When she recently hurt her foot, she was afraid to go to the hospital, afraid of what she might be told. The experience underscored the ways in which she and her children live on the edge, without options in a time of emergency. "What if I couldn't work for two or three weeks? You never can tell what might happen. I might lose my job. You know I don't want to hear that."

Yuvette repeatedly mentions that she wants to pay her own way. "I'm independent," she says many times. "I don't want my kids to say, 'My mom didn't work.'" Her income allows the family to purchase items such as a couch, a chair, a TV, and a telephone, hardly in the realm of luxury. Looking around the nearly bare apartment, Yuvette's wants seem so few, but they are important to her:

> I need furniture. I want something halfway decent. Not trying to impress somebody, you know, I want it for myself. That's why I'm working. I love this couch. I love to look at the color. I want to keep it so bad. I got it at the rental place. You know, pay so much a week and then you own it. But you know it takes forever. I know it costs more that way. I couldn't get credit to buy at the regular store. This store ad said, No down payment! No credit hassle! So I went there and they tried to get me to get a lot of things. I got this couch and chair, and the TV. For the couch and chair, I pay a little over $20 a week. I pay that for 78 weeks. But now there ain't so many weeks left and I hope I'll be able to see it through to pay it up. If I had the

money to buy it straight out I would do it. I tried _____ [furniture store], tried to get them to use my record at the rental place to get credit. They told me they don't count no rental place when they see about giving you credit. So what can I do? Anna says to put the money in the bank, every week, until I get enough saved. But it seems like every day when I bring home my tips, the kids need something for school, or something. It's hard. I hope they don't come for the couch. It's so embarrassing, it happened to me once before. They come to the door, say 'Miss Evans, we came after the table.' I hope they don't come. I want something nice so bad.

Yuvette's heartfelt desire to have a new couch and chair—a little piece of the American dream—saddles her with a debt and with a decreased ability to stop working long enough to participate in an education program that will help her prepare for her GED. One afternoon, we drove to the furniture rental store so Yuvette could make a payment. When she got back to the car, Yuvette told us that the clerk had tried to interest her in a bedroom suite. It was $880 for a headboard, chest, dresser, and mirror, Yuvette said, if you paid "straight out." The rent-to-own deal was $23.04 a week, for 78 weeks. "He wouldn't say how much altogether," Yuvette reported. We both gasped as Yuvette borrowed her daughter's calculator to figure it out—and found that she would be paying almost $1,800. "I'm going to try my best not to buy that," Yuvette vowed.

Everyday Literacy and Technology

Although Yuvette says she doesn't particularly like to read, she does read when it is necessary. She mentions filling out forms, helping the children with their homework, reading and writing on the job, and paying bills. She readily uses math in shopping activities and on the job.

I observed Yuvette read a Head Start parent's note aloud to her son, operate her daughter's calculator, and read the Shackney's menu. Lack of literacy skills does not appear to be a barrier to Yuvette's use of technology or to almost anything she attempts in her life. Yuvette usually pays her bills in cash:

I have a checking account, but I made a mistake with it. One time I called them to see how much I had. I wrote a check, but some of the checks hadn't come in when they told me I had enough. So now I have to get enough money to cover the check and the charge from the bank. It's put me behind. So now I leave my checkbook at home.

Yuvette doesn't have a car or a driver's license. She walks, rides the bus, or asks a friend to take her where she needs to go:

> Nobody showed me how [to drive]. My brother, he learn on his own. I could get him to show me, but he go too fast! I might ask my sister-in-law to show me. Yes, [I use a bus schedule]. Or sometime I just go up there and sit and wait.

Yuvette appears to depend on herself to figure things out. She does not seem to need a network of helpers to fill out forms, read directions, or carry out everyday responsibilities. She does seem to want and need support that she often does not have—in making decisions, in talking through her problems, in coping with life. However, these needs relate more to her social context and isolation than to lack of literacy skills.

Technology. Yuvette's lack of literacy skills is not a barrier to her use of technology. She has a programmable telephone, and she often records phone numbers that way. She learned to program the telephone by reading the owner's manual. She operates a tape recorder and uses a calculator. She mentioned operating a VCR and using a remote control for the TV. "It's no problem" she said when asked about learning to use the equipment. She learned either by reading the instruction manual or "Just looked at it and figured it out."

Every day at work, Yuvette must use the electronic preregister:

> At the end of the night, we have to do our tickets. We have to ring them up and add them and give it to our supervisor. The supervisor takes the report out of the preregister and does a match.

If the employee's calculation and the preregister statement don't match, the calculation must be done again. Yuvette was able to learn to operate the preregister easily, she reported.

Family Literacy. Yuvette's life is closely intertwined with her children. She spends much time and effort thinking about and caring for their needs. Yuvette is very concerned that they both get a good education. Both Jessica and Arliss have experienced speech problems. Jessica stutters, and Arliss had difficulties with delayed speech. Yuvette has sought help for these problems and is generally supportive of the children's schools. She especially likes Arliss's Head Start program:

At Head Start they really care about those kids. They're nice and you talk to them about something and they'll really listen. They asked me if I want to visit the class sometime. I want to go. They send home a little homework thing, and I read that to him. He talks better. Head Start helped him out a lot. He talks a lot now. Used to, he didn't really understand. They're having speech [class] with him and it helps a lot.

Jessica, born when her mother was 17, has had more difficulty in school. Jessica has been the center of a tug-of-war between Yuvette and Yuvette's mother, who appears to retain some "claim" on the little girl she helped raise. Yuvette's mother is critical both of Yuvette's child-rearing and of her life in general:

My mama likes to worry. She thinks I don't know how to take care of my kids. She don't give me credit. She thinks my boyfriend shouldn't live here. My mama gets up early, makes salmon patties, grits and biscuits, and sausage and gravy for breakfast. She thinks I should do that. She don't want me to work. She thinks my daughter shouldn't go out because we live in an apartment, too dangerous. I try to give her [Jessica] some freedom, let her meet her girlfriends and stuff. My mama don't want her to get out. She'll come up and get her, take her out of school and go to Georgia. And then she'll bring her back. You know my girl, she was having a problem. She was fighting. She don't like it [school].

Yuvette is very critical of her earlier involvement with Jessica's schooling. She tearfully described her shortcomings as a young parent:

This is one thing I regret. I really didn't go to the school much as I should, like the PTA meeting. I'm going to spend more time with them and I'm trying to do that now. And you know I can help Jessica with her work and stuff. [While I was in Even Start] she says, "My mama go to school too." You know she was proud of that.

Yuvette has dreams for her children, that their lives will be different from their mother's. More than anything, she wants them to be free from the need for government assistance, to "be independent." Yuvette pins that hope on education, believing that graduation will mean a good job. In contrast to her own upbringing, Yuvette does not make clear gender differences between her children regarding expectations:

I want Jessica to do good, I don't want her to have no kids [too young]. I want her to get a good job, rent her own apartment, you know, pay out of her pocket instead of someone else doing it for her. And get a car, be independent. I just want them to do for themselves.

Well, I hope he'll love to go to school all the time and that he want to do something with his life. I hope to Lord I won't see him out here drinking and smoking, hanging out on one of the corners. I want him to go to school and go to college or whatever, try to make something. I want him to get a good job and he'll have a good head on his shoulders. You know I don't want him to do bad, I want him to do good.

Summary

A few days after we finished the interviews, Yuvette was fired from her job at Shackney's. Yuvette reported that a customer complained to the manager that she had not refilled the tea glasses quickly enough. Yuvette said that even one customer complaint was enough to be fired over and that she had had another complaint about three or four months before. She was angry at Shackney's, because she felt they treated her unfairly. Yuvette also felt some panic about paying the furniture bills and buying her children's Christmas presents.

Yuvette found a job within a week, bagging groceries part-time at a national food store chain. Yuvette was happy to have this job, noting that again she had found work on the bus route. There were other benefits as well. "They have a union. They can't fire me for little or nothing like Shackney's did." For the first time, I heard Yuvette talk about making her boyfriend move out. "He laughed when I told him I got fired. I told him, I'll have another job before you. And I did. Seems like he just not trying. I think I'm better off without him."

Completing a preparation program to get her GED, raising her children in a positive and loving way, and finding skilled employment that pays above survival wages are important issues for Yuvette. Despite the social isolation and poverty of Yuvette's life, she manages to keep going.

LES WILLARD

By Kathleen P. Bennett deMarrais

Les Willard is a 36-year-old white man who lives in Knoxville, Tennessee. He works as a skilled electrician but is unable to read well enough to pass the written test required for an electrician's license in the city. Les is married and lives with his wife and two children, a 15-year-old stepdaughter and a 9-year-old son. Although he officially graduated from high school and has a diploma, Les is unable to read except for a few words he sees regularly in his work.

Much of Les's daily life is consumed with work in order to make enough money to support his family. In addition to his forty-hour-a-week job as an electrician, he has regular "side jobs" that he works in the evenings and on Saturdays. These jobs all involve electrical and plumbing skills, although he will do almost any work he can get if it will bring in money. He sometimes does yardwork for friends and family. Les keeps two nights a week free for bowling and on Sundays catches up on the work that needs to be done around his own house, such as car repairs or home maintenance.

Les's jobs are tied to his relationships with family and friends. He sees himself as someone who "holds up"—who takes his responsibilities seriously. If someone needs something, he'll make sure it gets done; so although he works to increase the cash flow into the house, he also works to help his friends and relatives. Les seems to have defined his "kin" as those relatives who are worth his time and energy. He has several brothers and sisters he chooses to have little contact with because of difficult circumstances in the past. For those he regards as kin—his own immediate family, a disabled brother, his aging father, his wife's mother, and so forth—he takes full responsibility to make sure they are cared for. He devotes time to these responsibilities.

Les is a tall, wiry man who regularly dresses in jeans and black T-shirts, usually with colorful slogans or pictures. His official work uniform also includes a pair of sturdy leather work boots and a leather "pouch," or belt, in which he carries all the hand tools he needs for jobs. Les's lifestyle, which consistently involves 60-hour (or more) workweeks, and his sense of responsibility for his extended family seem to have taken their toll on his physical well-being. He has been physically ill off and on over the past several years with an undetermined stomach ailment, colds, and viral infections. He does not generally seek medical help because he has no medical coverage.

Les and his family live in a small, one-story frame house in one of the poorest communities in Knoxville. Because the house is situated on a lot that formerly held two houses, the property is larger than others in the neighborhood, which are very small. The other house that had been on the lot burned down before Les and his wife bought the property from his wife's aunt. They paid $8,000 for the house by paying her at the rate of $160 per month for four years. Les believes she sold the house not only because she had a second house in another part of town but also because she did not feel safe in the neighborhood. Les' double lot is partially surrounded by a 4-foot chainlink fence that marks the property line. Les reported that his wife would like to have a new home built on the lot next to their present house:

> My wife was telling me about something she read in the paper or heard in the news about this company. If you make less than $16,000 a year, they would come in and build you a house for about $190 a month. She said "I'm going to do that and I'm going to tear this place down."

On the back portion of the lot is an unpainted, one-story, gray cinder-block building, which Les is improving so that his disabled brother can live there. The two-room building is now being used as a storage facility.

The houses around Les's property are much the same—one- or two-bedroom houses. Some are in better condition than Les's house. Others are in poorer shape and resemble tenant farmer houses. The street in front of these houses is lined with older cars and trucks belonging to local residents.

Les believes that the neighborhood is unsafe because it borders Western Heights, the second-largest housing project in Tennessee. When describing his community, Les mentioned with dismay that he lived "only three houses away from the projects." He is concerned with the safety of the community. Les tells a story of someone attempting to break into his home. He met the intruder at the door with a shotgun and said, "Come on in." Les says he has not recently been bothered by burglars.

The inside of Les's house is quite small for a family of four, with a living room, kitchen, and two bedrooms. Outside the house, the yard is as barren as the rest of the neighborhood. There is no vegetation except for weeds and occasional vines. An assortment of building materials and yard equipment are scattered around the property. Paper and plastic items collect against the fence, where they have been blown by the wind. In contrast, beautiful dark-purple morning glories bloom on the front fence, providing a splash of intense color.

Life and Work

Les was born in Knoxville and raised in a family of six children, but since his father was a worker on dairy farms, much of his early life was spent in different areas of rural East Tennessee. He helped his father with the milking from the time he was about 6 years old: "Ever since I was old enough to stand on a milk crate I been pulling on cows' tits—udders." His mother did not help with the farm work because she was not well: "My mother wasn't able. My mother, she's been in and out of Healthrest [mental institution] since she was 13 years old."

Les enjoyed farm life and speaks with fondness and pride of his work on dairy farms as a young person:

> I could drive any tractor, use any kind of machinery on the farm, milk any cow, hog tie any pig. We had chickens, eggs; had some prize cows we had to take care of—pretty cows—black-and-white Holsteins. The biggest cow gave over 2 gallons of milk.

When asked if he would like to return to this type of work, he replied: "Ain't no money in it . . . no money in it. They pay you like three bucks an hour."

Les was unsure about his parents' school backgrounds. Although he reported that both could read, he was unsure how far they had gone in their own schooling.

Les married his brother's former wife, after their divorce, and cares for the daughter of that marriage as well as the son of the present marriage.

Work History. Les's work history has been affected seriously by his difficulty with reading. When he finished high school, he went out looking for jobs, and when an application form was put in front of him, he left: "I would go into places and have to fill out applications and I couldn't do it. I just had to lay it down and walk out."

He worked at places where application forms were not necessary. He worked at a furniture company as a "delivery boy" and at a manufacturing company as a warehouse laborer loading tabletops onto trucks. "All I did was load them on the truck. The foreman says 'Get this. Put it here. Get this. Put it there.' There wasn't no reading in it."

Les then started working with his uncle, who had an electrical contracting business. He learned to be an electrician working in this job. He is unable to get an electrician's license because he cannot read well enough to pass the test.

Les now works with Dave, his aunt's husband, in Dave's brother Ed's small electrical contracting firm. Ed has the necessary state license to work in the county; he does not have the appropriate license to work in the city. Dave and Les at times work illegally in the city doing electrical work and are fearful of being discovered by the electrical inspector.

Dave and Les work exclusively on jobs for Royal Realty Company, which owns and rents many properties in the greater Knoxville area. Royal pays Ed directly for Les's and Dave's salaries at common laborer's scale plus 50¢

per hour per person and an additional small fee to cover the vehicle used on the job—a total of $6.25 an hour—rather than an electrician's higher wage. Les and Dave keep timecards and give them directly to Ed. Les fills out timecards for himself and for Dave, since Dave can read on about a second-grade level. Royal Realty is subcontracting their labor and does not pay health or any other benefits for these workers, nor does Ed. Dave has some health benefits through his wife's job, but Les does not; his wife is not employed outside the home. Ed has a good relationship with both Les and Dave and freely loans his tools to both men when they do side jobs. The kinship relationships among the three men are essential to this working arrangement.

The reason for the complex organization of his worklife is in part due to the difficulty involved in becoming officially credentialed to do electrical work in the city. When I did some research, I found that the test for an electrician's license is a written one given four times a year. Application is approximately six weeks in advance at a cost of $40. The *National Electrical Code* book, available for $30, can be used to review the material covered on the test. The only oral examination available is in Gainesville, Florida. Following successful completion of the test, the applicant must submit three letters of recommendation from people who are aware of his or her abilities. In addition, the applicant must have had five years of experience in electrical work. There is an additional fee of $350 per year for the commercial license to work in the city.

When I told Les what I had found out about licensure, he shook his head and remarked, "They don't want the little people to have anything."

Educational History. Les's early educational history is unclear. He went to many elementary schools but has little recollection about experiences in them:

> I went to a whole lot of them [elementary schools]—Riceville, let's see, I went to Carter. Carter had an elementary. That's where they sent me to seventh grade to ninth grade.

He does remember doing well throughout the elementary grades: "I was making A's and B's all the way up to the sixth grade." A pivotal incident for Les occurred in sixth grade when one of his teachers would not help him with his math assignments:

> In the sixth grade, this one teacher, I couldn't do the math and she grabbed the math book and started hitting me in the head with it and I said, "Well, I'm not doing this math" and she said, "Fine!" From then on I quit trying. That's the only thing I remember.

The rest of Les's educational history is best told in his own words:

> I quit school down in Riceville [in sixth grade] and moved back to
> Knoxville. My mother and my older brother made me go back to
> school and they took me up Carter High School and I enrolled in
> the seventh grade there. About a week and the following Monday
> they come to me and said I was too old to be in the seventh grade
> . . . I was 16. I come back to Knoxville when I was 16 years old. They
> said I was too old to be in the seventh grade, so they moved me up
> to the ninth grade and that's the only reason. They didn't give me
> no other reason why. . . . I went a half a year and again they come to
> me and told me I was too old. . . . One of my teachers come to me
> and told me I was too old for the ninth grade and I was in voca-
> tional rehab and they moved me up to the tenth grade. . . . So I
> finished that half of the year out in tenth grade. The next year I
> graduated to the eleventh and I done half of that year and again
> they come to me [and moved him to the twelfth grade].
>
> It was going kinda fast seemed like to me.
>
> And when they moved me up to the twelfth grade and I
> finished it out and they told me, says, "We'll mail you your
> diploma." I said, "Can't I go through the line-up?" And she said
> "No. We'll just have to mail you your diploma."
>
> They [his teachers] wouldn't try to help you. . . . Mostly you sit
> at your desk and do nothing. You wouldn't do no work. It wasn't
> learning. It was a story.

Despite this rather grim picture of school, Les did remember one
teacher whom he described as a "good teacher":

> There was one teacher that did [try to help]. Shop teacher. He got in
> there with you and showed you how to do things, but the teachers
> in the class, I only had one class, all she done was sit up and read a
> book.

Les seems to learn best when someone demonstrates for him rather
than explains it without a demonstration. Traditional models of schooling
in which teachers lecture and give assignments to students obviously did
not work with Les.

> You show me one time and you won't have to show me nothing
> else. . . . Anything I start, even though I don't know how to do it or
> can't read it . . . it *will* be done!

Everyday Literacy and Technology

Les can read some words and phrases. He says he can "relate to" (recognize) some words but has difficulty with long words. "I don't feel comfortable with none of it [reading]. It's kind of hard to do—hard to read. I just don't feel comfortable with none of it."

Although he reported reading a variety of materials on the checklist of everyday texts we used for this project, he seems to rely heavily on any pictures and diagrams to comprehend the printed material.

One of the hobbies Les has had since he was a child is building model cars. He described the process he uses:

> I put model cars together, but I never once look at the words. . . . I look at the picture, at the pieces and from there it goes together. . . . I put model cars together my whole life not by reading the instructions . . . by looking at the picture. . . . This is Latin to me [points to paper full of written text], but show me a picture and I can do it.

In addition to building models, he also enjoys bowling. He has been in a Thursday-night league with his wife and daughter for five years. It's a family outing that nothing seems to interfere with—even work. When asked about scorekeeping in bowling, he explained that he can add up the points for individual games, but since he can't divide, he relies on the league's secretary to do the averages. He recently joined a men's Monday-night league. He religiously keeps Monday and Thursday evenings free so he can bowl.

Les is not a total nonreader; he does enjoy cartoons and comic books. He reads Superman, Batman, Spiderman, Flash Gordon: "Hey, I read the funnies, comic books . . . I read the words in them."

He reports that he uses the phone book to look up numbers of businesses when he needs to. When asked if he can find what he needs in phone books, he replied: "Not really. I can, but it takes me a while." All the other phone numbers he needs to know—the three numbers for his boss and family members—he remembers. Les vividly described his experience in taking a written driver's license test. I was surprised that he took a written rather than an oral test, so he described the procedure he used to complete the task:

> You know it's got . . . you got a dot here . . . dot here . . . dot here . . . I went down through, I put dot, dot here, dot dot there [random filling in of circles]. . . . Yeah, that's how [I passed it]. I didn't know what I was putting down. I filled in the circles and I hand the paper

to her and she said come out here—we'll take your driver's test. She wrote me out this paper . . . said your license will be in the mail.

Les uses several means of compensation to make up for his difficulty with reading. He makes a point of memorizing what he needs to be able to write or remember later—such as the names and addresses of places he works for his timecard or directions that he will need in order to find a location:

I put it back here in the back of my mind and just keep it there. When I got to remember, then it comes forward. You got one handicap, you gotta fall back on something else. This is what I got to fall back on [memory].

At home, most of the reading is done by Les's wife. She takes care of the mail, bills, letters from school, and so forth. She reads to him when necessary—she reads instructions for appliances (such as the microwave) if necessary and tells Les what it says. She also fills out application forms for him. For example, she recently filled out a sanction card for him to join a bowling league. Les explained that it used to embarrass him that he could not read, and he would be ashamed to ask for help. Now he is able to ask someone to read for him without feeling embarrassed. "My daughter helps me a lot; my wife helps me a lot."

Although Les regularly watches television, he does not watch the news or listen to it on the radio. The family does not get any newspapers or magazines. When asked about how he keeps up with local or national events, he replied: "I don't listen to the news . . . I don't care. Long as it don't bother me, I don't care." Les has never voted. In addition to his lack of interest in current events, he explained why he had never registered to vote:

I don't vote. . . . Never been registered. The only reason I don't register is on account they can call you up for jury duty . . . I don't want that . . . I don't want to. I can't put people behind bars. I can't hurt people even though they hurt people; even though I did put one person behind bars, my sister, but she needed it—19-month-old-baby, 50% of its body scalded to death. . . . She's still in prison—99 years—and one day.

Family Finances. Les is able to perform basic mathematical computations but relies on his wife to handle the finances of the household. In describing his numeracy skills, he explains: "I can do some math. Division I can't do. Some multiplication I can do. I can do adding." Les and his wife deal primarily with cash rather than checks. Les explained that they used to have a checking account, but his wife, who wrote the checks, was unable to handle the account:

> Don't have one [bank account] . . . had one . . . the wife wrote the checks and she writes this number down on here and thinks that there's money in here [pointing to imaginary checkbook] and she writes another check. . . . Yeah, I said, "Baby, give me them checks, honey." She got to bouncing here and bouncing there. She couldn't manage that checking account . . . so I said, "The checks go, baby." From then on she don't put no more money in that bank. We still got the account [checking account].

It is still Les's wife who takes care of cashing his check and paying the bills. Les has very little to do with the daily finances of the household. He explained their system: "I sign it [his paycheck], put it in the envelope, put it on the bookcase, my wife comes in and picks it up, she takes it to the bank, cashes it . . . and spends the money."

Les's bills include the "light bill" and the "cable bill (TV)." He has no credit cards, and his house is paid for. He explained that he no longer has a phone in part because his daughter ran up the bill by making three-party calls. He also reported that sometimes when he is unable to pay his light bill, he borrows the money from his boss, Ed, who advances him the money and then takes it out of his next paychecks a bit at a time until it is paid.

In addition to using cash as a financial base, Les, his family, and friends use an extensive system of barter for labor, goods, and services. Recently he needed money to buy a new (used) motor for his truck, so Dave bought the engine for him. In return, he worked off the debt on Saturdays at the same hourly rate he would have made during the week at his electrician's job. He has traded his electrical services with other men for work they could do for him.

Les's wife has the responsibility for all the shopping, both for food and for clothes. This seems to go along with the way they have divided up the household responsibilities. He laughed when he told me that "she works inside and I work outside."

His wife sometimes shops for supplies he needs for his repair work as well. He sent her out one Saturday to get motor mounts so that he could finish putting an engine into his car on Sunday. He seems to be too busy working (60+ hours per week) to do any of the shopping or work around the house. When asked about what he does when he does go to a store for something, Les explained that he didn't need to read anything: "Well, I always know what I'm going for."

Les has a 1971 Chevy truck he uses for work. He is always working on it to keep it in running order. Since he has lived in Knoxville for approximately 20 years, he knows the community well and tends to use landmarks rather than street signs in finding locations. For example, in order to find our house, he remembered to turn left at Westwood instead of going straight, as he would to his boss's house, then go up the hill, turn left on the third street up, and go up the hill and around the bend. "When I'm on a job," he told me,

> I try to write the address down and the street name before I leave the job, and if I don't I'll have to ask somebody how to spell it 'cause I wouldn't know how.

Literacy on the Job. Les has little need to read on the job:

> In my line of work I don't have to read nothing. All I do is go to a job, put my nail pouch on, put my electrical pouch on and screw wires, take wires apart, pull wires. I write it [a timecard at work]. One timecard and that goes for both of us. I can relate to [recognize] some words—"dining room." I've seen that. I don't know how to spell it, but I've seen that. "Kitchen." I've seen that. And there's a bunch of words I've seen but don't know how to spell. I can relate to them—"fuse" ain't no problem. I know what "fuse" is—I can see the word and know what it is because I've been told what it is. "Circuit" I've seen. "Breaker" I've seen. Sometimes I would have to try to read. I can read some of it, but the two-dollar words I can't pronounce.

Despite his extensive knowledge of and comfort with electricity, Les is uncomfortable with computer technology. He has tried to use the automatic teller machine at the bank but was unsuccessful: "I can't get them things to work [laughter]. I push my code in it. Spits my card back out." He and his son both played Nintendo games until their machine and one of the games was stolen by a neighborhood child:

> I bought this game [Nintendo] for myself and he let this little boy borrow it and this little boy ain't brought it back yet. . . . All you gotta do is hook it to your TV and plug it in. It's got another load thing like a charger box. All you gotta do is plug that in the wall and hook the other side to your antenna.

In a discussion about computers, Les reported that someone gave him a computer to hook up to the TV as its monitor, but he has not yet done anything with it. He seems particularly hesitant when it comes to working with computers. He asked to bring the computer over for me to look at for him. He said that he was unable to work on newer cars where computer technology is involved. All the vehicles he deals with are older.

When he was working on the electrical outlets that would service my computer, he was fearful of doing anything to damage the machine. He had to be reassured that the computer was disconnected and could not be harmed. He made a point to put my computer on a separate electrical circuit to make sure nothing else would interfere with it. He explained: "I don't know anything about computers. I know electrical work, but I don't know computers."

Family Literacy. Les's wife graduated from eighth grade and is able to read. She does not read to their children but does do the reading necessary for day-to-day matters, such as bills, school reports, and so forth. Although the family does not have many books or subscribe to magazines or newspapers, there is a clear message to the children that education is to be valued.

From the time they were old enough for school, Les registered the children using his wife's mother's address in order for them to go to what Les considered a better school. The neighborhood school, like the projects, is predominantly African American. Les explained that because this school is "98% black," he did not want his children to attend; he did not think they would be able to get a good education at the school. Apparently other white families in the neighborhood have used the same practice to put their children in schools across town.

Since the school the children go to is outside the local neighborhood, Les's wife keeps her mother's car to drive the children to school everyday. Les and his wife want their children to be better educated and have more opportunities than they had and have taken deliberate and time-consuming steps to try to secure good schooling for them. Les feels that his children are getting a better education than he did. Their daughter, aged 15, makes A's and B's in her high school classes, with the exception of a recent C in geography. Les told me she wants to go to college to be a computer expert.

Their son, Little Les, is in fourth grade. Although he does not perceive himself to be a good reader because of his placement in a Chapter 1 remedial reading program, Little Les also has aspirations to go to college. He said, "I'm gonna try to go to college, no matter what!"

Les believes in pushing children and encourages his son's teachers to control him and make him work in class:

And I better not be hearing nothing this year. I want him to have a better schooling than I had. I was not pushed, encouraged to go to school. I want him to have better than I did. Him and my daughter both.

I Hold Up: Assuming Responsibility for Kin

Les is the only one of his family who has not been in prison. He has little use for his brothers and sisters except for his younger brother, who is disabled. He explains that he married his brother's wife after they had divorced and that his daughter is really his stepdaughter:

He [his brother] ain't got no responsibility to him. I've had her ever since she was 2 years old. I hold up. I don't try to run away from nothing.

His love for his daughter is clear when he describes her desire to be adopted:

There's one other thing she's wanting me to do. Her name is Willard, but it's not my name. She wanting me to adopt her. She don't feel I love her; she's always throwing that up at me. She's wanting me to adopt her. I said, "You'll always be mine, you got my name, what else you want?" She said, "I want it on paper."

Les explains his success in keeping out of trouble:

I think I was adopted [laughter] . . . I don't know. I don't like to go places. I don't like to go to bars. I don't like to smoke dope. I don't like to drink. I like to work. I don't like to be around a crowd of people, and I don't like to go to restaurants.

Les seems to take pride in family responsibilities and taking care of his "kin." In addition to caring for his immediate family, he serves as the legal guardian for his disabled brother. He moved his father from Loudon to Knoxville so he could help him get Social Security benefits and take better care of him. He and his wife regularly share childcare responsibilities when her brother's family come for frequent weekend visits. He brought the "cousins" over with Little Les on two Saturdays while he worked on our electrical system. He regularly does household repairs and yardwork for relatives who need help.

Summary

Despite the difficulties of poverty and limited literacy Les has to face in life, he definitely "holds up." He and his wife have managed to build a solid marriage as well as a supportive environment for their children and extended family. They have tried to secure a good education for their children. Les is dissatisfied with his current worklife and would like to "get out of this rat race." He would like to "better" himself by learning to read in order to become a licensed electrician.

LISA BOGAN

By Faye L. Hicks-Townes

Lisa is a 37-year-old African American woman. She was born and educated in the rural community of Bay Springs, Mississippi, and lived there until she came to Knoxville with her first husband in 1973. Separated now from her second husband, Lisa is struggling to overcome the effects of an abusive second marriage and provide for her two children with a job as a sales clerk in a department store. Although she has a high school diploma, her reading is at the fifth- or sixth-grade level.

It seems that every facet of Lisa's life is filtered through her strong belief in God. Take, for instance, her reaction to the Gulf War:

> And why does this person want to be, you know, ruler and take
> over and do, treat people the way he want to? But that's been going
> on ever since the Biblical days and I just still wonder why do people
> want to have power over another person? God give us all freedom
> to do as we please but in a peaceful, loving way, not evil. But a lot
> of us have this evil force going within us and want to rule every-
> thing and everybody. And you can't do that, not as long as God
> have a say in it.

Lisa has had some hard times in her life but has a strong faith in her God-given abilities to make life better for herself and her children. Lisa's hope and determination for a better life come from her Christian beliefs:

> But I guess God gave me that there because I've seen people
> whereas I have made less money and another person has made a lot
> of money and I seem to make it better with what little money I have
> than a person that makes a whole lot of money. And I'm like, how

could they let theirself go like that making all of this money and I
got this little amount o' money coming in and everything seems to
be so organized. And to me that's common sense of managing
things better than that person with a whole lot of money throwing it
away. Wisdom or something.

Lisa lives in a large, two-story white house that has been renovated
into apartments in the heart of the Five Points area of East Knoxville. Five
Points is an urban area that has recently been targeted for rehabilitation.
Once a thriving business center, Five Points is most recently known for the
number of murders, police raids, and drug deals that occur over any given
weekend. The largest business in the area was a grocery store that closed
several years ago. The building stands empty with boarded windows, and
the parking lot is a haven for drug and alcohol users. The population of
the neighborhood is predominantly poor and African American.

The yard is surrounded by a chainlink fence and abuts an alley. Lisa
keeps the backyard gate padlocked because her downstairs neighbors have
many visitors who like to enter from the alley to come and have a drink.

Lisa's apartment, with its three bedrooms, two full baths, an eat-in
kitchen, and a small living room, was clean, organized, and nicely furnished. Lisa and I settled in the living room for our talks. There were a sofa,
two armchairs, a commode table and lamp, an endtable and lamp, a bookcase with pictures and books (school yearbooks, a Bible storybook, a Jag-
uar automotive book), and, in the center of the room, a 17-inch color TV
and stereo system on an entertainment stand.

Lisa has lived in this apartment for less than a year. Before moving
here, she had lived in her own three-bedroom home in a residential section of East Knoxville. Lisa and her first husband purchased the house. After
they were divorced, Lisa, her children, and second husband lived there.
The second husband's alcoholism and the ensuing financial problems
forced Lisa to sell the house and move to an apartment. Lisa's former neighborhood was quite different, in appearance and atmosphere, from where
she lives now:

It was a nice little neighborhood. The children, my children could
play in the neighborhood. And the neighbors are all nice that live
there. . . . And if anything come up we would see after each other's
children in the neighborhood.

Since Lisa has been in the Five Points area, her associations with her
present neighbors are limited to simple courtesies and intercessory prayers.

Life and Work

Lisa grew up in rural Mississippi, the fourth of seven children. Her father had practically no formal schooling and could not read or write. Lisa's mother taught him to write his name after their marriage:

> My dad he never went to school. He went to school from maybe first grade or something. And what he learned was from his family, I guess, and that was math. And he met my mother, and she taught him how to spell his name. But other than that, Daddy didn't know much of anything. So he couldn't help me. But my dad, about him not going to school, he just said he didn't see no sense in no one going to school. He had his own business of piling pulpwood in his big truck and all, and he was doing pretty good at that.

Lisa's mother finished the eighth grade and was able to read and handle many household chores, such as electrical work and plumbing:

> And Mom just worked in the home, in the field, and in white people's home. And she kept the house up. Like if the porch needed repairing, my mom she paid for it to be fixed. She bought the lumber and everything from someone. And if the electricity or something had happened in the house, she would fix that herself. Mom was very handy around the house to do things and we had outdoor facilities and Mom wanted indoor facilities and Dad didn't believe in indoor facilities 'cause he had been used to outdoor all his life and he just didn't believe in having a bathroom in the house. And so Momma was determined to have this bathroom, so she worked and she had a lot of friends, too, and the white people that she worked for in the town, the town we lived in, I don't know, they was just good friends to us, too. So Mom she took care of things around the house all right, so she eventually got her bathroom. . . .
>
> But Mom read a lot, like she finished the twelfth grade. And she was left-handed. She could write and do things very quickly. And if my mom would have finished high school and college, I don't know where my mom would be today. She was real smart.
>
> My mom, she worked a lot. It was six girls and one boy. And she took out as much time as she could with us. And she asked the other kids to help the others that was slow or whatever, anything around the house, and we farmed a lot. So it wasn't that much attention on someone helping me study.

Only two of the children attended college, and neither of the two earned a degree. Lisa's first husband shared her background. He was a poor reader from rural Mississippi:

> . . . about like I was on reading because he come from a small town, Hazelrig, Mississippi. And I guess he, I don't know what his background was on it, or anyone ever helping him or what was with him. But he's also trying to better hisself in reading and spelling and what have you.

Lisa's first marriage ended because she felt neglected by her husband:

> What got it was, my husband, my first husband and being young, I felt like he wasn't paying me too much attention because he was always out with the boys on his spare time and left me home with the baby. And I would always have things prepared for him, oh gosh, I guess I was like a little puppy dog, ready when he come home just at the door there, so happy to see him. And I got the bath water ran. I got your plate fixed with food and everything, we made plans to go to a movie or something, a picnic or what have you, just did all these things together and then it slacked off and he started neglecting me I felt. But it just that he needed the time to himself to breathe. I guess I was smothering him with all this love and attention that I wanted to give him. And so I just got with some girlfriends and I start going out, having a good time and everything and then he wanted the attention and I just like I don't have time for you. . . . And it just went downhill all the way.

Lisa has two children from her first marriage, aged 19 and 15. Lisa is pleased with the job she has done raising her children and has high hopes for their future:

> And my children, I feel like they're going do real good because there're so many children on drugs and they abuse their parents, and my children respects me so far and not on drugs or anything and real mannerable children. And I think I have done a terrific job there, a terrific job. Sometimes I feel like well maybe my children will be something else in the world to contribute to the world, whereas I neglected my life to be there every second, every minute, every hour for them, 'cause at school they could reach mom at home if something come up. I took them to wherever they needed to go to different things. And whereas some parents are working

every day neglecting the children, they end up going astray, on drugs or whatever, and get in with the wrong group. But I had that problem with my daughter, but I was there to work with my daughter on that betrayal my daughter felt.

Lisa attributes the failure of her second marriage to her husband's alcoholism:

The drinking got pretty heavy 'cause he would drink sociable, I noticed that when we first met but never every day, and then it got to the place where it was all day. And he just kept things to himself no matter how much I talked to him or questioned him about things, he just wouldn't talk to me. OK, I just start saying to myself and getting more and more into the church with my children, and their school activities and ignored him. Well that's when he really got angry with me 'cause I wouldn't talk back to him on some things that he would talk to me about. . . . But it just got to the place where he would curse, I'd end up cursing, then I'd just say well that's no good 'cause God wouldn't have me to do this, so I shut up with that. And I couldn't go anywhere. It got to the place where I couldn't talk on the phone, "You're talking to some man, you're going out to meet some man," but he wouldn't say it in a nice way, he was always saying vulgar, hellacious ways and the children in all the midst of this. Let's see about three years and the last year it got so bad, so I had to call it quits and go our separate ways. I'm still married to him but I'm thinking of going through with my divorce in the month of March hopefully, if my financial status is a little bit better. 'Cause I know I'm going to have to pay for it.

Work. Lisa has held a wide variety of jobs. Her first "real" job after she finished high school was in a factory that produced thermostats for electric blankets and other things. She worked at the plant for about half a year until illness in her first pregnancy. Her next work experience was in Knoxville at a factory that produced fish hooks and bait, but after three weeks she quit this job because the cost of childcare and transportation took most of her salary. She worked at Levi Strauss in Knoxville, sewing jeans, but quit after three weeks because she believed her babysitter wasn't taking good enough care of her daughter. She quit her next job at a deli when she found there were errors on her check every payday.

After Lisa's second marriage, she got a job working in the cafeteria of a city elementary school. Lisa mentioned having worked in church-run daycare centers and selling Avon. She stopped selling Avon because she had transportation problems. Lisa described working for Kelly, a temporary service company that sent her to warehouses to work with clothes. Presently Lisa works for Best's, an upscale department store at one of the local malls.

Educational History. Lisa completed high school in rural Mississippi but says she stopped learning after the sixth grade:

> OK, I wasn't good in math at all. I guess when I got, sixth grade, that was it. I don't understand math anymore. My reading, I'm in sixth grade, spelling sixth grade. It was like I just couldn't learn anymore, when I reached that sixth grade level. But I did enough to make the grade. I studied. I understood some things, but some things I just didn't understand as I grew older in high school. So I guess I just give up on it myself.

Although Lisa's experiences in school were frustrating for the most part, she has fond memories of her teachers. She never blames them for her reading problems:

> I was kind of slow in school, but my third-grade teacher she pushed me to do things and my second-grade teacher, and I did good in a play, couple of plays that they pushed me at, but I was always very scared, nervous and didn't have faith in myself to do things.
>   Miss King, my eleventh-grade teacher, she said I could do better than what I was doing. So she was a special teacher. They all, all of the teachers that we had back in those days was real good teachers. They pushed a lot of kids, but it was so many of us in the class until they didn't have time to take out with the slower kids. They took out as much time as they could with us, but it was just pressing to them to go on and teach, you know, kids that could keep up and everything.

Lisa was far less understanding of her family's inability to take the time to help her with her learning problems:

> So it wasn't that much attention on someone helping me study. It just seemed like it came natural for the other kids in my home. It was just difficult for me. But everyone had their own thing, doing it, and working and what have you, 'til I just felt neglected. I said no one loved me. I never told my dad he didn't love me, but I always

told my mom she didn't love me, didn't care for me. I felt like I was the black sheep of the family.

Lisa does have one very fond memory of a learning experience: Her father taught her to tell time when she was in the eighth grade:

I was eighth grade until I learned how to tell time. And he taught me how to tell time. And I remember in school, in elementary, the teachers were helping us to tell time but I just couldn't get it. And I needed that special attention there that I didn't get and I just went on and forgot about it. And my boyfriend bought me a watch for Christmas when I was eighth grade and that's when my dad, I was asking my dad about the time a lot and he just took time out and took time with me and just showed me how to tell time. And, uh, that was amazing to me. I was just so proud of myself and my dad for teaching me that.

Lisa remembers the anger, frustration, and embarrassment that were a result of her poor reading skills:

There was some books that I looked at when I started to read. I enjoyed reading them. But when the words become hard for me, to pronounce the words, I get angry because I didn't know the words and I try to get by with "what's this word here?" They would tell me so many times on words that I didn't know until they would get frustrated with me on it. And I would get so depressed I would just put the book down. . . . I knew I was slow and sometime I was too embarrassed to admit that I was slow in some things.

Lisa has tried to improve her reading skills by enrolling in an adult basic education program that prepares adults for the GED. Although Lisa graduated from high school, she thought the program would help her become a better reader. She is currently out of the program but hopes to go back:

We had teachers and there was a group of people that come in and, uh, need their GEDs. And I was, I guess about the smartest person in the class there, because I knew how to read better than they would. And the teacher would take up more time with the ones that was slow this time than myself. But she also said if we had any problems to come to her.

OK, we started on our summer vacation and some of the parents and they're saying it's hard to come back to school once you stop, especially people, parents with children. And that's what happened to me. I didn't go back, but I'm still trying to get back into going. 'Cause I feel like I can get the pronunciation of words if I can just get someone to take out a lot of time with me, 'cause it's like they said if they just have to get one person to tutor you until you get that, they'll do that, 'cause they're determined to help you learn to read better if you don't know how at all.

Everyday Literacy and Technology

Lisa seems to handle her encounters with everyday literacy quite well. She is able to follow directions especially well if they are illustrated:

> I do good in reading directions on things. Even when I would buy things for Christmas and had to put things together, I could read the directions and put it together. And somehow I just look at it, uh, the way they have it drawn out and put it together. But with products and what have you, things, I do good in reading on that. And whatever it is I don't know, I go and look it up in the dictionary and I know the meaning of it.

Lisa, who is able to use maps and road signs effectively, attributes this ability to her gift of common sense:

> OK, it's like in a direction magnet to one city to the next, I feel like that's, once you get your little map or direction, it's common sense to go straight there to this place that you've never been before. I end up having to sell my house and trying to find a real nice place to live, I got this mapbook of Knoxville. And I got the newspaper, other clippings from someplace else that might have had some places for rent and the street that it was on. I got my little book, mapbook, and found out where the street was and went straight to it. So I just do good in reading maps and everything.

Lisa is very serious about her responsibilities as a voter. She doesn't let her poor reading skills keep her from being informed. She relies on the media, her church, and friends to keep her informed on issues and candidates:

> I registered to vote, and I try to get there every chance I can to vote. Uh, if I'm not, you know, keeping up with the person on TV, talking with someone about the candidate being a pretty good person to

vote for, it's like, I don't know who to vote for, you know. So I kinda go along with the paperwork from church, or a neighbor or a friend that is into it more so than myself, and they give me some advice on it and vote for that person.

Lisa also depends on the media, her church, and friends to learn about national issues:

Sometimes I pay attention to my phone bill. They have a thing that come in to your telephone bill that tells you things that happening. And television and our church and different churches when I visit churches, too. I find out about local events and what have you. Radio stations, gospel stations tell me about events or other stations that I may listen to. And friends, they tell me about some of the events that's going on.

Lisa is a good organizer. She lives on her salary from a part-time job, child support from her first husband, Social Security disability from her second husband, and a rent subsidy from Knoxville Community Development Corporation (KCDC). Her effective organizational skills help Lisa run her household efficiently:

I understand everything in the grocery store that I go into at. And it takes me forever to be in that store. I check the prices, the name brand, the non–name brand, what's a better buy. I may buy some off brands that's a little cheaper than the main product and try it. If it's OK, I'll keep buying that product. But if it have a funny taste to it or the detergent may not last and wash the clothes as clean as another product, I do not buy that product again. But I make my budget, I have a budget, I go into the store, and I deal with that budget that I have. And sometime I come out under my budget and that way it saves me money and I can pay a bill with it, you know. So I do pretty good in budgeting myself in stores and around the house, you know, paying bills and what have you, real good. My daughter say I can go to the store with 50¢ and bring back fish and toilet paper and butter and just everything for 50¢.

Lisa does not buy a lot of reading material now because she can't afford it. She does, however, take advantage of the public library:

So we end up going to the library where we got library cards. Oh, gosh, we went last month a great deal. We haven't gone this month.

But last month and month before last, we go pretty often, especially if the kids have school assignments and they need to use an encyclopedia or something, do some kind of research from school, we go to the library. And I may check out some books. I like animals and insects, what have you, and I may check out some books like that and read them here at home. I always try to get them back on time, being an orderly person.

Lisa makes a special effort to keep up with Sunday School lessons. Her poor reading ability may be an obstacle, but it is not one that can't be overcome:

> OK, if I participate in Sunday School, I do pretty good in that if I have my Sunday School book to bring home to read before we go in Sunday School class that Sunday morning. And I look up a lot of things in the dictionary and find the definition of it, and when questions are asked in the Sunday School then I can do pretty good in that. But if I do not have the Sunday School book, I participate a little because I can't answer the question. I just kinda learn from what's being said and taught, and reading over the Bible, and someone explaining that verse in the Bible, learning that way. And a lot of things that have been said in the Sunday School, uh, and lessons that we've gone over, I had when I was a child at home. And all the things that are being said I already know them. And there are some things that come to me that are new to me. . . . Or just studying, reading my Bible studying, I'll look things up.

Lisa is comfortable with technology in the home, but she does not come into contact with much technology now because she lost some things when she and her second husband separated. Others were lost when her home was burglarized:

> I've had all of this. I've had VCR, microwave, Atari games that my son had, and electric organs and microwaves, remote controls for the VCR and the television. Someone broke into my house and stole all of these things but the TV, so I have never just been interested in buying anything else because I feel like if I buy it someone will take it, and right now I just don't have the money to really get into buying these products and keeping up with them.

When I asked Lisa if she felt comfortable using these examples of modern technology, she immediately responded,

Oh, yes. I did real good with all of it. I'm a person that more so stay to myself to learning something. If I can't, I need someone to show me how to do this. And once they show me how and I can deal with it, but if I feel like I can do it on my own, I just need to get in a room quiet to myself and I can work with it.

Literacy and Technology at Work. Presently Lisa works at an upscale department store in a large mall. Her sales job involves only a minimal amount of reading and writing and poses little problem for her:

Yes, it's a little reading in that and writing. Because, OK, how I get back through that, if the customer want to hold something, a item, uh, I have to put their telephone number, their name, and address. OK, they tell me these things. And I do good on it. If I don't know how to spell their name, I just ask them to spell that for me. And they do. So I get by with that. And that's about it at work with Best's. And reading different things, I do good on the product that's in the store have a name brand they're looking for, I have learned that, I do good in that.

Technology is more of a problem. Preferring to work with the customers and clothes, she avoids using the computerized cash register for two reasons:

Well, that's where I do not have confidence in myself to work with that cash register. I have seen everyone say it's so simple and easy which it do seem very simple and easy. Uh, but I still thinking I may make a mistake on it. And I'll be responsible for it. And I just don't want that responsibility of something going wrong. But they say you can't go wrong. The computer tells you when it's wrong but. . . . So I'm still kinda holding off on the cash register. Eventually I might get brave enough to work with it and do good at it. But right now I'm just kinda staying away from the cash register because the fear of messing up.

Everyone wants me to, that works on the floor, want me to work on the cash register 'cause I'm good with the customers. And plus it would help out more if I deal with the cash register. But a lot of lady that work the dressing rooms and the floor, uh, we don't care to work with the cash register, to deal with it. We have had some people that will steal some kind of way with it and I, they fired some girls that done this and I just rather not work with the cash register.

Family Literacy. For her two children, Lisa has been an involved and concerned parent. Her daughter Toni is 19 and her son Benny is 15. Lisa read to them when they were young and had them read to her:

> Well, we have a gathering to the place where, when my children were small I would get the books out, now I could help them with things, their elementary books, and little storybooks that I would buy them in the store and read to them and they would go to school. I would let them read to me. And they did good. And I did good in helping them with that.
>
> But as they got older in high school and the work became that hard for me again, then I start asking help from the schoolteachers in the program they have and they've helped my kids at reading. I went to PTA meetings, if anything went wrong with my child or my child had problems here at home with their studies and I couldn't help them, I got them help at school, their teacher, I talked to their teacher, their guidance teacher, and I helped my children. And I just thank God that that was there for them as it wasn't there for me in my hometown. And I just felt comfortable going to the teachers telling them you know my problem here at home that I couldn't help my child. So can't you all help them? And I helped them, you know, to my best of knowledge that I could at home. That's what I did. I even had friends to help my children. OK, and after I remarried, their stepdad helped them a great deal 'cause he was real smart.

Toni has finished high school and is enrolled at a local community college. In Toni's attempt at higher education, however, she met some problems this past fall semester:

> But my daughter, she's 19, graduated from school and everything, goes to Pellissippi State, she's doing real good in reading and spelling. My daughter she's goes to Pellissippi, but it hurt my heart that she failed her English and math. She's not good in math. So the grant will not pay, you know, for your schooling if you fail. So now she's gonna have to work to pay for that and make up that grade. And then the grant will continue after she makes that on her own.

Benny, Lisa's 15-year-old son, does well in school in spite of being a slow reader:

> And [Benny] he's a little slow in his spelling stuff and reading, but he's a whiz in math. I mean 'cause he's always been up on time, up

early, get off to school ever since he was kindergarten. And he's smart at a lot of things, electronics, and he work with that real good. And I think that calls for math, too. But he's good in his math. But he's doing good in school. He always passed, made A's and B's and he made a D this past, no last week, and he was just like destroyed by making a D because he never made a D in school. So maybe it'll make him strive more to do better, study harder. 'Cause as I, you get high school it get kinda hard.

Summary

Lisa's journeys in life have taken her from a rural Mississippi community to one of the more violent urban neighborhoods in Knoxville. Despite limited literacy skills, a difficult marital history, and struggles to find employment that fits with her life as a single mother of two children, Lisa has managed to construct a rich life for herself. She hopes both her children will be able to finish college:

I have encouraged my daughter to better herself to the utmost, much better than her mom, and my son because if you ever marry a young lady you will be provider of that family, and that means you've gotta earn more than minimum wage.

Lisa is heavily involved in church activities, finding faith in God one of the central forces in her life.

MARÍA REYES

By Loida Velazquez

María Reyes is a 41-year-old migrant worker of Mexican origin, born in Mercedes, Texas, a small town near the border with Mexico. For the last 27 years she has traveled along the eastern migrant stream looking for a better life for herself and her five children. María left school before completing sixth grade, but her English reading skills test at the third-grade level. Her preferred language is Spanish, although she is not literate in Spanish. María chose to conduct the interviews in Spanish because it is the language she uses in daily communication with her children, friends, and fellow migrant workers. She uses a form of Spanish full of anglicisms. For example, she says "apa" for *papa* (father), "nohotros" for *nosotros* (us), "writiear" for *escribir* (to write), "piscar" for *recoger* (to pick). At the time of the interview, María was a resident of Valley View, a small town in North Carolina with a growing migrant community, and was enrolled in a high school equivalency program (HEP) for migrant workers.

> Yo trabajé en los campos en Ohio cuando me casé con mi esposo. He piscado tomates y cotton en Arizona. En California trabajamos en un packing house, en Chicago trabajé en un plastic plant, en Oklahoma trabajé en un dry cleaners, en Florida he piscado oranges. He vivido en Dallas, en Abilene, en Fort Worth. Este es el estado que me gusta más y este pueblo. Yo nunca he vivido en un sitio que me guste más. Me gustaría quedarme aquí.

> [I worked the fields in Ohio when I first got married with my husband. I have picked tomatoes and cotton in Arizona. In California we worked in a packing house, in Chicago I worked in a plastic plant, in Oklahoma I worked in a dry cleaners, in Florida I picked oranges. I have lived in Dallas, in Abilene, in Fort Worth. This is the state I like the most and this town. I have never lived in a place I liked more. I would like to stay here.]

María is less than 5 feet tall. She has worked hard all her life, and it shows. Life as a migrant means getting up before sunrise and working under the broiling sun until you are too exhausted to continue. You have to stoop and crawl to pick the crop, eat a fast lunch from a truck parked in the middle of the field, live in cramped and substandard housing, and move often to find work. For the last five years María has worked the fields in Florida during the winter and picked apples in North Carolina during the fall.

My first contact with this family came through María's son, Tito, a HEP graduate I interviewed for my research on dropouts and the culture of migrancy. At a certain point during that interview, Tito said: "My father is not like my mother; he even went to college for two years." He did not seem ashamed by his mother's limited literacy skills—he was just stating a fact. He later sounded proud when he told me he was the only child in his family who had finished high school requirements (by passing the GED test) and that this had motivated his mother to enroll in HEP.

The Migrant Community

The Trailer Park. "Trailer parks like these are all over town. They appear overnight and become a sore," said Jorge, the HEP coordinator who introduced me to María. He was driving me to her house because he was afraid I would never find it. The appointment for the interview had been set for

his classroom, but María had called that morning to say she had no transportation. She invited me to come to her house instead.

María's trailer looked recently painted in bright yellow and brown.
An old-looking blue VW van was parked by the porch. Behind the van was
a large car with the front two doors opened. We parked by the van and
approached the car parked behind it. Antonio, one of María's three sons,
greeted us. Jorge asked about the car, and Antonio explained that he had
taken the seats out to change the car's carpet. A young boy opened the trailer
door and stood there watching until María came to the door and invited
us in. Since Jorge had to return to the community college, I went inside with
María and her grandson.

The trailer looked small from the outside, but it seemed larger once
we went in. Although Antonio was working outside and had some tools
and two beer cans by the car, the porch was clean and tidy. María apolo-
gized for "the mess," but I did not see any. The room we entered consisted
of a narrow area that seemed to serve as living room, dining room, and
kitchen. It looked lived-in but not messy. A small sofa lined one side of the
living room area, with a two-shelved bookcase with a TV and a VCR on the
opposite side. María got a rag and cleaned a small round table that served
as the dining area. We sat at that table across from the kitchen.

María lives in the trailer with two of her sons and her youngest daughter. The oldest daughter and her two children live somewhere else in the
same town. Her oldest son lives with his father in Texas. María takes care
of the two grandchildren while the daughter is at work.

Valley View, North Carolina. Valley View, along with most of Western
North Carolina, was originally the land of the Cherokee. The town traces
its beginnings to 1787, when the first white settlers arrived in the area. The
land is very fertile, and the town is surrounded by apple groves and produce farms. The town government of Valley View, which is nestled against
the Smoky Mountains and surrounded by numerous lakes, is very interested in attracting tourists, but farming is still the main source of income
for its residents. A recent survey by the Department of Labor reported 350
apple and 250 vegetable growers in the four counties surrounding Valley
View. These growers depend on the availability of farmworkers to harvest
their produce.

Main Street is Valley View's business and commercial area. The street
was recently renovated by adding a brick sidewalk and planting trees along
both sides. Antique and curio stores attract vacationers visiting the Smoky
Mountains and give life to the town. North of Main Street is the town's
residential area. Most of the houses are surrounded by tall trees and well-
cared-for gardens. South of Main Street are two large car dealerships. To

the south of the car dealerships are several trailer parks. Some of the farmers provide housing for the migrant workers within the farms, but most, like María, live in the trailer areas.

Migrants in the United States. For the purpose of this profile, migrant workers are defined as those persons who are agricultural laborers and who travel within the geographic boundaries of the continental United States and Canada. Migrant workers move along three identifiable streams: the Eastern stream, the Mid-Continent stream, and the West Coast stream. The Eastern stream is made up of Puerto Ricans, Mexican Americans, Anglos, Canadian Indians, and African Americans. The stream flows up and down the region east of the Appalachian Mountains. The Mid-Continent stream traces the Mississippi River basin. This group is primarily composed of Mexicans, Mexican Americans, African Americans, and, most recently, Vietnamese and Cambodians. These migrants move in all directions to and from regions in Texas. The West Coast stream is the largest migrant movement, extending from California and Arizona to Oregon and Washington. This stream is comprised primarily of documented and undocumented Mexicans, Central Americans, Vietnamese, Filipinos, and other Western Pacific immigrants.

Mexican American migrants are predominantly from Texas, Arizona, New Mexico, and California. Undocumented migrants, recently arrived from Mexico, are incorporated daily into the families of Mexican American migrants moving through the streams.

Migrant groups differ in social and educational background. While many Mexican American migrants have some knowledge of English, others are not literate in any language (Prewitt-Diaz, Trotter, & Rivera, 1990). The social and educational background of migrants results in education-related problems for their children. Ignorance of the school system, difficulties in learning the language, and problems adjusting to the community environment are but a few of the reasons that many migrant children drop out of school. Many migrant children make a conscious and deliberate choice when they drop out to join their parents on the migrant stream and become an added source of family income.

Migrants live in isolation even when they are surrounded by people. They move often, and their involvement with the local community is limited and casual. María's experience is no different. She has lived in Valley View on five different occasions, but her circle of friends is limited to the other Hispanics living in the community and to the people working for agencies and programs to help migrants. They form her helping network and are her only contact within the community. She has never voted in local or national elections but would like to: "No, I have never voted because I don't know how to do it, but I would like to. I never know who the candidates are or anything, but it is something I would like to learn." When asked if she was involved with any local organization she answered: "No, I am Catholic and attend mass but that's all."

Life and Work

María is the fifth of nine children born to a first-generation Mexican American family. Her father was a hardworking migrant laborer who became a crew leader. He would contract to bring a set number of migrant workers from Mexico for farm owners from as far away as Michigan and Ohio. As with most migrant families, farmwork was a family affair that involved not only her father but her mother and all the children. During harvest time the whole family migrated north or east along the migrant streams. María started working the fields at a young age. Her parents were children of migrants who dropped out of school to help their parents and became migrants themselves:

> My father went to eight grade and my mother went less . . . I think she went to seventh.

> Mi apá era contratista, trayia gente para los trabajos.
> [My papa was a contractor; he brought people to work.]

María's parents spoke Spanish at home. She lived in a Hispanic neighborhood where everybody spoke Spanish. When asked in what language she preferred to conduct the interview, she chose Spanish, yet she went to a school in which everything was taught in English. "I was 13 when I first got married and 14 when my first child was born."

María divorced the father of her five children eight years ago. Although he had a high school diploma and two years of college, the couple became migrant workers when he was unable to find another kind of work. María kept the children after the divorce and joined the Eastern migrant stream, following a boyfriend who is a crew leader. This new relationship lasted six years. The day we first met, she told me they had broken up the day before because he physically abused her. A tattoo spelling his name covered each knuckle of the fingers on her left hand. They were visible the day we met but were covered by rings during our second interview.

Educational History. María attended school on a regular basis until she was in the third grade. Although she later continued until the sixth grade, she says her education stopped at the third grade:

I went only to sixth but you can say I went only to third grade
because—I couldn't attend for several years. When I went back I
was older than the other children and at that time they would
promote you because you were too old for the grade not because
you had learned, as they do now.

Her memory is vague about those years that she missed school. She
talks about an illness that paralyzed her face temporarily and about going
to the fields with her parents. "I only went to school when we were at home
in Mercedes. I missed school so often that by then I was too old for school
. . . I was about 12 when I dropped out of school."

From her school years María remembers only the strictness of the classroom environment:

They were very strict, very demanding, they [the teachers] would
raise their voices and you would tremble. They did not have
patience with the children. Everybody would behave because we
were scared of the teachers.

As in most small towns, the teachers were community residents who
had taught in the same school all their professional lives:

The one I remember best is the one who taught all the children in
my family from my oldest brother to the youngest. The teachers in
that school taught in the same school all their lives. When I went to
first grade my brother was 22 and his first grade teacher was my
first grade teacher.

María herself made the decision to drop out of school. She talks about
dropping out as something that had little to do with the school or her
parents:

It was my decision, but my parents did not oppose it because by
then my father was very ill and could not work the fields anymore.
I was expected to assist my mother and help her with the fruit stand
my father had by then.

The reasons María gives for dropping out are consistent with the reasons given by other migrant dropouts. Although María talks about illnesses
that kept her from attending school, she also mentions that she did not
attend school while her family went to work the fields in out-of-state farms.
These trips up the Mid-Continent and Eastern streams normally take three

to five months. Most migrant parents take the children along, and they might or might not attend school while away from their home base.

The records at the HEP show that María currently reads English at the third-grade level. They used the English version of the Test of Adult Basic Education (TABE) to determine vocabulary and reading comprehension skills. The Spanish version was not used, although it is María's preferred language of communication, because she cannot read or write in Spanish. Her spoken English is good enough for communication outside her Hispanic circle of friends and relatives, but she recognizes problems in reading and spelling:

> I don't know how to read and that is why I am going to HEP, to learn to read. I like math and I can do it, but I have a problem with reading and even with math when it is a word problem.

In addition to the HEP program, María attends an English as a Second Language (ESL) literacy class and a JTPA work experience program.

Everyday Literacy and Technology

María's low reading skills have forced her to develop other ways to deal with the reading and writing demands of her environment. She is not afraid of asking for assistance and relies heavily on her memory to learn job routines:

> Yes, that is something I have problems with [filling out forms and applications], for example, you have to report changes in income within five days—I don't put the information in the right place because they always have to ask me again—so I ask the person who is helping me to do it for me.

When María goes to the migrant clinic, she makes sure the doctors, nurses, and technicians explain clearly to her the tests and medicines prescribed. She cannot follow the instructions of a sewing pattern, but she uses a sewing machine to make her own dresses. She is concerned about retaking the driver's license test, but she has driven from Florida to Texas by herself.

The techniques María has developed to deal with her reading and writing limitations are assisted by "a good head for numbers" and "a good memory." About grocery shopping she says,

> No, I never look at the ingredients. I have to stretch my money and I buy only what I can stretch. . . . I go by myself because I know how

much money I have and as I select the items I add in my mind the amount. If I take someone with me they will distract me with conversation.

She has also developed a network of people who help her to read and understand important documents:

When I get mail, I try to read it. If I cannot understand it or it has too many words I can't understand, I don't leave the letter out of my sight. I take it to people I trust . . . and they will explain it for me.

Although María has migrated back and forth from Florida to Valley View for the past five years and admits that her involvement with the local community is very limited, the network of people who assist her with reading is well developed and stable. They are people familiar with the plight of migrants and who are in one way or another involved with the local migrant community.

María has learned to interact with modern technology by developing a support network and by sharpening her ability to retain information. She is not afraid to ask for assistance and is not intimidated by the instruments of technology:

That is something I have, I am not afraid of things like that [power tools and machines]. All I need is someone to explain to me how, and I will learn and be able to do it. I have yet to find something that I could say I have tried and could not do.

A VCR and a microwave are the most sophisticated appliances in María's trailer. The microwave is used only to warm food, and the VCR is used by her children.

Working the fields does not require any reading or writing. Most migrants are paid in cash at the end of the working day and will work without a contractual agreement. Between migrant trips, María has worked at jobs where the need for literacy was minimal: ironing at a dry cleaners, assembly work at a plastic plant, and canning at a packing plant.

Two months before the interviews, María had enrolled in the HEP for migrant and seasonal farmworkers. As part of the program, María was assigned to do work-experience at the local employment office. She received training to work as a receptionist. Her job is to greet the clients as they come in and assign them to the available counselor. María is very grateful for the opportunity to learn to use a computer at her work-experience placement:

I have been assigned to do work-experience at the employment office. The way I have done it is by memory. I have a very good memory. I had never used a computer but Vickie, the supervisor, is teaching me. It is not difficult, everything comes out as in a sheet of paper. All questions have a blank. Most of the things I learn are memorized. If things are explained to me clearly, I learn them. I just run them over in my mind [until I learn them].

Taking phone messages at work and spelling names are María's hardest everyday tasks:

That is new for me. I never write letters, but now at the work-experience training I have to write because the staff leaves me to answer the phones while they go for lunch and that is when we get a lot of calls . . . and I have to write [the phone messages] and it's very hard for me because I don't know how to spell.

Besides memorizing, María has developed other techniques to deal with the lack of spelling skills:

I write it as good as I can and make sure to get the name of the person who calls. I ask them to spell the name very slowly so that I make sure I have spelled it correctly. I take their phone number and the message and after they hang up I rewrite it carefully. If I don't know how to spell a word, I look to see if I can identify it in some of the books they gave me. Once I find a word, I memorize it and when another call comes in with a similar request, I am able to do it then.

The work-experience supervisor showed María how to use the computer to retrieve information on the clients. María explained to me in careful details the steps needed to retrieve information:

When people come in I greet them politely and ask if I can help them and they will tell me "I am looking for a job" and the type of work and I ask for the Social Security number and I write it in the computer and hit "Enter" and it will give me all the information on that person: where they live and what kind of work they are looking for. Every job is coded by numbers and if I want to know what the number stands for I enter "D", hit "Enter" again and the number, and it will tell me the type of job the person is looking for, and I enter "O" and "A" and the original information returns. If all they want is information on what we have, I send them to use the other computers by the wall. If they find something, they will give me the number and I find their name in the computer and I enter a key and the computer will make a copy for that person, then I will take it and put it inside a box. I have to check to see if they are veterans and put those apart from the ones who come to claim. Those will be placed in another place. I have to check all those things before storing the papers.

María's memory skills and her eagerness to learn seem to ingratiate her with her employers. She quickly memorizes the work routines and impresses her supervisor with hard work and good attendance:

She has me doing almost everything. She sometimes leaves and I stay by myself [at the JTPA work-experience]. In the last job I had, I was the best and fastest worker and my supervisor said I was the best hand he had. . . . He was the one who told me "you have a good head, you are a smart lady, you can do anything you set out to do."

In some ways María is different from the typical migrant worker, for whom fieldwork is the only available job. She has worked at a dry cleaners, done assembly-line work, served as a nurse's aide at a nursing home, and assisted a mechanic at a repair shop. When asked how she learned to do those things, she answered: "People would explain it to me and I would listen carefully."

Family Literacy. Only one of María's five children is still in school. Her youngest daughter is in fourth grade. The other four children dropped out of school before completing high school, although one now has a GED.

While María's former husband was still part of the family, he read to the children and helped them with homework:

Their father finished high school and went to a college for two years, and he did most of the reading. He used to read to me, too. He helped me to understand things before we got divorced.

Helping her only child left in school seems to be María's greatest concern:

I try to help my daughter with her school assignments. What I hate the most is social studies, but I try to help her by carefully reading a paragraph and trying to find the answer to the questions. We read together and try to find the answers together. I don't know if they are the correct answers, but we try.

She is very concerned about her youngest daughter and seems to blame herself for the other children's school failures:

> My oldest son never finished. He had completed eleventh grade and attended twelfth grade for a few months and he dropped out. It made me mad. Then came Tito, and [he] did the same. I know it was my fault, because I would take them out of school to take them with me to Florida and they would miss school for a while and they started to get behind. . . . Sometimes I think it was my fault that she [my older daughter] left to get married, because she was very private and quiet. She had a good head for school like her father, but I could not stop her.

Summary

During her interviews María expressed interest in making Valley View her home, but three weeks after our last meeting I learned that she was back with her boyfriend and had left with him to go to Florida for the winter harvest. She left her youngest daughter with relatives in Valley View so that she can continue in school. It seems doubtful María will return to the HEP program or the work-experience at the employment office.

At the same time, María's newfound interest in education has filled her with hope for the future. She is fascinated by computers and carefully described the steps she took to learn how to use them. She sees learning how to read and write not only as the means for personal liberation but as the way to fulfill her desire to help others:

> I see people who read and read and I want to be one of those people. I want to be able to take a book and not be ashamed. Because I want to be able to open a book and be able to understand it. I am the kind of person who sees someone with a problem and wants to help that person. I want to be able to help others and if I know how to read and write well, I will be able to help others. That is what I want to do. I tell myself if I try hard I will be able to do it.

✽ 3 ✽

Learning from the Appalachian Profiles

THESE APPALACHIAN PROFILES contain powerful images of people's lives. We met Tom, whose ambition is to move up in the world to be a sharecropper—a role that many would think at the bottom of the labor market. María's boyfriend's name tattooed on the knuckles of her hand is a symbol of permanence in her world, which is constantly on the move. Marcy's children went to bed with their shoes on, ready for her to take them away if her husband came home drunk and abusive. Yuvette worries over being able to keep up the payments on her couch and chair, little enough to ask for in twentieth-century America. Les continues working, working, working, to take care of the many people he calls family. Lisa, who has lost her house to the debts of an alcoholic husband, lives across the street from drug dealers but works in an upscale department store.

These profiles paint a picture of adults who are doing their best with what has been dealt out to them. But their lives are on the edge. Most of us these days are one major illness away from economic crisis. These people are even closer: the loss of a part-time job, a large repair bill, a child's illness, especially divorce—any of these can destroy the fragile security they have tried to build up. Literacy is only one factor in the complex social and economic interrelationships in the lives of poor and working people.

In this overview, we summarize the role of literacy and technology in everyday life for these Appalachian people, their expectations and beliefs about literacy and technology, and how they view the demands placed on them by their social and personal contexts. We outline the barriers and incentives they identify to furthering their own literacy skills and examine how literacy affects their social relationships.

ATTITUDES AND EXPECTATIONS
ABOUT LITERACY AND TECHNOLOGY

A common stereotype is that those with limited literacy hide their lack of literacy and at the same time do not value literacy and education, at least for their families. There are internal contradictions in this stereotype—why hide a lack of literacy if you place no value on literacy? There is some indication among these six adults that the former may be true to some extent. But there is no evidence that the people we profiled do not value literacy and education—indeed, there is a great deal of evidence to the contrary. The two men are the poorest readers and the two who expressed the most embarrassment about not being able to read. Les was hesitant to apply for jobs that involved a written application. Tom has never gone back to take the driver's license test after his first embarrassing failure. Lisa, too, talked about feeling bad at not being able to read the books she wanted and the frustration she perceived in others when she asked for help.

In contrast, neither Marcy, who reads quite well except for some "long words," nor María, who reads poorly, expressed any embarrassment about their literacy limitations. If they need help in reading, or more likely in writing, they ask for it. In general, it seems that their limited reading abilities and lack of a high school diploma are perceived by all these people as problems, at least in terms of employment, but not as really debilitating factors in their lives.

In contrast to this perception of their limited literacy being a problem in their lives, most of the people we profiled have confidence in their ability to learn practical skills and have positive feelings about their abilities in everyday life. Tom knows he can learn from others how to do things he needs. Lisa is proud of her ability to organize her budget and run her household. These are people who do "function" well, and know it.

All the people we profiled value education and literacy, perhaps having unrealistic expectations of the difference it could make in their own and their children's economic situations. In a variety of ways they are working to promote their children's education: transferring their children to what they perceive to be better schools, looking over schoolwork, helping with assignments, visiting the schools, taking their children to the library. All these parents not only love their children but also want them to have a better life, and they value education because they see it as the key to that better life.

EVERYDAY USES OF LITERACY AND TECHNOLOGY

Those of us who read fluently often assume that people with limited literacy skills do little reading in their everyday lives. We also assume that their use of technology is affected by their literacy limitations. Deprived of the capacity to read manuals or instruction booklets, how could anyone master new technology such as computers or vcrs? In fact, our profiles show that everyone does some reading in both their home and workplace and that literacy limitations do not seem to affect technology use, at least directly. The people we profiled make limited use of new technology such as VCRs or computers, but this seems to be primarily because of their low incomes.

What do people read in their everyday lives? The literacy skills among the people we profiled vary quite widely, and so do their literacy practices. The more fluent readers were not always those who read the most. In every domain of their lives—home, work, community—everyone we interviewed did some reading and each used reading in several ways. Table 3.1 summarizes the text materials that each person reported reading as well as the technology they said they use. This table is probably not an exhaustive list, particularly for those who read a lot, but it indicates the kinds of things people remember and report when asked.

At home in their families, the uses of literacy are similar for everyone. All have children in school and do some reading related to their children's schooling. For Tom this is limited to papers his son brought home from kindergarten, while others also read the various forms and communications from the schools. Everyone does some financially related reading, but it is rather limited in every case—paychecks, prices, money orders, catalogues, bills. They don't invest, don't have savings accounts or even checking accounts. They do have to deal with the paperwork of various bureaucracies—schools, the welfare system, housing programs, medical bills, adult education programs. Almost everyone reads in connection with shopping and consuming. This may be very limited, such as Tom's reading mainly brands of pop and candy bars. Or it may be quite complex, such as Yuvette's reading the manual for her programmable telephone.

Only Marcy, Les, and Lisa report reading anything for entertainment, but reading skill does not seem to be the determining factor here. Yuvette, who is one of the more skilled readers in this group, does not read for pleasure or much at all, while Les, with very limited reading skill, enjoys the funnies and comic books. Most report some reading in their work, but it is quite limited. Tom probably does the least—only incidental reading of names of machinery or seed. The rest write names and addresses or read menus or labels, but none mentioned reading reports or manuals, and they learned their jobs by watching and doing, not by reading. Reading that relates to their community or to the broader world—church, other organizations, politics, and news—is also fairly limited for everyone. Only Marcy regularly reads local newspapers, only Lisa regularly attends church and reads bulletins and Sunday School lessons, only Les is part of a regular recreational group that involves some use of literacy.

The uses of writing by the people we profiled are much more limited than their uses of reading. Few send notes to school or write messages, send

Table 3.1.   Everyday Uses of Literacy and Technology in Appalachian Group

	LITERACY USES	TECHNOLOGY USES
TOM	Children's books Food labels -- candy bars, soda pop Letters from wife Routine bills Child's school papers Prices in stores Road signs Bible	Farm equipment -- tractor, chain saw, loaders Television Stereo
MARCY	Newspapers, True Story, tabloids, Reader's Digest Grocery lists, store signs, prices Mail-order catalogues Birthday cards, letters to sister Money orders Food ingredients Brochures from Health Department, doctors Materials from nurse's aide course Bible Medicine labels Papers from son's school	Satellite dish Television Intercom Mother's pacemaker monitor
YUVETTE	Menu at restaurant where she worked Customers' bills Papers from Head Start, child's homework Bills, forms Bus schedule GED class materials	Preregister at restaurant Programmable telephone Tape recorder VCR Calculator TV with remote control
LES	Timecards from work Names and addresses of jobs Some work words -- "fuse," "kitchen" Cartoons and comic books Phone book Paycheck Bowling league scorecards	Tractor, farm machinery Mechanics of cars and trucks Electrical work -- wiring etc. Nintendo Microwave TV with remote control
LISA	Forms, labels from work Brochures, fliers from church, Sunday School Fliers, bills Prices in stores Directions for assembling toys etc. Dictionary, maps Bible Newspaper, classified ads Children's books, library books for pleasure	Cable TV TV with remote control Stereo VCR Microwave Electric organ
MARÍA	Some mail, forms, bills Child's schoolwork Phone messages	TV, VCR Microwave Power tools and machinery Computer at work

letters and greeting cards to others, make grocery lists, or write down phone numbers. It is worth noting again that, within this group, literacy use is not consistently related to literacy skill. Nor is schooling closely related to literacy skill. Both Lisa and Les have a high school diploma but quite limited skills. Marcy and Yuvette did not graduate but seem to have quite high literacy skills.

As we examine the relationship of literacy and technology in these six people's lives, we see few ways that technology either substitutes for literacy or demands higher literacy skill. Their use of technology is limited, but not necessarily by lack of literacy skills. All have some consumer electronics, if only a television and stereo. Most also have used, if not owned, a VCR, a microwave, video games, and remote-control devices. Tom, María, and Les said they could operate equipment or power tools. But none seem to use automated bank teller machines or computerized information systems (such as card catalogues). Their experience with computers is minimal. Only María and Yuvette have used computers at work in a very limited way. Les and Lisa expressed discomfort with computers. Marcy and Tom do not ever seem to have been in a situation where they came into contact with computers. Income seems more important than literacy in limiting people's use of technology. Many of those we interviewed simply cannot afford VCRs, microwaves, computer games, and the other technological trappings of our age. The use of automated teller machines in banks is irrelevant to those who live in a cash-based economy and have no bank account.

Nevertheless, several people have experienced another revolution in technology use in their lives. Some of the people we profiled, although not very old, have moved in their lifetimes from an essentially nineteenth-century agrarian world into an industrialized one. Marcy grew up, as she says, "back in the sticks." No TV, an old battery radio, wood stove, carrying water from the spring. Lisa and María grew up in similar rural situations. The technology in Tom's present life seems little different from that Marcy describes from her childhood. The stove is electric, a TV and refrigerator have been added, but there is still no inside water, no bathroom, no car.

Although literacy difficulties are not in themselves necessarily a major barrier to technology use, there may be specific barriers erected by limited literacy. For example, Tom's limited literacy is a barrier to his use of a car, because he cannot get a driver's license. But on the whole, the adults we profile have learned to operate most of the technology they need or to which they have access.

A potentially important role of both literacy and technology in people's lives is as a source of information. TVs, radios, computers, telephones, and vcrs enable people to gain information. So do books, newspapers, magazines, owner's manuals, food labels, prescription labels, maps, and phone books. The people we interviewed vary in their ability to use these sources of information, although for the most part their access to and use of print-based information is fairly limited. There seems to be a pattern: Those who desire information about news and current events both read and watch news shows on TV. Those who are not interested in the ways of the world do neither.

Although Les watches television, he does not watch the news or listen to it on the radio, and the family takes no newspapers or magazines. Tom reads little, has no newspapers or magazines in the house, and watches only a little television—baseball or football games. Yuvette can read but doesn't care to. She watches the news occasionally on TV but does not read newspapers. In contrast, Marcy regularly reads the two local newspapers, a weekly tabloid, and *Reader's Digest*, and she also watches the news on television. Her main interest in the newspapers is not in current world events but deaths, horoscopes, and court cases.

Although Lisa's literacy skills are limited, she has no problems getting the information she needs. She reads directions on things she buys as well as church bulletins and the news insert that comes with her phone bill. Although there are few print materials in the home, if her children have a school assignment that involves research, she takes them to the library. María uses a variety of means to get information she needs. Of all the people we profiled, she is the best "plugged-in" to a network of helping agencies. But María also has other, more independent, ways of getting information, which are primarily oral. At the migrant health clinic she is careful to get the doctors and nurses to explain to her clearly the tests and medicines prescribed.

Information comes to the people we interviewed, as it does to most of us, in a curious mixture of the modern (electronic media) and the archaic ("show me"). Most of them have telephones and use them to stay in touch with family (and since they do not write letters, the telephone functions as a substitute for literacy). Their use of electronic media may not be very different from that of other Americans. There was no reference to the use of tape recorders as a memory aid or listening to "books" on tape. None expressed concern that their access to information is seriously limited by their lack of literacy skills. And although we may perceive their access to and use of information to be rather narrow, it reflects the way they see and live their lives in relation to the outside world.

In a print-based society, almost everyone experiences some literacy demands that they have difficulty meeting. It may be tax returns or warranty deeds, scientific articles or medical records, but most of us are "illiterate" in something. The people we profiled also identified literacy demands that they have difficulty meeting. However, these literacy demands seem fairly limited.

Les is hindered at work by his limited reading ability. He is able to handle the reading and writing he must do as his job is now arranged, but his inability to take the electrician's test places severe restrictions on how he works and how much he is paid. Tom is able to do the farm work he encounters, but he says he guesses at times when applying fertilizer and pesticides. He certainly does not read the safety information on the labels. Lisa and Yuvette both have sales forms and computerized registers at work. Yuvette seems to have had no trouble, but the written work is a challenge for Lisa and she avoids the register. Marcy's work has few literacy demands and she meets them easily.

In both work and everyday life, situations that might seem to demand higher literacy skills than these adults possess are dealt with through "practical problem-solving" strategies. These include the educated guesses Les makes in measuring electrical cable. He "walks it" out the length of the room, or the area across which it is to be run, and adds what is needed on the walls. It usually comes out quite accurately. Tom makes similar educated guesses in estimating his bid for cutting a field of tobacco.

Both Lisa and María get a sense of achievement from their ability to work out their household budget and shop effectively. These adults with limited literacy skills appear to use most of the same strategies for grocery shopping used by the more middle-class, educated shoppers of Lave and colleagues' research (1984). They go to familiar stores, buy familiar goods, and do price comparisons on selected items. Tom usually goes to the grocery store himself, because he thinks he gets better bargains than his wife can. Despite his very limited reading skills, he compares prices, and he knows the words for familiar products.

Indeed, literacy may not increase their ability to solve problems in their lives. Yuvette knows that buying her couch and chair via a rent-to-own company is costing her more than if she had the cash or could get credit from a furniture store. But she cannot get credit. She was shocked when she and the interviewer used a calculator to get the total cost of buying an $880 bedroom suite through rent-to-own—a whopping $1,800. Yuvette vowed she would "try my best" not to buy that, but with her strong desire for some nice things, and with few options, she recognizes that she might well be tempted.

These six people have largely worked out ways to meet the literacy demands in their everyday lives. However, these demands are quite limited, especially in the domain of work. A bigger question is how much they have limited themselves or been limited by their lack of literacy in their expectations for themselves, in their jobs and income-generating capacity, in their readiness to engage in further education and training, and in their social and community relationships.

All the people profiled in Appalachia work and have tried a wide variety of the less skilled jobs available in their communities. But for the most part they have not held jobs that enable them to live with even a margin of comfort. They may not be underemployed in terms of hours worked, but they may well be underemployed in terms of their needs and abilities. The impact of literacy varies from one to another. As Tom says, "It's kinda hard on me every day, 'cause I never know where I'm gonna get ahold of the next penny at, and I know they [the children] need something all the time." His part-time and sporadic farm work keep him on the margins in terms of cash income. He says that it would help him, in tobacco farming, to be able to read the names of the chemicals that have to be applied, but it seems that literacy is not his major handicap. Usually he works with someone who does read—his crew boss, who is an old school friend, or his father. To become a farmer, rather than a farm laborer, he would need not literacy but land.

For Les, his literacy difficulties have proved a decisive limitation to advancement in his job. Les could earn much higher wages as a certified electrician, and his lack of reading skill is all that prevents him from passing the required tests. His practical skills as an electrician are high, but he cannot get the certification.

Lisa talks about her hesitation to use the cash register at her department store, although it is not clear that her literacy limitations are the major reason (since she also expresses concern about handling cash and being accused of theft). Nor does this avoidance seem to endanger her job. Her encounters with technology at home (VCRs, microwave, Atari games, electric organs, and remote controls) have presented her with no problems. She generally learns slowly and requires extra time and attention to learn new things. Perhaps she has not had the individual teaching she would need to use the cash register at work.

For the others, the work-related impacts of literacy limitations are less clear. Although María's husband had completed two years at a community college, lack of jobs in their hometown forced him into the migrant stream. Her own more recent experiences demonstrate how hard it is to leave the migrant stream, settle down, and find a good job. None of the people we profiled have encountered the substantial technological changes at work that others in this country have experienced over the last few years. The literacy and technology demands of all their jobs are very limited.

LEARNING AND SCHOOLING

In order to understand barriers and incentives to learning, we look back at the school experiences of these six people and at how they came to be adults with limited literacy skills despite many years of schooling. We also look at their hopes and aspirations, their plans and attempts to meet society's demands for higher skills and credentials.

Their schooling experiences will be familiar to many participants in adult basic education programs. Pregnancy and family moves had an impact on schooling, childhood illnesses took their toll, and teachers for the most part paid little attention to those who were falling behind.

Marcy grew up back in a "holler" (hollow) and had to walk two miles to get the school bus. She and María were both often sick as children. And María's migrant life also disrupted her schooling repeatedly. Even for those who were not migrant farmworkers, family moves had a major effect on their schooling. Tom's family moved to Ohio and then back to Virginia. Les's father worked as a dairyman on several farms, and Les attended "a whole lot" of elementary schools.

Although the problems may have begun in elementary school, the people we profiled often remembered the transition into middle school as being a turning point in their schooling. Sixth grade was a pivotal time for Les. He was having difficulties with math, and his teacher started hitting him over the head with the math book. From then on, Les stopped trying. Yuvette made good grades in elementary school, but she didn't like school later and didn't go a lot. Lisa, too, says she stopped learning after sixth grade, although she received a high school diploma. "It was like I just couldn't learn anymore, when I reached that sixth grade level . . . I guess I just give up on myself."

Tom, like Lisa, describes himself as a slow learner. They both remember being willing to learn in school but felt the teachers did not have patience enough to teach them. Tom was often sent out on menial tasks, like raking the ball field. "They just passed me to get rid of me."

For Yuvette, getting pregnant at 16 was not the precipitating factor in her attitude toward schooling that it might have been. She hated school before then, she hated it afterwards, and she avoided it as much as she could.

All except Les have participated in adult education programs, although we made our contact with only one through an adult education program. Like many adults, they move in and out of programs, impelled by other factors in their lives. Their incentives to enroll in adult education programs have been primarily, though not solely, job-related. Tom's experience was not voluntary, and he did not continue with adult education once he left the correctional institution. But Marcy, Lisa, Yuvette, and María hope that working toward their GED will help them get a better job and a more stable, less marginal life.

Nevertheless, despite the incentive, a complex assortment of barriers stand between them and participation in literacy programs. Time is a premium for several of them: They work long and irregular hours, and they have family responsibilities and many problems to deal with—Tom says, "I ain't really got time to sit down." For Tom, lack of independent transportation is also a factor. Both Tom and Les would like to learn to read better, but a sense of pride and a reluctance to admit their reading difficulties to others get in the way.

Yuvette talked of the striking contrast between the Even Start class, where she felt part of a "family" with other parents of young children like herself, and the Job Training Partnership Act (JTPA) class where she could not connect with either teacher or students. In Even Start, she says, "You know when we do the work, we help each other, it being like a group thing. The teacher, she help you, she be right there helping you." In the JTPA class, however, the teacher "would explain a little bit, and then we have to do the work. Maybe if I had another teacher . . ."

Adults with low literacy skills face many problems in the rest of their lives that make a commitment to their own education difficult for them: Their time is stretched, their family economy is on the edge, they focus on their children's needs rather than their own, and their self-esteem is easily damaged by being made to feel stupid. Literacy programs need to provide an encouraging environment for adult learners. Above all, they need to feel support, to be part of a "family" or community of learners, and to have the personal attention of a teacher.

Patterns of Intergenerational Literacy

The overall absence of pattern is striking as we examine the literacy and schooling of three generations of the people we profiled. At the level of their parents' generation, there does seem to be a pattern. All of their parents' generation had limited schooling, most less than high school level, and usually also limited literacy skills. Limited schooling was probably the norm at that time for residents of the rural communities from which most of these people come: Whether in Mississippi or in Appalachia, most working-class people did not complete high school in the 1930s, 1940s, and 1950s.

Furthermore, as is true today, limited schooling sometimes masks well-developed literacy skills. Lisa's mother "read a lot," although she had left school in eighth grade, and was well able to take care of a wide range of the family's needs. Tom reports that his parents could "read pretty good."

If there were a pattern of intergenerational lack of literacy, we would expect that all the siblings of the people we interviewed would have literacy difficulties. This is not consistently true. Tom's sisters all graduated from high school, but his twin brother dropped out at the same time as Tom did, although with somewhat better reading skills. None of Marcy's sisters graduated, although one sister has higher skills than Marcy does and helps her with filling in forms and with getting around. Lisa's siblings graduated from high school, and three attended some college. None of María's siblings graduated from high school. There is not a clear pattern in this generation.

Nor is there a distinct pattern among the spouses of the people we profiled. The two men have wives who are the "readers" of the family although they did not graduate from high school. Lisa and María had husbands who were much better educated than themselves. Marcy's husband spent fewer years in school than she did, and had skills lower than her own.

Among the children of these people, there is great variation in terms of their success in school. Some are still too young to tell whether they will do well in school: Yuvette's son is still in preschool; Tom's children are in kindergarten or younger. Those who are older have not consistently had problems in school. Lisa's children are both college-bound and have done well in school. Marcy's oldest daughter left school to get married before graduation, although she was doing quite well in school; her middle daughter did graduate; and her son will graduate this year. Les's daughter makes A's and B's in high school.

But some of the children have had problems. Yuvette's daughter has been the center of a tug-of-war between mother and grandmother, and she has had problems in school as well as speech problems; Yuvette's preschool son has developmental delays. Les's fourth-grade son is in a Chapter 1 reading program, although he plans to go to college. None of María's children have graduated from high school, although one got his GED. She pins her hopes on her youngest daughter, now in fourth grade.

Among this group of adults with low literacy skills, we find no consistent patterns of intergenerational transfer of illiteracy. While we studied only six adults, the lack of a clear pattern does suggest that the reality may be more complex than conventional wisdom suggests.

LITERACY AND SOCIAL NETWORKS

These lives are focused on family and kin. They demonstrate that while the forms may be changing, family values continue to be strong in this society. The form of the family may be multigenerational (as in Marcy's three-generation family), the traditional nuclear family (Tom) or extended family (Les's immediate family together with his handicapped brother), or single parent with children, sometimes with a boyfriend (Lisa, Yuvette, and María). But whatever their concept of family is, all the people we interviewed focus primarily on that family. They all value their children and want something better for them than they have had themselves.

In some ways their literacy limitations tie them even more tightly to that close family network. Many depend on family members for help in meeting literacy demands and for other kinds of help, including finding jobs. Marcy found her present job through her ex-brother-in-law, who happened to live next door to one of the children of the elderly woman whom she looks after. In small rural communities, it is common for "who you know" to be more important than "what you know" in getting a job. Even in a large city, Les, severely limited in his ability to seek jobs, found work through similar means. Lisa, the most outwardly involved of those we interviewed, is also the only one who does not have an extended family nearby. The others depend on extended family networks for much of their lives.

Beyond the family, most of the people we profiled have little interaction within their communities. Most neither vote, participate actively in a community organization or church, nor appear to have much interest in the rest of the world. Only Lisa votes regularly, attends PTA meetings, actively seeks news of the world, and participates regularly in church. Marcy has voted twice in her life but sees little point to it. She has a passive interest in the news of her small town (scanning the deaths and court cases in the local newspaper) but apparently little active involvement. Yuvette is perhaps the most isolated. Although her two best women friends are active members of a neighborhood organization, Yuvette has never attended a meeting or even the community festival that the group organized. In a community that she feels is alien and threatening, she sees it as a virtue to stay home and stay out of trouble.

Limited literacy may limit these six people's access to and use of information about the broader world. However, everyone also devotes substantial amounts of time and energy to surviving—working long work hours, raising families, shopping for bargains, taking care of others. There is not much time or energy left over for citizenship.

But perhaps more than time and energy, it is the perceived lack of efficacy of citizenship activities that prevents people from becoming involved. Like many poor people, they feel quite powerless and do not expect that their voice, their vote, or their actions could make any substantial difference either in their own lives or in their communities. Marcy sums it up when she says "Why vote?" People with very limited time and energy do get involved when they think it makes a difference. Most of the people we profiled don't expect to make a difference.

CONCLUSIONS

These profiles provide an in-depth view of the lives of six people in our region who have limited literacy skills. They offer a rich description of their uses of literacy and technology in everyday life, the ways in which their lack of literacy skills limits them, and the strategies they have devised to cope in a print-based world. The profiles support a social contextual view of literacy: What literacy means for each person varies, and their literacy demands and uses vary according to their context.

These individuals vary in how, where, and when they use literacy as well as what they use it for. Different demands and uses of literacy may exist for the same person in different domains of their lives—work, family, church, social group—and at different stages of their life history.

The patterns of literacy practices we found do not seem to be closely associated with literacy skills, although clearly skill level plays a role. Someone like Yuvette may have fairly high-level skills but be almost a-literate. Someone like Lisa may have much lower-level skills but may need to use text or may even read for pleasure. Literacy skills, literacy demands, cultural and social contexts, expectations, and attitudes are all interconnected in quite complex ways.

All the people we interviewed would like to improve their skills and get more education. Not all can find a way to do so without other changes in their social context. Such changes vary from solving transportation problems to finding time between working and caring for family. Their experiences suggest that adults with low literacy have considerable practical skills at managing their everyday lives, that they have developed their own ways of learning new skills and new tasks, and that the formal education system does not fit these ways of learning very well.

Our profiles put literacy in its place as only one of the factors affecting people's lives. It is not clear for most of these people that a gain in literacy skills alone would make substantial differences in their lives. Perhaps it would help them get a better job and thus enable them to move out of poverty. That is most likely to be true for Les, if gains in literacy skills enabled him to get an electrician's license and command higher wages. But without some major changes on a national level (for example, national health insurance and a minimum wage that is a living wage), they would most likely simply move from one sector of the working poor into another.

4

California Profiles

THE SIX PROFILES from the West Coast offered here represent the individual lives of immigrants now living the complex, multicultural reality of California. Migration, adversity, bilingualism, cultural domination, underemployment, cultural isolation, limited English language proficiency, and hope are living issues for these new residents of the most populous state in the country. Due to a historically massive, sustained influx of immigrants and the consequent rapid expansion of its culturally diverse population, California is no longer what it used to be, and no one is sure what it will become. What is certain is that a complex process of economic, social, and cultural change is well under way, occurring too rapidly to be well understood or accommodated by public policy makers or service providers.

The *San Francisco Chronicle* (December 23, 1991) sought to characterize the magnitude of the cultural shift currently under way in the state:

- By the year 2000, there will be no cultural majority in California—all cultural groups will be "minorities."
- Latinos will comprise about one-third of the state's population in the year 2000.
- Almost two-thirds of California's legal immigrants in the past 10 years have come from Asia, while about a quarter have come from Latin America.
- Legal and illegal foreign immigration to California was estimated at 2.3 million in the 1970s and 3.1 million in the 1980s; it is projected to be 4.1 million in the 1990s.
- From 1990 to 2000 graded enrollment in California's public schools is expected to grow by 48.1%, from 4.8 million students to 7.2 million students, many of them children from immigrant homes.
- Many adult schools and community colleges throughout the state have waiting lists of hundreds or even thousands of immigrants waiting to enroll for ESOL instruction.

- More than 1 million illegal immigrants granted legal status under 1986 "Amnesty" legislation will soon be eligible to bring parents and children to the United States.

The six individual profiles presented here offer a profoundly human view of what it is like to be on the inside of a major cultural and demographic shift. They also offer a picture of the complex and important interactions of literacy and technology in these immigrants' lives. Without ethnographic profiles such as these, it is difficult to gain a sense of the nature of life as an immigrant in California, even if one is inclined to do so. Simply reading the statistics cannot suffice. The impact of this massive cultural shift can remain largely invisible for many "regular, mainstream" Californians, for it is their culture that remains dominant, their culture that the TV broadcasts, their culture that the print media largely present, and their culture that the workplace rewards. But cultural boundaries and cultural changes clearly exist and present powerful barriers to immigrants, often serving to hamper the human growth and development that are needed for collective economic growth and development.

These profiles offer insight into patterns of literacy and technology in the everyday lives and worklives of members of some very diverse immigrant communities in the San Francisco Bay Area in northern California. The profiles come from several of the major immigrant groups that have had an impact on California in the last decade or more. The people profiled range from Oliver Gonzalez, an urban Latino youth who loves video games, to David Wong, a middle-aged Chinatown fish-seller who is a former agricultural engineer; from Nura Tola, a nonliterate North African refugee who now cleans homes for a living, to Michela Stone, a Russian bookkeeper who used to teach college-level accounting; and from Alicia Lopez, a widowed, "newly legalized immigrant" Latina who studies building maintenance, to Sokhhoeun, a Cambodian refugee who helps other refugees as a bilingual aide in a literacy program.

The people of these profiles inhabit realities so diverse that it is hard at times to believe that they could live in the same time and place. But they do, and this overwhelming diversity must be accommodated through new and innovative ways to use—and to learn to use—language, literacy, and technology.

ALICIA LOPEZ

By Mari Gasiorowicz

Alicia Lopez, age 47, migrated from her native Mexico to the San Francisco Bay Area in 1981. Widowed, she lives with her sister's family and raises her 6-year-old grandchild. Alicia is a generous, thoughtful, and determined woman. Her family situation challenges her, and her limited English presents barriers to her ability to progress. Nevertheless, she approaches her life with the attitude that "you can do anything you really want to."

Alicia lives in the city of South San Francisco, with a population of 55,000 in 1990, 27% of whom are Latino. (In contrast, San Francisco's population is only 14% Latino.) "[In this neighborhood,] more than half of the families are Latinos—families that have been here 20 to 30 years, some of them, so of course there are children, and adults, various ages . . ."

Several blocks from her home is a small downtown area. A restaurant, a bakery, two bars (all Mexican), a Chinese restaurant, a Burger King, and two discount stores share two short blocks. Alicia lives approximately one hour by bus from downtown San Francisco and the job training program in which she is enrolled.

Alicia's family makes up her social world. She lives in a house with her sister's family and an adult male cousin. Alicia shares a room with her granddaughter, Carmina, whom she cares for as if she were her own. (It was only when the child left the room that Alicia identified her as Maria's daughter, not her own.) Alicia's daughter Maria, age 29, came to the United States after Alicia had been here more than four years. Maria now has five children, and her life has brought Alicia much pain:

> My daughter—it's been six years since I brought her here. She was married in Guadalajara and her husband treated her badly so I asked, "Do you want to come [to the U.S.] with me?" I went to Guadalajara to get her and a couple of months after I brought her here, Carmina was born. And a couple of months later, she went to live with her boyfriend and left me with the baby. And now she has other children. He got her into the habit of using drugs and because of that, the children have problems. The children are in the hands of the government [foster care]. They told her she had to go to school but she didn't go. It's been more than a year.
>
> I want a good job for them in another state on a ranch, or where there is space. I want to adopt them. If she can change, that's better. If she were clean, she could get the baby back. She has help [recovery] in her own hands. But, if she doesn't want to . . . it's a tragedy, but . . .

Alicia's two sons, ages 23 and 27, live in Mexico. Until a few years ago, she sent them $500 each month so that they could go to school and start their own professional careers. At that time, she was earning only $1,200 per month. "They want me to come [back to Mexico to live]; they'll help me. But you get used to supporting yourself and you don't want anyone to help you."

Until recently, Alicia has worked—often two jobs at once, and usually at least 10 hours a day. Five months ago she enrolled in a job training program that she attends weekdays from 8 A.M. to 4 P.M.

> I don't go out dancing or anything. My world is Carmina and the other children. My family . . . I go to Mass on Sundays. In Spanish, or English, whichever. It's the same. I keep the faith, the Catholic church.

She mentions only one person with whom she socializes outside of her family. He is an old boyfriend, now friend, whom Carmina refers to as "Papi." A poster-sized picture of him with his baseball team hangs on the wall in her bedroom.

> I got to know him when I first got here. So, we were together. He's from where I'm from. The only problem is that he drinks a lot and at some point I said, "no." I said, if you don't want to change, then you'll have to live your life without me . . . now he is a friend.

Alicia's social world is much narrower than it was a few years ago. Her fear that her two youngest grandchildren could be adopted by strangers provides strong motivation for her to focus on her own employability because she needs a steady income in order to be eligible to adopt:

> There is a Mexican saying, a drop of blood weighs more than a pound of meat. People who are not related by blood don't care as much. Parents adopt a child and then they have their own and they love the first one less.

Life and Work

> I was born in Mexico, in the state of Zacatecas, in a small town—Nochistlan. My childhood was good. We were a large family. We're 11—6 girls and 5 boys. We were many, so we couldn't have anything we wanted but it was good, my childhood.

Alicia's mother gave birth to 22 children; Alicia was the fourth of the 11 children who survived. Her mother ran the household; her father had a series of small businesses, including an ice cream store, a janitorial service, and several real estate ventures. "He was very hard-working. All of the businesses that he had made money. It was that he didn't know how to take care of it. And he had other women . . . "

Her parents were both from middle-class families, and since her mother was an only child, she inherited the house in which she had grown up:

It was a nice old house—seven, eight rooms, a large area with big trees, fruit trees, a beautiful yard. My mother was born in that house, and almost all of us. We had a radio by the time I was 15, no television or blender or stove. We cooked on charcoal. We used a stone grinder [for grains] . . . we washed clothes by hand, with a scrub board.

Alicia grew up in a household that supported education. Her father had been in the seminary, and her mother had a third- or fourth-grade education:

My mother believed in education; she sent me to school. . . . [My parents] read at home. They had very nice books—stories for children—different stories. Now I have to look everywhere for nice stories for her [Carmina].

Alicia attended a small public elementary school. She liked school, but during her seventh-grade year she dropped out, primarily to help her mother raise her seven younger siblings:

I left school at age 13 to help take care of the other children. I can't blame my mother. She had so many children that she couldn't really pay attention to all of them. . . . I regret that I didn't study more. People who study more, work less and earn more, and people who study less, earn less and work more. So I regret it.

Because the family was so large and because her father "was careless with money," Alicia grew up in what she described as a lower-middle-class household. Her father controlled the household: "He was very strict with us. We couldn't go out; couldn't go to parties. He was strict about every-thing, had to have his way. That's why they had so many children."

Partly to escape her father's harsh discipline, Alicia married and left home at the age of 16. She had her first child when she was 17. At the age of 26, with children ages 4, 8, and 10, Alicia was widowed; she did not want to remarry. She moved in with her mother and younger siblings. In the intervening years, her mother had also been widowed and had moved from Zacatecas to Guadalajara so that her other children could attend high school. Alicia's mother looked after her children while Alicia took a full-time job at a Kodak store selling cameras and supplies. With the exception of a brief employment training program at Kodak, she had no formal education as an adult until recently. But at this job, she became familiar with photographic equipment and had a chance to practice her math skills. "If it cost 860 pesos and there was an import tax of 20%, I would calculate that [on paper]. I could do it very fast." She stayed at this job for eight years.

Migration to the United States—"Then I Came Here." In 1981, at age 37, Alicia migrated alone and undocumented to the United States. She went to South San Francisco, where she had extended family.

> Then I came here. I've been here 10 years. You can earn more. I came, I came, I wanted to come. I was the first one [of my siblings]. I came to work—to earn more. [My] children stayed with my mother.

Initially she lived with an aunt, but she felt constricted. "I liked to go out, and she wanted me to be back at a certain time." Then she lived with a friend, and then in an in-law's apartment in the house of another aunt. Five months ago, she moved into her current housing situation, sharing a room with Carmina in her sister's house.

During her first seven years in the United States, she worked for a company that prepared food for Price Club and other discount stores:

> I made salads, soups, macaroni, tortellini, alfredo sauce, pesto, tabouli, elbow macaroni, minestrone, lasagna, chicken noodle, beef noodle, salads—Waldorf, coleslaw. . . . They gave me the formulas and I did everything—cooked everything.
> The manager wrote in English. He'd give me the formula—all the powders and they all had a name. Six ounces of this, 6 ounces of that. And I'd try [the powders] and then I'd memorize the names.
> He'd give me a list to do for that day—25 lasagnas, 5 black bean soups, 140 pounds coleslaw, and I'd write it down [in Spanish].
> When I was making salads—120 batches of a certain salad—I would figure out how many ounces of this powder and this one.

With the exception of the manager, who was Anglo, the companies employed only Latinos; her co-workers were all Spanish-speaking. She managed to do her work with a knowledge of English limited to the names of foods, but she believes that she could have progressed much further if she had spoken English:

> It would have been better if I had spoken English. I could have learned many more things. I could have gotten a better position. In

other companies, there are people who know less than I do and have higher positions because they speak English. . . . Also, I couldn't ask for a raise. English is very necessary.

She used some large but simple machines to mix foods but prepared most foods by hand. There she worked 10 to 12 hours a day. Her starting rate was $3.50 an hour and, by the end, she was earning $6 an hour:

Almost all were Latinos—people who didn't have papers. And because we didn't have papers, they paid us $3.50 [an hour]. They got us good and cheap because we didn't have papers.

The company moved to a city 45 miles away. She decided not to stay with the company. Commuting was out of the question: "It's far—I'd be gone from 7 in the morning till 11 or 12 at night. That's a lot—then you have to pay for babysitting and you're never home."

Relocating did not make sense either. She had always lived with family members or rented from other Mexicans who had not required the usual last month's rent and security deposit, but she anticipated that that would not have been the case if she had moved. She also believed that babysitting costs in a new location would be prohibitive. "If they would offer me good money, I'd follow the company, but for $6 an hour, it's not worth it."

She packed spices for $5 per hour in one factory and then added another nearly full-time job in a ravioli-packing factory for $7.25 per hour, until the company relocated to Washington State last year. In each of these jobs, she worked long hours and found herself too tired to go to school, although she twice signed up for ESL classes.

Also during that time, Alicia became a legal resident of the United States through the 1986 Immigration Reform and Control Act (commonly known as "Amnesty"). Gaining legal status relieved tremendous stress about the possibility of being deported:

When I arrived, without papers, I was afraid of just waiting at the bus stop. People said—I heard from friends that sometimes someone at work with a bad disposition would report a company. . . . It was very ugly. Really horrible. Now it's different, but before I was legal, I would always be afraid that I would be walking and they'd grab me. It's an ugly fear.

Her new status also made her eligible for benefits, including unemployment compensation, MediCal for her grandchild, and government-funded employment programs like the one she enrolled in five months ago.

Adult Education: Employment Training. About the time the ravioli-packing factory relocated to Washington, Alicia learned of the job training program that she currently attends. "I heard about it on the radio [in Spanish] and I went to find out. It didn't cost me anything. I qualified. So I started."

It is a private, nonprofit employment training program that offers instruction in ESOL and four skill areas: facility maintenance, shipping and receiving, accounting, and office skills. The program is funded partly through Amnesty, partly by an insurance company, partly by Pell grants (government-funded student grants), and partly through a bank loan. She enrolled in the facility maintenance training track—instruction in plumbing, carpentry, painting, electrical work, and janitorial work. Her English skills, both written and spoken, are minimal and not adequate for the other tracks. "If I could understand more English, I'd learn something more . . . something better, but since I don't, I'm studying this."

She is in the fifth month of an eight-month program. She attends weekdays and is quite enthusiastic about the program:

> The teachers are very patient. They are very good. I like school. It's not easy for us—those of us who are older. We don't learn as fast as the younger ones, but the teachers are very patient. When I think about all the time I lost . . . but you can't regret . . .

By her instructors' and her own accounts, learning English comes slowly to her but she performs exceptionally well at facility maintenance skills. She provided the interviewer with a 45-minute tour of the work area, demonstrating with comfort and care the proper use of each tool. She also described the skills that she must demonstrate in order to graduate from the program. "I have to take out the toilet in the ladies' room and put it back so that it doesn't leak. I have done it twice already, but the third time is one that counts."

After she finishes the program in three months, she hopes to be able to find an apprenticeship (unpaid) where she can improve her skills. Her next goal is to find a job, and then she hopes to continue her schooling. "If I have a job—more or less good—and I have time, I'll continue classes in English. It's because of the language that I can't do other things."

Everyday Literacy, Language, and Technology

Alicia's uses of literacy and language in her daily life are characterized by three themes: First, she reads and writes Spanish well. When she can obtain information or services by conversing and completing paperwork in Spanish, she manages without difficulty. Second, her written and oral language skills in English are very limited. She is hampered by her lack of English and ultimately avoids many situations in which using Spanish is not an option. Third, in her words, "If I want to learn something, I can." Alicia is skilled at making use of the resources she has access to. She offers an example of successful problem solving:

> Three years ago, I had a niece who is a doctor who wanted me to send her some books and I didn't know where to buy them. I looked in the phone book for different bookstores and I found a big one on Market Street and I went there and bought them and sent them. If you want something, you'll find it.

In her conversations about her job training program, Alicia identified three strategies she uses for learning the maintenance skills, some of which involve literacy. First, she pays close attention to the skill instructor's lectures and demonstrations, for example, as he explains watts and volts current in black, red, green, and white wires, and the uses of various types of nails. Second, she has found books in the library to help her understand electricity, although "The one in Spanish was so old, so out of date, that it didn't serve me. The one in English, I understood only a few words." Her third and primary strategy has been to work with the other women students:

> The women get more than 90% on the tests. The test is on electricity, I got 93% and the men got 70%, 72%, 75%. The women work together more than the men. For example, there's a Salvadoran woman. We work, this is this; that is this. We work together—it's better—you can talk. And the men don't really work together. They say "good morning," but that's it. It's better—working together.

Alicia finds learning English to be harder than learning maintenance skills, and studying with other women students is not as effective here. "[The most difficult] is speaking. I want to learn, but you have to practice. I am ashamed to speak." She borrows books and tapes in English from the library and follows the text with the tapes. She also looks up common words and then copies them many times in her notebook. "And I get these newspapers from my neighbor's recycling bin. I can pick out a few words," but she cannot understand the whole article.

Most of Alicia's literacy strategies follow this pattern: (1) She uses her native language whenever possible, (2) she avoids situations that make extensive demands on her limited English proficiency, and (3) she employs creative problem-solving techniques, sometimes using text selectively (dictionaries and phone books).

For the most part, her use of public services falls under the first category; Alicia conducts most of her business and communicates almost entirely in Spanish because Spanish-language services are often available. Carmina's school caters to the many monolingual Spanish-speaking parents by offering a Spanish-language call-line at the school and sending all information to parents in both languages. Alicia also has had no trouble finding bilingual staff and forms for legal and social services. This includes the staff with whom she dealt during the Amnesty application process, the social worker assigned to handle her grandchildren's foster care, and the employees who process MediCal forms.

Alicia uses two public libraries about once a month; they both have bilingual librarians and large (if sometimes out-of-date) collections of books in Spanish and simple English. She discovered the public library system only a few months ago when she started the employment training program. "I can get the books out of the library and use them for a month and then renew them and not pay anything! These books are very expensive; I can't buy them."

While in most cases she has been able to receive adequate services, she does mention having had to go to a family practitioner who spoke Spanish rather than a specialist doctor who spoke only English. She also faced language barriers in trying to participate in union activities at one of her previous jobs:

> This [letter] is from the union but I can't read it. . . . They don't speak Spanish at the union. I didn't go to meetings because they didn't speak Spanish and I didn't speak English. Oh, I went once or twice and I tried with someone translating this and this and this but no.

Public transportation has not been much of a problem for Alicia. She has a monthly pass and uses the bus exclusively. She has always been able to find out from Spanish speakers which route to take:

> I called up [the employment training center] and they told me [in Spanish], "It's on this street and this street and do you have a car? Where are you coming from?"
>
> Before, if there were people here longer, or now I've been here longer than other people . . . I teach them what bus. My aunt taught me; she spoke English and everything. She would take me and show me. . . . Now, on the bus that I take in the morning, the driver speaks English and Spanish and so I can ask him how I get somewhere.

Right now, the cost of owning a car and carrying insurance is prohibitive, but Alicia hopes to buy one eventually. Since she has had some practice driving and the driver's license test is available in Spanish, she does not anticipate any difficulty in passing it.

Restaurants also present little difficulty. She seldom eats out, but that is because of the cost rather than her discomfort with the language. "For example, I like Chinese food. I know the names of the main foods [because of work] so I know I like [this dish], and this I don't." As for calculating the tip: "If they treat you well, you leave two or three dollars. If they don't pay attention to you, you don't leave anything."

Shopping for food items is easy because "There are many products that are the same brand in Mexico. And well, milk, cookies, bread, pastas, it is obvious." Cleaning products present dangers that she was not even aware of until recently:

> I know how to use bathroom cleaner now, because I've learned in school. But before I didn't and it's dangerous because it has a lot of gasses, and if you mix it, it's dangerous. But it's in English and I couldn't read the instructions.

There are circumstances in which her limited English presents some problems in everyday living, but they are fairly minor. In reviewing the mail she had received, Alicia described her attempt to follow up on a coupon (entirely in English) for carpet cleaning. She was able to read the basic information:

> Carpet cleaning. $24.95 for five rooms. A good deal. I called for information and no one speaks Spanish. They say, "Do you want to make an appointment? What day?" I can't understand her; she doesn't understand me, so I didn't do it.

Finances. Alicia has never used banks in the United States. Before she became a legal resident, she limited her financial transactions to cash in order to protect her undocumented status. At two of her three jobs, she was paid in cash because the companies hired undocumented workers and operated under the table. Now she receives an unemployment check and cashes it at the local meat market. She has few bills since her sister owns the house. She pays her bills using money orders—usually two each month. She is also trying to establish a credit rating:

> I have credit cards from JC Penney's, Mervin's—to try to develop a credit rating. . . . I always stay within my limits. I know what my

balance is. If I go the store to buy a pair of pants, I buy [only] what I need.

She added that she is only able to obtain credit cards when the sales clerks speak Spanish or the form is available in Spanish.

In her room at home, Alicia has a television, a VCR, and a tape recorder. The stereo in the living room belongs to her cousin, so she prefers not to use it. Kitchen appliances available for her use include a microwave, a blender, a stove, and an oven. They also have a washing machine. She finds new appliances quite simple to figure out:

> Actually, these days, the instruction manuals for things are really very clear. They have pictures for everything. . . . Now things are much more modern. There are the buttons. It's just a matter of trying them.

In her former jobs in food-preparation plants, Alicia made use of fairly simple technology, primarily mixers; much of the work was done by hand. In her current job training program in facility maintenance, she uses a variety of hand tools. Her low-wage, low-skill jobs brought her into little contact with sophisticated technology: Although some food-preparation plants are becoming increasingly mechanized, the ones for which Alicia worked relied more on cheap labor than computerized machinery.

While she exhibits no discomfort or fear about using technology in her daily life, her broader views seem to reflect society's love–hate relationship with technology:

> What's modern is good—to be able to heat food in the microwave—it's good, but at the same time it's the same technology that's destroying us. It's bad for you, that it gives you cancer.
>
> And modern things, machines—they displace people in their jobs. At ____, when they got a big packing machine, it replaced eight or ten people; now four people do that job.

Family Literacy. As a parent, Alicia is thoughtful about her role in the formal and moral education of Carmina and the other grandchildren. "I always go to her school. With the other children, I wasn't as careful. Now I pay more attention; I'm more careful."

She emphasizes two themes in discussing how she raises Carmina—her desire for Carmina to "become someone" and the value of retaining the language and culture:

I tell her to study because people who study work less and earn more. [To Carmina] You have to study because the people who don't end up cleaning bathrooms, and I don't want that for you. I want you to work in an office—to do something positive.

I want Carmina to speak two languages. For her to speak English and not Spanish—that I wouldn't like. I want her speak both. I don't want her to lose her roots, her customs. I want her to love Mexico. I know many friends of the family who have children 14 or 15 years old who have disdain for Spanish. I try to inculcate that in her—to love Spanish. English, too. She must speak both.

Spanish is spoken exclusively in the household. With the exception of her cousin, who is rarely home, the adults speak little English and, except for Carmina, the children are not yet of school age.

Summary

Alicia approaches new experiences with confidence and determination. She has faced difficult times—as an undocumented immigrant, in her family, in unstable and low-paying work. But she is successful at a wide range of activities—from learning facility maintenance skills, to mastering new technology in the home, to deciphering the child-custody system. Learning English presents her with her greatest challenge. She sees her limited English as also the greatest barrier to her being able to get a better job—the key to her being able to adopt her grandchildren. She is determined to keep studying English until she can achieve her goal of gathering all her grandchildren under her own care and love.

DAVID WONG

By Chui Lim Tsang and David Hemphill

David Wong is a 53-year-old male Chinese immigrant. Born in China in 1938, he immigrated to the United States in 1983 with his family. Since his arrival in the United States, he has worked and lived in San Francisco's Chinatown. He lives with his wife and his two children, a son age 22, and daughter age 19. Both children are pursuing a degree in business at San Francisco State University; the son is a senior and the daughter is a sophomore.

The Wong family has lived for about six years in a two-bedroom apartment in an older building. The rent is reasonable. The apartment is small and crowded, packed with furniture, a TV, radios, a microwave oven, a

VCR, a computer, and other electronic products. By U.S. standards, it is a small area for a family of four—two parents and two grown children. Yet its location means a short walk to work for Wong. Shopping and social networking in the Chinese community are convenient as well.

Wong has worked in a fish and poultry market for several years. Before that, he worked as a meat cutter in another market nearby. In his current job he serves mostly Cantonese speakers, selling them fish and cleaning the fish for them. The market where he works is located on Stockton Street, the major shopping street in Chinatown. It is a small store with seven employees and the owner. Wong works from 8:00 A.M. to 6:00 P.M. every day, six days a week, making $5 per hour. He gets time off for lunch and time off for breaks when the store is not too busy. The job does not provide medical coverage of any kind. Although his salary is low and the hours long, Wong considers his job to be one of the better ones available in the Chinatown labor market. He notes that overtime is compensated in this shop. He likes his employer because he is kind and treats his employees fairly. Wong describes how his boss encouraged him to get a driver's license:

> I have a driver's license. But I don't have a car. I took my driving test three times before I passed the test. After I failed my test the second time, my boss said he will give me $50 so I won't give up. I passed it on my third try. He's a nice guy. He's the lean one [points to him], about 60 years old, working on the opposite poultry counter.

Wong's wife also works outside of the home. She is currently working in a garment factory in another part of the city. She makes about $5 an hour doing clean-up work. Before this job, she was unemployed for a few months and found it very hard to find work, although she searched actively. She works hours similar to Wong's, also six days a week.

On his days off, Wong usually goes shopping with his wife, and they sometimes eat out in Chinese restaurants. Now that his children are grown, they no longer go out much with their parents, except on special occasions such as Chinese New Year, Christmas, and Chingming (ancestor memorial day). Wong's friends are all Chinese and Chinese-speaking. He also socializes with his wife's family, which is well represented in the local area. On occasion, he goes to the headquarters of his family association in Chinatown and talks to friends from his part of China. Chinese family associations, formed over generations by Chinese immigrants from the same clans and regions, have traditionally served as centers for community and cultural maintenance. The surname "Wong" is one of the most common in China, and the Wong family association is accordingly one of the largest in Chinatown.

Most of Wong's social network consists of people who are recent immigrants. Many were educated in China, but few have received formal education in the United States. Many have to work long hours like Wong and base their social network in the Chinatown circle. Few venture outside, for it is here that they find understanding and friendship in their newly adopted home.

The San Francisco Chinatown community contains one of the highest concentrations of Chinese in North America and has one of the highest population densities in the United States. San Francisco's Chinatown is an economic and social center for Chinese and Chinese Americans from throughout the San Francisco Bay Area. In many ways, it is a self-contained, self-supporting community within which immigrants can subsist, making only limited contact with the English-speaking world. There are also Chinese newspapers and radio and television stations. Until recently, the local Chinese TV stations mainly broadcast imported programming from Hong Kong and Taiwan. However, with the San Francisco earthquake of 1989, Chinese-language news broadcasts became a priority as it grew evident that reliance on the English-language media in a time of crisis was difficult for many members of the Chinese community. Now one of the Chinese-language channels offers a locally produced news show in Chinese.

San Francisco's Chinatown is located in one of the oldest parts of the city, and it has been firmly established for well over a century. This section of town consists largely of older brick buildings and relatively narrow streets. Streetcars inch their way through narrow lanes lined with double-parked cars and trucks unloading visitors and commercial goods. Produce shops, meat and fish markets, Chinese delicatessens, restaurants, dry goods stores, herbal medicine stores, Chinese banks, and souvenir shops line the streets of this area. On smaller streets, behind the main shopping avenues, there is also considerable economic activity, with small garment factories predominating. Family associations, social clubs, churches, and religious associations are also frequently seen on these less crowded, back streets.

Life is rapid and quintessentially urban in San Francisco's Chinatown; work is hard and long. Ten-hour days working for piecework or close-to-minimum wages are common for the members of this immigrant work force, and health insurance and paid vacations are all too rare. Asian immigration into the San Francisco Chinatown area continues at a high rate, fueled by continuing uncertainty over the future of Hong Kong and economic and political difficulties throughout China and other parts of East and Southeast Asia.

Life and Work

David Wong was born in Hahksan, outside the city of Canton (Goangjou), in the province of Guangdong in southern China. Hahksan was a rural town with about 2,000 inhabitants, most of them farmers. They worked their own land as well as lands owned by others. Wong was the fifth child in a family of six children, which included three girls and three boys. His parents were small farmers who owned their own land. When the Communists took control of the government of China in 1951, many of the large landowners lost their land holdings. However, farmers like Wong's father with small plots of land were left to continue what they and their ancestors had been doing for centuries. Besides farming, Wong's father sometimes went to markets to sell his farm products. According to Wong, life in the village was poor. Children usually went without shoes in the fields. Wong's family wore clogs made by Wong's father at home. When children reached school age, they walked to school barefoot. Only in winter did they wear shoes, mostly ill fitting and handed down from older siblings.

The house Wong lived in as a child was a simple farmhouse with a mud floor. The only items of technology in the home besides manual farming tools were a clock that required winding and a manual, Victrola-type record player. As Wong puts it,

> It was an old-style hand-crank machine that looked like an attaché case when folded. Before you play the records, you take the hand crank and give it a number of cranks. Everyone in the family knew how to use it. We had a supply of records—Chinese opera—that came with the recorder. My father bought it. It was made in China.

While his mother did not read or write, Wong's father had five years of classical educational training. He also served as a teacher in the village school at night. Wong's father loved to tell stories. It is common in the Chinese educational tradition to employ parables, aphorisms, and traditional sayings, and he often used such devices to educate his children. As Wong notes, "Because my father was a learned man, he liked to tell us stories to make us understand things." Wong recalls fondly his times as a child when his father told such stories. One story he remembers had the following message:

> mh   pa   loufu   ji   pa   louh.
> Not   afraid   tiger   only   afraid   leak.
>   [One doesn't fear tigers or violence as much as leakage or losses.]

Education and learning were emphasized in the family. Education was only supported by the government up through the sixth grade and was not mandatory, but all of the children in Wong's family were sent to school. As Wong notes,

> I was the only one in the family who was successful in education. My oldest brother quit after only two years. My second-oldest brother managed to stay in school for six years. He never made it to secondary school. All of my sisters went to school for only three to four years.

Wong attended elementary school and junior high school in his native town. His record of academic excellence earned him scholarships, and his high school years were spent in a boarding school because there was no high school within easy distance of his home. All of the instruction up through high school was delivered in Chinese. Once in high school, he studied English as a foreign language for three semesters.

After high school, Wong was fortunate to gain admission to the agricultural technical college in Siuhing, not far from his home—quite an accomplishment. After he graduated, he was assigned by the government to work in the nearby town of Toiseng, the county seat of Toishan. His responsibilities included directing a project to control pests. He also conducted research on the effectiveness of plant fertilizers for different crops.

Wong came to the United States in 1983, immigrating under the sponsorship of his wife's brother. His reason for immigration was simple: There were limited opportunities in China for himself and particularly for his children. This reason—to provide opportunities for the future of one's children—is frequently cited by immigrants as key to the decision to emigrate to the United States. When he first arrived in San Francisco, Wong wanted to return to China. It was a very difficult time for him and his family. He had no job and no income, and he did not speak any English. He had no access to any public assistance programs of any sort. He had no unemployment insurance and no local experience, and taking welfare is frowned upon in the Chinese community. He thought that his best plan would be to work hard for a few years, save some money, and then go home to China. "Today I no longer plan to go back to China to live. It's not too hard to work here. There is no use returning to China. My children are here, and there is no retirement in China."

It was not until his move to the United States that he saw the need for further formal education as an adult. But Wong did not start attending adult education programs in the United States immediately upon his arrival. It was not until 1987, four years later, when he felt his economic situation was under control, that he began to take adult education classes. Since 1987, Wong has attended about four years of English classes, all offered by the local community college. The last English class he attended was an ESOL 300-level class, which is designated a "low-intermediate" level according to the local community college district. He repeated the course at this level three times. In between, he also attended for several semesters a janitorial training program offered by the community college on Saturday mornings. He also took part in janitorial training offered by the local union. Wong's goal is to obtain a janitorial position somewhere outside of Chinatown.

Currently Wong attends a citizenship class offered by the community college at the YMCA a few blocks from his home. He attends classes Monday, Tuesday, and Wednesday evenings. Class begins at 6:30 every evening. This means that Wong has to rush home after he gets off work at 6:00, take a shower to wash off the smell of fish caused by work at the market, and run to class in order to make it on time. On the nights he attends class, Wong does not eat his dinner until after class, around 9:00. He hopes to be able to use the knowledge gained from this class to pass the test to become a U.S. citizen.

Everyday Literacy, Language, and Technology

Wong and his family speak the Toishan dialect, a subdialect of the Yue language, when they communicate with one another. This is the language that Wong spoke in his home village. With their friends and neighbors, they use mostly standard Cantonese, the lingua franca of Chinese immigrants in North America. Wong's children speak fluent English, but Wong's wife speaks practically no English at all.

Wong reads the overseas version of the *Tsing Tao Daily* newspaper from Hong Kong every day. This is one of several Chinese-language daily newspapers that are widely available in San Francisco's Chinatown. He does not usually read the local English-language newspaper. His son, however, reads it every day. When he does look at the English-language paper, he focuses on the want ads, scanning them for janitorial openings. When he reads the English-language newspaper he uses an English–Chinese dictionary.

Besides reading the Chinese newspapers, Wong watches TV in the evening to get his news. He watches the Chinese TV stations when he has time. He sometimes also watches English-language programs which his children have selected that come on after the Chinese programs, although "I can't understand all of the dialogue. I can probably understand 30 to 40% of the programs my children watch."

Wong is also working on a novel that he has written in Chinese, which he completed earlier this year. In his free time, he now works on revising

it. This novel combines his personal immigration experience and his knowledge of the village in which he grew up.

Other reading materials in evidence in the Wong household include
such items as utility bills, telephone bills, bank statements, and tax forms.
Wong usually deals with these himself. He learned long ago that these can
be deciphered once he figures out the way the information is laid out. The
regularity and fixed format of these documents make it relatively easy for
him to deal with them. He sometimes consults his English–Chinese dictionary when handling these documents. He does not, however, like to ask
his children for help:

> I don't ask him [the son] to help. I can do it myself. He is busy most
> of the time, and it's easier for me to handle these matters myself.
> Yes, I can handle these myself. I really don't need his help.

Wong says this in a way that indicates he feels it is probably more work
for him to ask his children than it is worth. He expresses the same feelings
about filing his income tax. He takes care of it himself. And if it becomes
too complicated, he asks his friends or an accountant. As an example of
this, Wong notes that he needed his relatives' help when he first applied
for his immigration papers. The letters he got were too complicated for him
to decipher, so he sought the help of his contemporaries.

Wong keeps a family checking account in a local bank, which is located about a block away from the market where he works. He goes there
to deposit his paycheck and withdraw money. Workers in the bank can
speak Chinese, a common practice in the plethora of banks and thrift institutions in San Francisco's Chinatown. He writes the checks and mails the
bills in himself.

Wong doesn't go to many places outside of Chinatown. He sometimes
goes shopping in the large chainstores; when he does this, he takes the bus.
Occasionally he has to go across town to visit his wife's family. For most of
the places he needs to go in his everyday life, he goes on foot. He has never
had to ask a stranger for help in finding his way around the city:

> I can read the bus schedule and I can read the signs. I can also
> drive. Do you know that after one week in this city I could already
> figure out where things are? I could read a map. I went everywhere
> with the map. I could tell how to get from one place to another.

Wong does most of his shopping in Chinatown. He does not have much
trouble shopping, even in large mainstream department stores such as
Macy's. Sometimes he and his wife go downtown to the department stores

to shop. He can read the labels and the price tags. When he really needs something in a store, he asks. He recounts how he once asked for help in a large supermarket:

> Like the other day I went shopping at Cala Foods. I wanted to buy some game hens. I saw an ad in the newspaper. I couldn't find any in the store, so I had to ask. But they couldn't find any more. They told me they will have more next Friday. That was not a problem for me.

Technology. Wong can use most of the appliances that are in his family's apartment, including the TV, VCR, radio, and tape recorder. Generally speaking, he has learned to use them once their operation has been demonstrated to him by his children. The family has two microwave ovens. One is for the children and the other is for Wong and his wife. The one used by his children is more modern and complex, and Wong cannot figure out how to use all of its functions and features. The one he and his wife use is a more basic model that is easier to handle.

Wong's wife takes care of the family's laundry. Small items such as underwear she washes at home. Larger items she takes to a nearby coin-operated laundromat. She has been shown how to use the machines, and using them does not present a problem.

Wong uses his family's VCR and the TV extensively. Like most of his friends, Wong and his wife are avid followers of programs produced in Hong Kong and Taiwan. They rent videos frequently from any of the numerous Chinese video rental stores that have proliferated in Chinatown. In addition, Wong and his wife tape Chinese TV programs. Wong also uses his tape recorder quite often. He has obtained taped material to help him review the facts he must know in order to pass the U. S. citizenship test. He reviews these materials at home, using the tape recorder and earphones, when he has time.

Wong has a bank card that he has received as a feature of his checking account at the local bank he patronizes. The card allows him to withdraw money from automatic teller machines, but he does not use it. He has given it to his son so he can have access to cash whenever he needs it: "I give it to him so he can get money if he wants to. He carries it with him. He took it with him when he went to Los Angeles. I don't need it. I don't know how to use it."

Wong has a personal computer at home. His children often use it, but he has never thought of doing so. He does not view it as a tool that can help him in his daily life or help him achieve any of his goals.

Literacy and Technology at Work. The fish market where Wong works sells live fish to customers. The only tools the workers use on the job are knives and wooden sticks to slaughter and clean the fish. Hand trucks are used to transport the goods, and ice is kept in a large freezer in the back. Besides cleaning and selling fish, Wong has to help clean the store and sometimes he cleans the big fish tanks.

Wong speaks mostly Cantonese at work, since most of the customers who come into the market are Chinese Cantonese speakers. But not all of the market's customers can speak Chinese, and Wong describes how it often falls to him to handle these English-speaking customers:

> There are some American-born Chinese who cannot speak Chinese. I have to deal with them. In fact, there are quite a number of clients who cannot speak Chinese. Then there are non-Chinese clients. I will have to speak to them. I don't have much trouble. I can say "Hi," "How much?" "What kind of fish?" "May I help you?" "Thank you," and all that. There are only two people at work who can handle English. Besides myself, there is another person. The others cannot speak English at all.

Wong does not deal with written English at all at work. Some math skills are required because the workers have to collect money from the customers and make change for them. This does not present a problem for Wong. A typical math transaction involves figuring out the amount owed by multiplying the cost per pound or per ounce of the fish purchased by the actual weight of the fish. Then the total purchase is added together. Wong then has to collect the money from customers and give the proper change.

Goals and Expectations

Wong has a limited set of goals and expectations for the immediate and not-too-distant future. Each of his goals is framed in terms of a unique set of expectations that reflect his perspective as an immigrant and one who is not a member of the dominant culture in the United States.

His first, and most consciously pursued, goal is to get a janitorial job. He is not completely satisfied with his current work in the fish market, and he believes that securing janitorial work will lead to better pay, medical benefits, and a shorter workweek. His expectation appears realistic, inasmuch as service trades such as building maintenance are heavily unionized in San Francisco, with relatively good pay and benefits. He has been trying to achieve this goal for two years. He recently took a test for custodial positions offered by the San Francisco civil service system. These jobs pay about $9 per hour with full benefits. He passed the test and is now 125th on a list of 200 candidates: If the city continues to hire janitors at its current rate, he may be hired in about three years.

Before taking the civil service test, he tried numerous times to secure a janitorial position in various places. He applied at three large San Francisco tourist hotels but was not hired. He believes that his lack of English communication skills was a key factor in these hiring decisions. He thinks that he probably made errors in filling out the application forms, or that his writing and the information he put down were not judged adequate. He enrolled in a union janitorial training program, but after finishing he was not able to become a union member until he put in a minimum number of hours working a union job, and he could not afford to take time off from his job at the fish market to take temporary work. So the civil service appears to him to be the best alternative for janitorial employment.

Wong has made a hard-eyed and pragmatic assessment of what he can do and what sort of work will support him and his family in the new cultural context in which he finds himself. His assessment reflects the dual filters of his own cultural perspective and his limited English-language proficiency and literacy. He shows little awareness, for example, of the fact that biotechnology is one of the growing, most promising industries in the San Francisco Bay Area. He sees no link between his own background as a trained and experienced agricultural engineer and the employment possibilities in this new area, for example, as a lab worker in a biotechnology firm. He also sees no direct utility for him in learning to use the personal computer he has in his home. He cannot think of how the use of a computer may help him with his dream of getting a janitorial position, or with a job search, or with any sort of creative function.

Wong has other goals as well. He wants to obtain his U.S. citizenship and he wants to buy a house. His pursuit of the citizenship goal would appear to be well under way. His enrollment in citizenship classes in the evenings and his regular audiotape study of citizenship questions enhance the likelihood of his becoming a U.S. citizen in the near future. It is also likely that Wong and his family will be able to buy a house in a few years. He and his wife both save regularly, and housing prices have started to fall in the local housing market. So this goal, too, appears achievable in the near term for Wong.

Wong's final goal is his intention to complete a novel in Chinese about his immigration experience and to have it published. Despite the fact that cultural and linguistic barriers have caused him to pursue work that ignores his education and experience, Wong has nonetheless found a more aesthetic means of employing his Chinese education, intellect, and literacy: his novel. In describing his novel, he expresses his hope of recording and sharing with others—in other times and places—the unique nature of his life and his experience, surely one of the most basic and moving purposes of literacy:

> This story is about an immigrant Chinese who returned to China after spending years in the U.S. After returning to his native village with money he managed to save with his hard work in the U.S., he built a nice little house in a remote part of the village. There he married and planned to live his life in the quiet company of his new family. One day, he was found dead. The suspected cause of death was murder. The story kind of dramatizes his experience in the U.S. and the events that led up to his death. I wrote it for fun. It's about 30,000 words in length. I am recopying it now. I don't know if anyone will want to publish it.

MICHELA STONE

By Tom Nesbit

Michela Stone is a 32-year-old single woman, a refugee from Byelorussia in the western part of the former Soviet Union. She has lived in San Francisco since 1989 and hopes to gain American citizenship. She works as a bookkeeper/accountant in the immigrant department of a community center. Michela lives alone in a small, third-floor apartment in a four-story building. She doesn't know many of her neighbors. Her mother is dead, and she has a younger sister who is married and lives with her Russian husband and child in New York. Her father, who emigrated with Michela, also lives in San Francisco, in government-subsidized housing:

> I still cook for him, so I see him three to four times per week. He is also learning English, so he comes to where I work for classes. I spend one night a week at his apartment so I can cook or clean for him. He can look after himself, but I need to do this. In Russia, family is very important.

Her apartment is close to her work. "I have a nice apartment near this job. It's just seven minutes by walking. It's very nice. It has a security system, which is very good. And my spruce tree—it's my friend." She doesn't know a lot of people in her apartment building or outside of the Russian community:

Most of the people I know are Russian. I do know more Americans than my friends, partly because of where I work. But also, my friends, they have family and more obligations to kids. They don't have time to spend outside home. I have very few good friends. In Russian a friend means a lot. It's one who shares your bitterness and your happiness, you can share anything. Here you don't have quite the same sorts of friends because you don't live in your community like you used to. When situation is hard you need to find a way to survive. Some people find an honest way to survive. Some people just cheat and lie. Especially here, society gives people such a good field, such a good opportunity to lie. This is true. So making friends is hard. I have a lot of acquaintances. Especially working here, I know a lot of people and they know me, know who I am. Everyone comes for money or for favors. I try and help them.

As for free time, I love to cook. As you can see I'm very—I eat too much. So I try not to cook, but . . . I like to dance also, but I don't have much time. If I had a car it would be easier. My hobby, it's photography. I have a camera but it's not very good. Here the equipment is very high-quality but I can't afford it.

I also get together with my friends and I try to find an American friend. This is most important problem. Finding American friends. Male or female doesn't matter. I don't look only for romance. American men are not so romantic. I decided not to have a boyfriend right now. It's totally different values.

Michela is not a member of any community groups. "No time!" However, she once joined a choral society. "I went with my friend. She had a Chinese boyfriend, and it was Chinese group though most had been born here. We sang in English. I didn't like it much. I just liked people."

In order to feel more assimilated into American life as well as to improve her learning of English, Michela began to teach Russian to three Americans:

I started to exchange Russian to English, English to Russian. Lessons just for exchange, you understand. Not for money. We read and write and speak Russian and English. Maybe one hour, two hour a week. Then I learn something about American lifestyle. Cultural exchange. To meet American people, to learn something from them.

Her students are two Americans who want to learn Russian so they can visit and an American-born Lithuanian who wants to keep his cultural heritage. "You see, Russia and news about Russian federation has been a lot in the papers. This wakens interest. People want to go there, to see for themselves."

Michela's apartment is designed for one person: a bathroom, a small storage area, and a carpeted oblong room that is bedroom, living room, and kitchen. The cooking area is sectioned off by a counter that serves as a table. Michela's kitchen area has a small refrigerator/freezer, an electric cooker, and a microwave. Her living room/bedroom contains a bed, a small low table, and a bookcase with some books, photos, a small TV, and an FM/AM radio. There are pictures on each wall, although one of the shorter walls is taken up by a window that looks out onto a mature spruce tree. The overall impression of Michela's apartment is of functionality and practicality.

Most of the area where Michela lives is filled with similar apartment buildings or small family homes. There are not many trees or gardens, and Michela's building faces onto one of San Francisco's commuter corridors. There is a university close by, and every other street corner contains a small grocery store. There are banks, supermarkets, laundromats, cafés, and restaurants within a 15-minute walking distance as well as frequent public transport to other parts of the city.

Michela Stone is part of San Francisco's Russian immigrant population. She has lived in the area for two years. The community center where she works is an integral part of a wide community network, meeting many of the housing, education, and social needs of both recent and more established immigrants:

> I think there's about 10–15,000 emigrants from Russia in the area. There's been four waves of emigration: around the time of the revolution, after World War II, about 1973–74, and then after 1987. . . . Each wave helps the next settle in. It's like family. We're very tight.
>
> Most recent Russian emigrants to San Francisco are Jews, though it's not a religious thing. It's more cultural, you know? It's how we grew up. We want to keep it. The center where I work is not a synagogue. Most people who use the center are Russians. It's just a local place for Russians to go, to keep our traditions, to be together.

Many have a college education and come from the Russian professional class: university teachers, businesspeople, doctors, or scientists. They come mainly from the Ukraine, Lithuania, or Byelorussia. "They're the ones with the knowledge of European countries and cultures. They know about other ways to be, rather than just Soviet way."

Most Russian immigrants come to the United States for two main reasons. The first is the poor living standards in their country of origin. "Even if you're wealthy it's hard. You can't buy or do much. There's not a lot of foreign currency in Soviet Union, so most things are for tourists." Second, immigrants desire to live in a more open society:

> They also dream about living in a free country. Where government does not lie to the people. It's like prison sometimes. Where you go, what you do, it's watched. And for Jews it's worse—there's persecution. There was a lot of trouble. Like for me and my father. Our name, it's _____. It's Jewish. We didn't do anything. But we have to think one thing, say another thing, do a different way. It's hard. I worked with teenagers. When you know young persons and they ask you some question and you have to say certain things and not say certain things.

Life and Work

Michela was born in Gomel, a city of 500,000 people in southeastern Byelorussia. She lived there with her parents until she was 17.

> My mother live there all her life, but my father came from a smaller city. My parents weren't so young when I was born. The war you understand. My father was 34, my mother was 29 when I was born. This was quite old for Russians.

Michela has one sister, younger by two years. The family lived with Michela's paternal grandmother all the time that Michela was a child. Michela's parents both worked:

> My mother first she was a math teacher in the local high school. But then she was an executive director in a secondary school in a military base. When I was born it was hard for her to find a job. So she enrolled in a correspondence course from Kiev and she graduated with a diploma in foreign languages. My father, he was the first in his family to go to college. But he did not complete his undergraduate education. So he did not change jobs too much. In fact, he stay in the same job for 42 years. He was accountant. It was a trade union company, and he eventually got a trade union position as a financial manager. In Russia you know that a trade union's task is different. It is not only to protect workers' rights but also to provide welfare for the people. Trips to resorts and taking care of

workers' health and welfare. So my father organized that for the union where he worked.

Michela went to a local school in Gomel until she was 16. She remembers it fondly:

It was easy for me to learn to read. I could read before I went to school. My mother and my grandmother help me. They would read to me, and I would follow the words on the page. Writing—that was harder. I could print, but my calligraphy was not so good. I had no patience with this. We had ink and a quill pen. My mother always say, "Michela has great patience." If I make mistake, I start again from the beginning. I found school easy—apart from chemistry and algebra. I love physics. I was a good student, not because I am quick learner, but because I studied a lot.

She took her high school exams a year earlier than her contemporaries and then moved away from her family home to go to college in Moscow. She lived there for two years.

It was great experience. I lived in dormitory and was near the theater and movies. I went out all the time. I used to skip my lunch and go. I was a full-time student as well, so it was a busy time. I never missed any school.

When her mother died, economic hardship caused her to move back home to live with her father and her newly married sister. "My father he didn't force me to move back. But I thought it was necessary. We were an established family, in terms of the money situation, but still it was hard for us. It was expensive to stay in Moscow." She completed her bachelor's degree (in accounting) at the local university and enrolled in a correspondence course to get a master's degree in accountancy teaching.

She remembers her parents (her mother especially) being very supportive of education, partly because of their own educational experiences:

My father, his family, was not so clever, so educated. He was the first in his family to get a higher education. Before the revolution, for Jews—it was forbidden to live in a city. Just in the country where schools were not so good. My mother's family was very well educated. I know this for three generations. Her mother was a governess and could speak seven languages.

Michela feels that her mother's being a teacher helped form her own attitude toward education and learning:

> When I was little I remember being read to a lot by my mother and my grandmother. Not only in Russian. My mother would read me stories in French and German. Fairy tales and historical stories mostly. Lovely printed books with colorful pictures, special editions.

She doesn't remember her father helping so much: "Of course, he was working man. Sometimes 18 hours a day." There were always lots of books around the house:

> Russian history, classical literature like Pushkin, math books—my mother was a math teacher, foreign language books—mainly in French and German, and crossword puzzle books—my mother used to love doing crosswords. No English books, though—I don't know why. Perhaps no one could read English. My father certainly couldn't.

When she left Russia, Michela had to sort out her family library:

> There were over 2,000 books, most of which my mother had collected. All sorts of books. All had to be left behind—I brought only 40 books with me. Some cookery books, a collection of Pushkin, some history. I don't have any kids, but I brought at least a couple of history books to let the children know about Russian history.

In Gomel, Michela worked as an accountant/bookkeeper in a wholesale company.

> It was boring for me. I was only 20 years old and it wasn't very exciting. No computerized accounting. We used abacus and calculators. I had to supervise three older women, and they made it hard for me to do that. So I was very depressed and decided to get another job.
> I should add that I was a camp counselor for five years each summer for violent kids from bad families. We would go away into the country and do education and workshops, help the children, they were aged about 14 or 15, feel good about themselves. So I realized that I liked to teach, and I applied for a job teaching basic

statistics and simple accounting in a college. I did that for seven years. During that time I also did a correspondence course and got my master's degree in accountancy teaching.

In January 1989, Michela and her father got their permits to leave the Soviet Union. They moved first to Italy and then (after two months) to the United States. She has lived in San Francisco ever since. She plans to stay in the United States. "I lost my Russian citizenship—I am a refugee. I want to be a U.S. citizen. After five years I can apply." Moving was challenging and frightening:

> I didn't know what we would find. We were lucky. My sponsor found us a place to stay. You need to have a sponsor to come here. Our sponsor was my father's friend's son. He was financially responsible for first few months. He gave us an apartment for me and my father. Two beds in one room. But it was cheap. We stay there one and a half years. Then my father got a government-sponsored apartment and I move to my own place.

Initially, she worked "as a cleaner in an apartment house, then in a hotel doing office work. Then I got a job here at the center." She'd eventually like to move to a job teaching in a local college. "I need to learn economics, though." When she moved to the United States, she found people were not particularly helpful with advice about work:

> People would tell me that I couldn't get a job as an accountant. You can get a job at a hotel or cleaning up someone's mess. Why they did that I don't know. It was misinstruction. It made me think I was nothing.

When she moved to the United States, Michela couldn't speak any English at all—only a little German in addition to Russian. "At first I forced myself to read for one hour per day. It was the rule. I just did it." Since she's been here, Michela has already enrolled in several adult education classes: basic literacy, accounting, and two English classes. "The literacy class was the most helpful. Probably because I'd just moved here and needed to know the most."

This basic course developed practical literacy skills in simulated real-life situations. "I remember we were taught how to use the telephone. To talk faster and not so loud. You see, in Russia we shout. Really loud." She concentrated on using simple English words and phrases:

That was so helpful. The teacher wasn't American. He was Chinese, I think, and had graduated from a school in France. And he did not have such good English. We had to listen to him very hard. But that made it easier for us to learn. Just simple English. I wasn't so afraid of making mistakes when the teacher made them too sometimes. He was OK.

The course was held in a community-based organization in central San Francisco. Most of the other students were recent immigrants (though by no means all Russian), and one of the main objectives of the course was "learning how to do things the American way. So we can better get jobs." The students learned a lot from one another:

At first I thought I don't want to be doing this. So many different languages, you understand. I want to learn American and be in class with Americans. But after a while I liked the other people better and saw that they had many of the same problems I had. We talked a lot about that. We had a lot of fun laughing at everyone's mistakes.

The accounting class and the other English courses were held in more traditional college environments and were less enjoyable:

The first course was about listening and grammar. I thought the teacher was very good and helped us a lot. But the course was more expensive and not so fun. A lot of written tests and corrections. And passages, you know? Reading passages. You have to understand direct and indirect questions. You could not use your previous knowledge and experiences to get a correct answer. It was hard. Even for Americans.

Michela's goal is to improve her English to such a degree that she could pass the TOEFL (Test of English for Foreign Learners):

I'd like to be able to go to college here. Enroll in a business program. Get an MBA. Nobody thinks my MA from Russia is worth much. I took TOEFL once and scored only 10 below. That's just one or two answers. I'll certainly take it again when I have time to study.

Everyday Literacy, Language, and Technology

Michela works as a bookkeeper/accountant in the immigrant department of a large community center. Her office is tiny and crammed with files, two desks, computers, and a giant refrigerator leaking ice. Papers are strewn over every surface. The office feels cluttered but friendly. Her co-workers are constantly in and out of one another's offices. They use Michela's office to play computer games. On a wall near her desk, Michela has pinned a list of tenses of English verbs. "It's my homework."

Neighboring offices of similar size serve as a reception/counseling area and the editorial office of a Russian-language newspaper put out by the department. She works with two other people, both Russian, although she has sole responsibility for the department's financial recordkeeping. She is clearly skilled at her work and enjoys it, despite the meager salary. To supplement her income, she also works for seven hours per week as a bookkeeper for a small dental practice near her apartment.

At work, Michela reads in English. "Papers related to accounting, program services. I don't know every word. Some very technical. My co-workers help me a lot. I also have dictionary on my desk. I use every day." She also writes in English. "Just short letters and notes. To be honest, my writing is not so good. My co-workers have to correct it. Syntax is different between English and Russian."

One of the drawbacks of her job is that she doesn't get to speak a lot of English. She does, however, use computer technology:

> With my co-workers I speak mainly English. About 85 percent of time. With clients I speak mainly Russian. Their English not so good. Most of my work is with figures, and it's in my head. As well, a lot of the people who use the center are Russian and can't speak a lot of English. I can't improve my English very much.
>
> I use computers here for the bookkeeping and for typing letters. I did use computers in Russia, too, but they were more outdated. Different machines. Slower. Some of the computer language is hard. I thought "goto" was a strange word. I couldn't find it in the dictionary. Only now I know it is two words, "go to."

Because of her two jobs and having to cook for her father, Michela doesn't have much free time. Most of what free time she has is spent reading:

> Not as much as my parents did, though. They had more settled lifestyle. I don't have time. I read both English and Russian. In Russian I read Pushkin and Russian history. These were the books I brought with me. In English I read accountancy books and love stories. Love stories are easy to read. Short, simple words. Accounting books are technical, not so much interest. But with dictionary, it's OK.

I also read magazines about the [movie] stars. This help me participate in some conversations amongst my friends. In the dentist's office where I work, they have magazines like *USA Today* and *People*. If I have 15 minutes off, I try and read them. To understand what's going on in the country. It's interesting for me to read about Soviet Union. It's hard to understand the changes in Soviet system. I sometimes see a Russian newspaper—my father subscribes. For him it's his life.

Michela gets most of her news from TV, which is also a good source of entertainment and learning about "American" culture:

I have a small TV which gets local channels. My father—he has a cable TV with 35 channels so he can watch Moscow news every day. He watches a lot but doesn't understand much. I watch the news and soap operas. "Young and Restless" is a favorite. There's a lot of stories. It helps me find out about American life. In Soviet Union the soap operas are more about crime and cops.

I like "Jeopardy" because it's written, you know? Of course, I don't know many of the answers but I like reading. I also watch programs called "Donahue" and "Geraldo." They are talk shows, with different guests. That's really interesting. Always some aspect of American life is on. People are very open with their feelings and opinions. Not like in Russia. I usually find the programs very interesting. Most of the general ideas I understand, some of the words are hard.

Michela doesn't have a VCR: "If I did, I could tape these shows and discuss them with my father and friends. Only so much time though." At the moment, she doesn't want other technological equipment either. "When I have more money, I buy. Better kitchen equipment. Make life easier."

Shopping presents little difficulty for Michela. When she first came to the United States, she would carry a dictionary with her—"Always with me. For two years, in my purse." Now she doesn't use one when she goes shopping:

I can usually understand. You don't need English to buy food. You just walk in and they serve you. In Chinese store, I ask how to cook certain vegetables. Usually they tell you. Some don't know English. It's hard to find right person to explain.

Sometimes I don't know products. When we went shopping, I didn't know different kind of tofu. I didn't know you could get different sorts, like "hard." Sometimes I use dictionary to find out what's in canned foods. And for recipes.

She doesn't use food coupons, not because she doesn't understand their language or use but "I don't have the time. At first I think 'Why do Americans try to save money?' Although I do try to buy cheapest. I always buy brand name of store. It's less money."

She has little difficulty with written instructions for household appliances. "If I don't know, I try to just use and see how it works." She can readily pick up how to use most machines, although "When I first came, I couldn't understand the ATM machine at the bank. People from my class show me. Now it's no problem." Her only serious difficulty was with a newly purchased telephone answering machine. "I didn't know how to set it up. I don't understand the word 'rings.' I knew which buttons to press but not how to save. I use a dictionary. Then it's not so difficult."

Buying clothes can be more troublesome. "In Soviet Union, sizes are different. For example, I don't know what is 'petite.' I cannot ask the salesperson. So I try on. I usually go with friends and they tell me."

Michela doesn't have a car and gets around by public transport, although she has passed her California driving test: "That was easy. No trouble with the words." Public transport is readily available and easy to use: "For first few days it's hard. I don't know ways to go. No problem now."

Menus are only a minor problem:

I sometimes eat out. I like Chinese. Though I find it hard to understand the menu. Not words like "spicy" or "pork," you know, but specific names of dishes. Sometimes I ask, or point. Sometimes I choose what I know. I try to read. I usually get what I ask for.

In general, Michela has little difficulty with written English. What she doesn't understand immediately, she remembers or writes down to look up when she gets home. "You can pick up most from context." Because of her greater difficulty with understanding social contexts, spoken English is generally harder to pick up:

I try to understand what people say on the bus. But it's hard. People use a lot of slang. In Russia, too. But you use slang without thinking. Here I try to use at right time, but the words are different. If you try to understand just the words, it's hard. I cannot participate in conversation about the movies—I don't have time to go often and I can't understand much when I do. At first, I tried to speak English with my Russian friends but we jumped back. We didn't know enough words. But we tried.

Talking to other people I find hard. People don't always show you. They behave not nice. They don't want to teach you because they're afraid you're going to take their jobs. They're not always sympathetic when you don't have good English. For example, there was a counselor at the local college. When I met him, he was very rude. He didn't give me any information. He just kicked me out and didn't explain. All because I had poor English. I understand he has more people apply than places, but . . .

Michela doesn't have any children of her own, but she spends time with her friends' children:

Most of my friends have kids, and they ask me not to speak English to their children. They are frightened they will lose their Russian. Then parents will lose family connections and influence on their children. I think they are right. If I had kids, I would be same.

Retaining and sharing aspects of her own culture is very important to Michela:

It's strange. Americans are more competitive, more individual. In Russia we are more together. We help each other. We are more social, more sharing.

You see, with my students—the ones who learn Russian. We have lesson outside—in bar, or beach, or sometimes in my apartment. This helps me learn English better. I'm not afraid to ask some question. Because my student, he or she feel the same way I do. Because we don't know a lot, we are not ashamed to ask each other. Personal contact and exchange has helped me the most.

SOKHHOEUN

By David Hemphill

Sokhhoeun is a 38-year-old Cambodian man who has been in the United States since 1981. Sokhhoeun is married with three children, ages 13, 11, and 9, and lives with his immediate family in the Asian refugee and immigrant community in East Oakland. He came to the United States as a refugee after a harsh six-year odyssey following the rise and fall of the Khmer

Rouge in Cambodia that took him through the experience of forced labor, de facto imprisonment, exploitation on the Cambodian–Thai border, and further incarceration in refugee camps in Thailand.

Sokhhoeun describes himself as someone who likes to help others. His first job in the United States was in warehousing, but after being laid off and falling ill, he started to volunteer with a refugee resettlement agency, helping newly arrived refugees connect to social service agencies. He was soon asked by an agency administrator if he wanted to work further in this area, and he agreed. He has worked for six years as a bilingual teacher's aide at three sites of an ESOL adult literacy education program. The adult refugees with whom he works are predominantly from Vietnam, Afghanistan, China, and Laos. He works mostly in the classroom helping individual students or small groups with particular lessons being taught by the instructor. He also helps adult refugee students with individual problems such as social service referrals. He finds that informal chats with students at break time are an effective means of establishing friendships and gaining confidence.

His neighborhood has seen substantial changes in the last 10 to 15 years. Formerly a predominantly African American and Latino community, the area now has become considerably more complex. There are signs in Chinese, Vietnamese, Lao, and Cambodian advertising "banh my" (Vietnamese pâté sandwiches), coffee shops (serving strong Vietnamese coffee), hair salons, auto repair, video rental (dubbed in Chinese, Vietnamese, Cambodian, Lao, and Thai), groceries, fast food, and legal services. Many of these businesses have grown up surrounding the Clinton Park Adult School site, a main ESOL center.

Sokhhoeun lives with his family in a two-bedroom apartment in a small, pastel-colored, stucco apartment building in a residential section. Most of the other tenants in his building are Mien people from the hills of Laos with whom he communicates in English. When he was looking at the building before moving in, he introduced himself to his prospective neighbors and offered them his help should they need it. Now he is often invited to his Mien neighbors' social gatherings.

According to Sokhhoeun, most Cambodian families living in Oakland are members of a formally structured community mutual support system, organized by neighborhoods. Sokhhoeun is the leader for his neighborhood. The 15 such Cambodian neighborhood groups in Oakland maintain a mailing list of all Cambodian families. A primary function of this support system is to support individual families when a member has passed away. When a death occurs, neighborhood leaders canvass their members for monetary contributions, which are presented on behalf of the entire Cambodian community to the bereaved family at a formal funeral ceremony.

Sokhhoeun stresses the importance of this community support function in time of family bereavement.

Life and Work

Sokhhoeun was born in 1952, the youngest in a family of five children. He had two brothers and two sisters. Both brothers are now dead, killed by the Khmer Rouge in 1975.

> I was born in Cambodia and I grew up in Cambodia also. When I was a child . . . my family is very poor, and I don't have a chance to go to school in my country. I never been in the school. So when I was . . . 13 years old . . . I became a monk. Then I learned my language from that. . . . After that, when I was 18 I got married. . . . After I got married two or three years, then I had one child. . . . Then my family moved down to a different city, because my family [was] very, very poor. . . . When I was 25, then my family moved to another city, too. That was called Battambang city.

When Sokhhoeun was young, his family lived in rural areas of Cambodia. The whole family worked to help his father, a rice farmer. The family moved around frequently, seeking situations in different regions of Cambodia where they could make enough of a living to survive.

> [We worked] very, very hard every day. . . . In the morning we get up at six o'clock . . . and when we got to the farm, you know, it's around eight or eight-thirty something like. It's not very close . . . the field is very far. . . . We walked two or three hours sometime. . . . It's my own [family's] farm . . . because . . . when we move from another city we have to buy land, you know, buy the land from someone else.

His family lived in simply constructed homes, which they rebuilt themselves whenever they moved to a new area:

> We live in a house together, one house . . . but it's not really, you know, good house. . . . They used hay to make a roof. . . . The walls just bamboo, they use bamboo. And for the floor they use the bamboo, too. . . . We do have the stove, but it's not a stove like we have it right here [in the United States], electricity stove, gas stove, whatever, we just [use] the . . . cement to make it don't burn the floor, because the floor we make from the bamboo. So we . . . just

make three leg like this [gestures like a tripod] . . . and you put the pot and . . . we go cut the wood and make a fire. . . . When we grow rice . . . we use the cows, pull the . . . plow . . . to make the ground . . . open and we can put some rice in.

We do have radio. . . . We have small hand radio like that [points to tape recorder], we use battery. . . . Once awhile we go to the city to the market . . . and we buy the battery from there.

His father knew how to read and write, but his mother did not. He doesn't know if his parents ever went to school, but he doesn't think so. He remembers his father reading Buddhist texts every day at home:

He had a book at home and he liked to read the—what is that called in English—you know, when you become a monk, you study that word [Buddhist scriptures]. . . . So he likes to read that every day. . . . But he's not become a monk.

Sokhhoeun had no formal education until the age of 13, when he became for a time a Buddhist monk, a common practice for young males in Southeast Asia. At his mother's urging, he went to live for two years in a nearby temple.

Life in the temple was rigorous, an unvarying schedule that began with prayers in the main hall at five o'clock, running for one to two hours. This was followed by food gathering. Monks split up and went in teams in different directions carrying begging bowls to gather food for the day's meal from people in nearby villages. On return to the temple, a meal was prepared and eaten, and the remainder of the day was spent in prayer, study, and chanting.

Formal instruction in Buddhist ritual and doctrine was conducted orally by chief monks at the temple, followed by exposure to the written texts of particular rituals, one at a time. In this fashion, after a few months' time, Sokhhoeun learned to read and write the Cambodian [Khmer] language:

When I first became a monk . . . they just brought me the book. . . . OK, you study this. . . . And you just look at every day, every day, every day . . . if you have any question, just go there and ask, what is that, what do you say . . . how do you pronounce that? It's just word by word, or something like that. . . . So, very difficult to read that Buddhist word, very difficult . . . not like everyday [words]— special word. And they [the words] have a tail, they have a head, or whatever . . . [laughs]. It's very difficult, but when they tell you . . . one time, then you just try to remember yourself, you know. . . .

But we don't write very much. Just used to read and, you
know, to practice by orals. . . . But if you want to study like . . . more
education about Cambodian letter, you have to go to the city and
study at school. . . . I decided to go into the city and study, but at
that time the Khmer Rouge came into my country, so I don't have a
chance to go. I just quit.

Once Sokhhoeun had learned to read through his studies at the temple,
he was then able to transfer the skill of reading to other texts of a secular
nature, although doing this kind of reading often required additional
independent study or questioning of others:

So when you want to study about politic, about . . . something else,
you have to use another book, and learn that by yourself. Sometime
. . . if you don't know you can ask people . . . like the people that
[have] high education or whatever.

When Sokhhoeun was 15, his family moved to a region of Cambodia
known for its diamonds. For the next eight years, until 1975, the family was
relatively prosperous. Their work involved careful prospecting in isolated,
forested areas where diamonds were known to have been found.

In 1975, with the fall of the Cambodian government, the Khmer Rouge
took control of the country. Sokhhoeun and his family were forced out of the
area where they had been living and sent to work on a sugar cane plantation:

The Khmer Rouge . . . they force you to the countryside. They not
let you stay in the city. . . . They told everybody to move out. . . .
When the Khmer Rouge took over, the Khmer Rouge . . . leader, the
boss or whatever, they ask you to do what they want to ask, you
know. . . . So we have to do for them. No choice. If you say something, they kill you. So we have to do what they ask you to do. . . . I
stayed there since 1975 to 1979 . . . four years, right . . . ? Just
working, the same work, the same job . . . no choice.

In 1979 Vietnamese troops entered Cambodia and drove the Khmer
Rouge out of many areas they controlled. This was the start of a period of
chaos and extreme deprivation for Sokhhoeun and his family. At first the
Khmer Rouge ran away from the plantation, and the refugees used knives
to stop them from taking all the vehicles with them. The Khmer Rouge
returned well-armed the following day to identify and punish the leaders
of the previous day's uprising:

They pulled that guy to the front of the people that sat. . . . So they used the handgun, a very small one and shot it right here [points to his temple], "Boom!" He died right away, and the brain blow in front of everybody. So, very, very, very scary. . . . Nobody say anything, just, oh my God . . . God help me, [chants a Buddhist phrase] God help me, something like that.

After the killing, the Khmer Rouge told everyone to go back to work and left, promising to return with food. After a few days, the community of about 300 people held a mass meeting at night and concluded that if they did not leave, everyone would die. The group split up into small parties of about 15 people, each to head off in a different direction. The remaining food in the village was divided up among all the families. The next evening, Sokhhoeun's family left, traveling together by foot with several others. They went to another village about five or six miles away. It was also controlled by the Khmer Rouge, and they were told to go away. But as a final act of desperation, Sokhhoeun threatened the village chief: "If you won't accept me stay here, please kill me, my whole family." They were allowed to stay, but their time there was brief, because the Vietnamese army came through again and the family left. The trip to the city took about five days, during which time Sokhhoeun's family had no food.

After considerable effort, Sokhhoeun's family finally reached the city and lived there for a time. Food remained incredibly difficult to obtain, and most energy was taken up with forays of several days' duration outside the city to find food. Abandoning hope of any life in Cambodia, Sokhhoeun's family decided to leave the country altogether. The walk to the Cambodian–Thai border took about a week. At the border the refugees discovered that they were virtual prisoners of the Cambodian border guards and the Thai merchants who crossed the border to sell food and goods to the refugees. The refugees were not allowed to cross into Thailand, nor did they wish to return to Cambodia. In order to get food, the refugees had to work—either for the Cambodian border guards or for the Thais. They remained at the border, working for food and trying to make things to sell to the Thais as a source of subsistence. Conditions were terrible.

Ultimately, word of the plight of the Cambodian refugees who were being detained and exploited at the border reached the American embassy in Thailand. Arrangements were made to send trucks to ferry large numbers of refugees across the border to the recently established refugee camp at Kaui Dang. While greatly relieved to be crossing into Thailand, upon arrival at the camp Sokhhoeun found that few preparations had been made:

When we got to Kaui Dang camp, it's very difficult too, the first time—we no house, no everything. Just like a forest, like all the tree. . . . Nothing when we first came. We just use the tent again, before the American embassy help to build the house.

Gradually, as shelter facilities were constructed in the camp and as food became available, the refugees began to feel better. They remained prisoners, however, subject to brutality at the hands of Thai military guards.

While in Kaui Dang, Sokhhoeun had his first opportunity to learn English in classes set up by other refugees as profit-making language-teaching businesses, but he decided against it because he saw no practical value in it, having no reason to hope that he or his family would be granted refuge in the United States. Instead, he devoted himself to supporting his family by evading camp sentries to go outside the camp perimeter to purchase goods from Thai merchants in nearby villages for resale within the camp. Many refugees operated such small businesses in the camp.

Sokhhoeun's father-in-law, who had been a soldier, applied for resettlement in the United States and eventually the application was successful:

They put the name on the [bulletin] board in the section [of the camp] and a lot of people they . . . run . . . to see the name . . . to go to the United States. So I didn't go [to see the names] . . . I didn't do anything. So I felt, oh, nobody take us. You know, it's very difficult, you have to have . . . a lot of money to go there [to the United States]. . . . So finally then my father he went, he went to the section to read [the names] . . . and when he came back he said, "Oh, we have name! We have name!" We feel happy, you know. All the family, we very excited. So we have name, go to United State.

After a series of interviews with American authorities, Sokhhoeun's family was moved to another camp at Mairat for refugees preparing for resettlement in the United States. There he began to study English in earnest:

I study there about three months. . . . When I first came I didn't know anything—A, B, C, D, or whatever—I didn't know. So they [teach] very beginning, like children. . . . They teach me about the sound of the letter, OK, the consonant and sound of the vowel. And it's very good teacher. He's very slowly and very . . . do again and again, you know, until the student remember. . . .

So I learned very fast, because when we know all the sound and all the consonant and put together, it's very, very easy how to . . . read and write. . . . So that's the way I learned. Just only three month I can read, you know, what they call "Book One," something like that. . . . It's very beginning. . . .

Talking . . . the teacher taught us, too. . . . They practice. They wrote the question, like "What is your name?" OK, and, "Where are you from?" learn how to practice in pair, and stand up. Sometime the teacher call two people to the front, in front of a lot of people . . . so you just asking and answer, something like that. It's very, very, very good.

For three months he paid to attend English classes. Then the family was transferred to Bangkok and boarded a plane for San Francisco. At that time, Sokhhoeun was the only member of his family who had studied English. Now, in the United States, his children and his younger siblings speak better English than he does, but his parents, older siblings, and wife still speak little or no English. He studied English in several literacy programs and community college programs in the United States during his first few years in the country, and he also participated in a bilingual vocational training program for electronics assemblers.

Adjustment to the United States. Sokhhoeun and his family of five arrived in San Francisco on September 21, 1981. After a long wait for their sponsor to arrive, the family was taken to a hotel near the airport. They stayed in the hotel for a few days until a Cambodian-speaking caseworker arrived to transport them to Oakland and to begin the resettlement process. They lived for about three weeks with another Cambodian family until the sponsoring agency helped them find a one-bedroom apartment.

After moving into their own place, the family began to feel a little better and more settled. In the next few days, Sokhhoeun had to ask a Cambodian friend to help him apply for identification papers, a Social Security number, refugee cash assistance, and medical care. He felt quite uncomfortable having to be so dependent on someone else for help, because in order to help them, his friend had to apply for time off from work two to three days in advance:

So, it's very very upset for me about that. . . . I didn't speak English myself, so [it was] very difficult to ask somebody, you know? They are working, right? So when I ask, they didn't say anything, they say. Oh, you know, I have to get permission from my boss first.

This caused Sokhhoeun to hesitate before asking for help. He was determined to become self-sufficient as quickly as possible.

Everyday Literacy, Language, and Technology

Sokhhoeun demonstrates understanding and skill in employing some forms of literacy and various forms of technology in his current work and life. He uses literacy when he needs to: in his daily life at home, in his community, and at work. He values and respects literacy as an important tool. He feels similarly about education.

Soon after his arrival in the United States, Sokhhoeun developed an important learning strategy using text as a storage and modeling device. It enabled him to achieve rapid self-sufficiency in his interactions with bureaucratic agencies:

> So when I went to apply for welfare, I have to watch them [his friends]. This is my idea. I have to watch them. How can they do, how . . . can they fill out the form, what form they do . . . the word they use . . . or whatever. Then, after he help me to fill out the form . . . I take it home, I not just [turn in]. . . . I just make a copy first. That's my idea. I didn't know anything, but I just make a copy. . . . Then later on . . . if I want to do that again I know, oh, maybe I can make copy from the old one. So that's my idea. I think that way, I do that way. . . . So I just keep the old paper. When I have something problem, the same situation . . . I may copy from that. . . . Later on, then I don't need help.
>
> I make up [this idea] myself, I do myself. Nobody tell me. I just, you know, use my brain to do that. Because I didn't know the English, I cannot read the English. But if I have a copy, I can follow, I can copy do the same thing.

Sokhhoeun is clearly proud of this strategy, proud that he devised it himself, and proud that it lessened his dependency on others. This example also suggests one important way in which he views literacy: as a practical tool for storing and retrieving important information.

On his current job, Sokhhoeun is required to read and understand the English lessons that the teachers are assigning to literacy students. He prides himself on always taking each lesson home and making sure that he understands every word, should he be called upon to explain any elements to students. On his job he also reads and fills out attendance forms that must be submitted to funding agencies. In addition, he has to read and understand internal memoranda and other agency-related procedural materials.

Sokhhoeun also has to do some math on his job. He is required to total the attendance figures for daily, weekly, and monthly attendance and to transfer the figures from individual teachers' attendance sheets to central files. He generally uses a calculator to do the math, although he points out that he could do it by hand if necessary. He does indicate that he does not understand fractions, although he can do percentages. He can do no algebra or more complex mathematical operations. In his home life, Sokhhoeun has had a checking account since two or three months after his arrival in the United States. He does not do his own taxes. Like many Americans, he pays someone else to do them.

When asked what he reads at home, Sokhhoeun responds that he likes to read a Cambodian–English medical dictionary. He wants to expand his medical vocabulary, for he hopes to be employed eventually as a translator in a hospital. He also reads the English teaching materials used in the classes in which he works. He sometimes helps his youngest child, the 9-year-old, with his homework, but his older children do not ask for this assistance.

He speaks Cambodian at home, as do all the members of his family except for the youngest, who speaks English but does understand Cambodian. When asked if he reads for pleasure, he says that he does not. Occasionally a friend might share with him a Cambodian-language newspaper, but he points out that he and many other Cambodians have so many painful memories about life in their country that they may display little interest in hearing of its current conditions. He does write letters to a few cousins who remain in Cambodia, perhaps once every few months.

Sokhhoeun seems to have adopted a view of literacy, language, and text that might be described as utilitarian. When he sees a pragmatic benefit to be gained from using text, then he does so. When he recounts his consistent pattern for learning new technical skills [such as operating a VCR or ATM], he reports that after the new technical skill has been visually demonstrated and orally described to him, he then insists on writing [or having written for him] the procedural steps he has just learned. He then refers to these notes when he needs to perform the function in the future. He does the same when he goes to a new place that he wants to remember how to find again. For example, his class went on a recent fieldtrip to a regional park. He wanted to remember how to go to the park later to take his family, so he drew a clear and detailed map (labeled in English) in his personal datebook to record this information for future use. He often uses his datebook (and seems to save the old ones) for this information storage purpose.

Thus Sokhhoeun seems to have rationally assessed the functional utility of text for himself and assigned it a role in his life that is indeed one of its most basic uses for humans: to somehow "fix," or make permanent, information and knowledge and to retain it for future retrieval. The notion of reading for aesthetic, pleasurable, or nonpragmatic cultural purposes does not seem to be a part of Sokhhoeun's life.

Technology. Sokhhoeun's family has a car, stove, refrigerator, television, telephone, vcr, and typewriter. He displays considerable respect for the technology he possesses or has learned to control, as well as pride in his ability to use and maintain them. His automobile and vcr are two prominent examples of this. When he lived in Cambodia, driving was considered to be a valued, socially desirable skill. Usually only men drove, and the profession of "driver" was a respected one. It may have been this set of values, plus his own innate pragmatic curiosity, that motivated him to teach himself to drive a tractor while working under the Khmer Rouge on a sugar plantation. He notes that he always rode next to the tractor driver when the work crews went out to the fields, carefully observing the shifting, acceleration, braking, and backing techniques employed. He asked incessant questions of the driver. Ultimately, the driver let him take over, for it allowed the driver to sit in the shade eating sugar cane while watching others work.

When he came to the United States, both because of the inefficient public transportation system and because of the value he places on driving a car, he strove to get a car and learn to drive it as soon as he could. Within six months of his arrival, he accomplished this, buying a 1970 Pontiac. He displays considerable pride when talking about his current car. He describes how he has changed the plugs, points, oil, starter, and battery, and proudly points to a new set of steel-belted radial Dunlop tires. He describes in detail how he diagnosed the problem when his car had a dead battery. He asserts the virtues of changing oil regularly.

He displays similar pride in his vcr, which he has owned since 1983. He describes how, after he first played a few tapes, the TV picture got "snowy." When he asked a friend, he was told that he had to get a vcr cleaning tape, which he did. But when he smelled the head cleaning liquid (acetone), he decided that it smelled a lot like fingernail polish remover (also acetone). So he went to the drug store and bought some of the cheaper nail polish remover, invented a head-cleaning tool made of a chopstick with a cotton ball fastened to it with a rubber band, and began cleaning his vcr's heads with it. He now notes that his vcr picture is consistently as clear as when the vcr was brand-new.

Sokhhoeun reports that he employs the same strategy of careful observation and questioning when he is learning a new skill—whether it is a literacy skill or a technical skill. His process for learning new skills—

including driving a car, opening a checking account, ordering from a restaurant menu, using an ATM, or operating a VCR—follows the same basic pattern:

1. He asks someone to describe the process orally for him and visually show him how to perform it.
2. He then performs the task under that person's supervision, usually several times.
3. He asks the person to write down the steps, or he writes them down himself.
4. He performs the task repeatedly on his own, until he is comfortable with it.
5. He relies on the written text of the steps the next time he has to perform the task, to refresh his memory.

In discussing this relatively invariant learning format, Sokhhoeun notes that no one taught it to him; it was simply something that he invented to solve problems. He also reflects on his own learning processes and needs by noting that it is not possible for him to learn a new process when only a written description is presented: He needs first to see something and to have it explained to him. Only then does text seem to have use for him— as a reminder and reinforcer of the process that has initially been acquired through other modalities. It is interesting to note that this process to some extent parallels the way in which Sokhhoeun first learned literacy in a Buddhist monastery: through oral presentation, followed by presentation of text as written reinforcement.

Literacy and Technology in the Future. In talking of the future, and specifically of literacy and technology in his future, Sokhhoeun speaks in general terms of his need for further education. He thinks that at some point he will need to move to another job and that doing so may require further education. When asked about other forms of technology that he might want to learn to use, he mentions the computer. He thinks that he could learn to use a computer, but that it would have to be through individual tutoring, perhaps with another Cambodian staff member who works at one of the agency sites. He does not identify any particular functions that he would be able to perform with the computer to help him with his home or work life. He thinks his children should and will learn to use computers. He notes that he has bought a typewriter at home, primarily for his oldest son's use for school assignments.

Sokhhoeun is a vibrant, expressive, attractive individual. He is warm and sincere, and he displays a strong attitude of independence and self-reliance. He has taught himself many things of a technical and intellectual nature—as well as having had brief occasional exposure to formal instruction—and he displays a pragmatic, self-reliant problem-solving rationality.

NURA TOLA

By Lensa Gudina

Nura Tola is a 29-year-old woman, an Oromo refugee from the southern area of Ethiopia who came to the United States in 1990. Nura is married and lives with her husband in San Jose, California. She had no formal education in her country and is literate in neither her native Oromo nor in English. She is currently studying ESOL. She would also like to learn sufficient English to work in the health care field.

Nura has experienced considerable change and adversity in the course of her life. She grew up in a village with no electricity and with mainly traditional forms of technology. She fled her home in southeastern Ethiopia in 1982, with the other women and children of the village, because of the war between the Ethiopian government and the Oromo liberation movement. She spent eight years in a refugee camp in Somalia, experiencing many brutalities that she is reluctant to talk about. Finally, her husband was able to get a visa to emigrate to the United States, a country of whose existence they had never known. A year later, Nura joined him in San Jose.

Nura's husband now works as a security guard at a nearby hotel, and Nura works as a cleaner. She is enrolled in an ESOL class, but because she was not literate in any language and because no Oromo–English dictionary exists, Nura is struggling to learn English. Her husband was educated and already literate in two languages (Oromo and Arabic) when he came to the United States and because of this had an easier time understanding ESOL classes.

Nura and her husband live in an apartment in the Alum Rock area of San Jose, a neighborhood largely populated by immigrants, most from Mexico and Vietnam but some from east Africa. Two other Oromo families live nearby, and Nura keeps in close contact with them. Her contact with other neighbors is minimal because of the language barrier. When they occasionally see each other in the hallway, they smile and say hello, but that is all. Nura is struck by the differences in social and cultural life between her present community and the one in which she grew up. She has no children but plans to have them once she gets adjusted to the lifestyle in the United States:

I would like to know the language well enough before I have children. I see the difficulties some of the Oromo women with children go through in this country. Life in this country is not like back home, where you leave your children with your relatives or neighbors if you have to go to the market or do something else. There are no relatives here, and, as you know, your neighbors don't even greet you, let alone take care of your children. You know how we take turns back home to get together at each other's house and drink coffee every morning. That's one thing I haven't been able to get used to—drinking coffee on my own or eating alone.

The Oromo community in San Jose is quite small. The number of Oromos residing in San Jose had reached 400 at one point in 1990 but decreased to about 100 when most of the community members moved to other states in search of affordable housing and better employment opportunities.

Life History

Nura was born in 1962. She had thirteen brothers and nine sisters. Half her family was killed in the war, and the whereabouts of her parents still remain unknown. Her father was a sheik with Islamic education who could read the Koran in Arabic. She grew up in a mud hut with a thatch roof. There was no electricity in the whole village; at night, they used kerosene lamps for light. One of her brothers had a transistor radio that he had brought back from the town where he went to school. Since her father was a religious man, he didn't allow Nura and her sisters to listen to the radio. They had no clock in their house; instead, during the day, they looked at the position of the sun to tell time:

> The sun rose at six in the morning and set at six in the evening throughout the year. You know, we don't have long or short days like they do here. We woke up when the roosters croaked and set out for work. By looking at the sun, we knew it was midday and time for lunch. And in the evening the animals would start heading back home—the cows would lead and the donkeys would follow, never the other way around. We depended both on the sun and our animals for time-telling. And there are the "ayyaantuus" [spiritual leaders] who can tell the time of the year by looking at the position of the moon and the stars.

Nura's father was a prominent religious leader in the village and relatively better off than most of the other villagers:

My father had four wives. Each of his wives had her own thatch hut with the kitchen built separately from the house. Children lived in their mother's hut. But every night we all gathered at the oldest wife's hut. All huts were located in the same compound. The men worked on the farm and the women took the produce to the market. We cultivated fruits, such as oranges, pineapples, papayas, bananas. We also cultivated vegetables and coffee. The men used oxen to draw the plough and a sickle for harvesting grain or crops. Women were not supposed to work on the farm, but sometimes we would help with the weeding.

Nura didn't receive any formal education while she was at home. She remembers being taught her genealogy as a child. She could count up to twelve generations on her father's side and up to seven on her mother's side. Learning one's genealogy is a very important part of one's identity in Oromo culture. The European method of using last names does not have a parallel in Oromo culture. Women never take a name from their husband—they retain the same name from birth to death. Oromo children take their father's first name as their last name. Each child is coached to recite the first names of his or her grandfathers for as many generations back as possible. She was also taught arithmetic through games and through counting the family members and cattle in the neighborhood.

Every night, when the men came back from the farm and the boys returned the cattle to the corral, we all would sit around the fire and listen to the elders as they told stories about the olden days. The stories were usually about animals, explaining why, for example, hyenas and donkeys became enemies or why zebras have stripes. Numbers were taught to us through songs or games. I don't remember being taught anything else; other things you just learn by watching others do them.

I watched my mother and one of my stepmothers as they cooked and learned how to cook. I also went to the market with them and observed how they sold the produce we had carried to market. We also did our shopping while we were there. I always followed one of my stepmothers who was known for her bargaining ability and learned how to shop wisely. A neighbor taught me how to spin cotton and weave the yarn into cloth. My oldest sister taught me how to weave baskets. After she showed me how to do the basics, I started using my own imagination to combine different colors and weave various designs.

One of the factors that prevented Nura from attending school was that her village did not have a school of its own:

Our village was surrounded by mountains. The rainy season lasted four to six months. There were no schools in our village; the closest one was located in another town across the river. Due to the rains, the river remained full for most of the year, which prevented us from going across to attend school. My father sent my brothers to go stay with relatives and attend Islamic school; but we, the women, couldn't leave unless we were married. As you know, once a woman gets married she has no life of her own. Her time is divided between taking care of her husband and raising their children.

The thought of going to school never crossed my mind until I left my village and went to Somalia, where I saw some Oromo women attending class. At first I was ashamed at the thought of a woman going to school, especially a married woman. But as time went on I got used to the idea and started going to one of the classes myself.

Flight and the Refugee Camp. In 1982, during the war between the Ethiopian government and the Oromo liberation front, Nura's village was raided and the women and children hid in the mountains:

Our village was raided one night by militia men from the government, who looted and killed. We [the women] took the young ones and headed toward the mountains to hide. We could see from afar when our huts and crops were being burned. We were also told that our water wells were poisoned. So we began the long walk to Somalia that took 14 days. We walked at night and hid during daylight. We lost half of the children on the way due to the heat and lack of water. Just within a day nine children died on us—there wasn't much we could do. There was no help to be found in the middle of the desert.

We didn't realize where we were going. We were looking for another village like the one we left. Instead what we found was a desert with no water or food. We walked from sundown to sunrise; our feet were bleeding. But we had no choice—we either had to keep walking and find some food and water or die in the desert. When we came close to the refugee camps we were surrounded by Somalian soldiers who accused us of spying for the Ethiopian government and put us in jail. Terrible things happened to us that I don't even like to talk about . . . but after a while they had to let us go. The jails were too crowded and people kept arriving by hundreds and thousands as the war kept getting worse and worse.

She spent eight years in a refugee camp in Somalia. Nura had never dreamed of coming to the United States, but eight years of hardship from living in refugee camps in Somalia and the dim prospect of returning to her home village motivated her to find a way of getting out of the camps.

We had no idea that such a country even existed before we left home. We knew that there were other countries, such as Djibouti or Somalia, but not the United States. I knew about those two countries, because they said that things like radios and watches came from there. Maybe the people who went to school knew more about other countries—I didn't.

Nura's husband found out about the possibilities of migrating to the United States through a relief worker. He applied immediately, but the process took four years. His visa came first and he had to leave right away, without his wife. She came a year later, in 1990:

Due to health problems I had to stay behind for one year until the problem cleared. The day I was supposed to depart, one of the Oromo relief workers explained to me about getting on an airplane and flying. I didn't like the idea, but he told me that was the only way to get to America. Planes remind me of the war. After four years in Somalia in the refugee camps, war broke out between Ethiopia and Somalia. The Ethiopians flew across the border and dropped bombs on some of the refugee camps. Many refugees died by the bomb attack. I can still hear the sound the jets made as they dropped the bombs. You can hear them come from far away, but before you know it they are right above you. I don't even know how we survived that. The God of our ancestors delivered us.

The relief worker explained more and told me not to get off the plane until it arrived in San Francisco, without mentioning anything about changing flights in France. When I got on the plane I sat there the whole night with my eyes wide open. When we arrived in France, everybody got off the plane but me. The stewardess came and talked to me, I think she was telling me to get off. I asked, "San Francisco?" She shook her head. I said I wasn't going to get off the plane until we got to San Francisco. She wasn't understanding what I was trying to say; she went and got other stewardesses, they all tried to explain, but I was determined to stay in that plane. They were very upset that they couldn't communicate with me. I started to cry, not knowing what was going on. Finally they all got up and left and I followed them. Right there I realized the importance of going to school and learning other languages. I was happy when I finally arrived in San Francisco and saw my husband.

Adult Education. Nura attended classes on how to read and write Oromo while she was in the refugee camps in Somalia. Since the classes were inconsistent, she still has a difficult time reading Oromo.

The Oromo organization at the camps sent their people around to talk to refugees, especially women, about the importance of education. They told us that unless we got educated we would spend the rest of our lives in those refugee camps. We were all determined to do anything to get ourselves out of the camps. Along with other women I started going to a certain location where we sat under a tree and recited the letters of the alphabet, one by one. Sometimes I sit in my English class and think about the situation in the refugee camps. Here in San Jose each student sits on his own chair, with a desk attached to it. There, in the camps, we sat either on the ground or found large rocks and used them as stools. Our laps were our desks. We didn't mind it, though; we were so excited that we were learning something.

I still try to improve my reading ability, but since I came to this country and started learning English I have a hard time differentiating between the rules of reading the two languages. I keep getting mixed up by the rules of reading and writing Oromo versus English. English is a difficult language to learn. The other students use dictionaries to translate new words, but there is no Oromo–English dictionary. If my husband doesn't know the words, then I will never find out. And sometimes, even after they are translated, they don't make much sense. Even worse, some words in English don't even exist in the Oromo language and vice versa.

Both Nura and her husband have attended ESOL classes, but learning English is very difficult for Nura. She has little opportunity to practice:

My teacher says that we should be in contact with Americans to practice our English, but I hardly come in contact with Americans. There aren't any in my neighborhood. The only time I see them is when I watch television or go to the store. But at the store they have no time for discussions. My husband and I were advised to talk to one another in English, which we tried for a while. But since we kept running out of English words, we cut down on communicating with one another. That made us feel even worse, so we gave up on the idea of communicating with one another in English.

Literacy, Language, and Technology in Everyday Life

Nura hardly uses literacy in her everyday life. Her cleaning job doesn't involve any reading:

> I know which cleaning detergent to use and how much of it through practice. At home I only write when I take down telephone numbers or when I do my homework. I also have to read the bus numbers when I catch the bus to go to work or school. I would like to be able to read the newspaper or storybooks, but that will take a long time. If I get letters or bills, I wait until my husband comes home from work. I do open the bills and I know where to look for the amount, but I still don't know how to write checks. My husband takes care of that.

Nura gets most of her news from other Oromo friends and some from television and radio:

> Our Oromo community holds a meeting once a week. Those who know English would tell us about what is happening in our home area or other countries. They get their news from the paper or BBC radio, and some of them call their families back home to find out what is going on—those who have family members left. I don't, so I don't call home. My husband and I watch the news every night. Sometimes I can tell just by looking at the pictures, but not all the time. I can understand some of the spoken words, but since they talk very fast I don't understand most of it. I also like to watch films; my teacher says they help one learn English faster.

Nura and her husband own a VCR, which they use to watch videotapes of Oromo cultural shows that were taped on different occasions. Nura seems comfortable operating the VCR. She knows how to turn it on or off if she wants to watch a videotape but doesn't know how to record shows from television. Nura and her husband also own a tape recorder:

> I use the tape recorder to tape my voice and send it to my friends and relatives, since I can't read or write well enough. I also use it to listen to tapes they send me. It's just like how you would write a letter. I always start by saying greetings and go on to tell them about my life here and ask them how their lives are going. It is nice, I enjoy doing it. But I would like to improve my reading and writing so that I can send them regular letters. I would also like to write down everything that we went through after we fled our home. I seem to have forgotten some of it. I think this country makes people forgetful; I have become forgetful since I came here. It's probably because of having to learn so many new things within such a short time.

Her lack of English proficiency creates problems for her in many ways. She must use a translator when she goes to the doctor, and this can be embarrassing when the translator is a man. She would like to be able to write letters to her friends and relatives. Above all, she would like better English skills so that she could get a better job.

Technology at Home. Everyday technology for Nura Tola is fairly basic by American standards. Her apartment has a refrigerator and an electric stove for cooking. She uses the oven only occasionally, for baking bread— one of her Oromo neighbors showed her how to set the oven temperature and the timer. She remarks on the contrasts between this technology and that with which she grew up:

> Another appliance I had to learn using was the stove. My husband instructed me on how to use it. I think it's amazing how you could light fire without doing much. You know how it is back home: You have to walk to the forest and gather firewood and pile it outside. Then you have to build a fire from the embers you left covered under ashes the previous night. To start cooking, you have to use three fire stones to put the clay pot on. Most of our time was spent cooking. In this country everything cooks fast.

She also uses a blender to mix the batter for the traditional thin, pancake-like bread that she and her husband eat every day. She has used a red and green marker to mark the buttons she needs to press to start or stop the blender.

When shopping, Nura selects only items that she is familiar with. She prefers to go shopping with her husband, but since her husband is not always available she does most of the shopping alone.

> When I first arrived here I was told a story that I can never forget. An Oromo man who had recently arrived went shopping by himself and ended up buying dog food. He kept eating that until other Oromos came and told him that what he was eating was dog food. I always buy fresh vegetables, never canned food. If I have to buy meat, I wait until my husband can come with me. The most difficult part is when I get to the counter to pay. I still don't feel comfortable using American money, especially the coins. I can't understand how a dime, which is a lot smaller in size, is worth more than a nickel. It's getting better now, but I have to think hard when using American money.

Technology and Work. In her cleaning job, Nura has had to find ways of learning unfamiliar technology. She has to punch in and out on a timeclock, but that created little difficulty for her. She uses a soda machine occasionally, identifying the type of soda she wants by the color of the can, not by name. She has learned how to use the vacuum cleaner and washing machine at work:

> Of all the equipment, I found the vacuum cleaner easy to learn. You just have to switch it on; the rest is just like using the broom. What I found difficult was using the laundry machine—setting it to cold or hot and adding the right amount of detergent in the right place. But when you compare it to going down to the river, as we did back home, it's much easier. Easier but not as enjoyable. Going to the river to wash our clothes was one of the happiest times, since all the girls in the neighborhood went together. We bathed in the river until the laundry dried.

Another machine she found difficult at work was the machine used at the hotel for ironing bedsheets, which requires setting at a certain temperature and adjusting where necessary. Now she has learned to use it on her own; but sometimes when she feels unsure, she calls her supervisor for help.

When cleaning bathrooms at the hotel, she used to spend quite a lot of time trying to get the right water temperature. A fellow worker eventually explained that the blue color represented cold and the red color hot. The water faucets they have in their apartment are not marked with colors, and her husband had told her to turn the faucet right for hot water and left for cold.

Goals and Aspirations

Nura's immediate goal is to improve her English so that she can go to the doctor on her own and fill out job applications without depending on others:

> You see, I developed health problems while I was at the refugee camp due to lack of food and water, so I need to go to the doctor's quite often. At times I don't feel comfortable telling my health problems to the interpreter, especially when you have a male interpreter. It can be embarrassing. I would like to call the receptionist and set my own appointment to see the doctor; but it seems to me that English becomes even more difficult over the phone.
>
> I would also like to get a better job. The one I have right now is physically demanding, and with my poor health condition it's difficult to do it. But everything here requires a good knowledge of the English language.

Nura's long-term goal is to get training in the field of health education and become a health worker:

> When I fled my home village and took refuge in the mountains, we lost nine children in one day. At that moment, I wished I knew more about medicine and how to treat people. In our village there were a few individuals who knew traditional medicine very well. They say that it was taught to them by their family members who were also medicine men or women. They used herbs for those who had internal problems, massage for those who might have hurt their backs through hard work or fell off a horse, and several other methods for other health problems. The medicine people never accepted money. If they accepted money from a sick person, the healing power left them. People didn't get sick in my home village as much as they did when I was in the refugee camp. There were no medicine people or herbs to cure the sick; people would die without getting any help. I would like to learn about medicine and help those who are sick. But I sometimes wonder if I am going to learn enough English to understand all these things. But I see you and other Oromos around here. You don't seem to have much problem understanding English, do you? One day I will be able to understand everything in English and say everything I would like to say.

Nura dreams of going back to her home village, but she is afraid to go back and face the changes that have taken place:

My home is always on my mind—when I wake up or even when I am asleep. People always ask me about how it feels to be away from my home. Taking someone out of his or her village is like taking a calf away from the mother cow. If you grew up in the village, you would know what I am talking about. But I am afraid of going back. I don't know what has been happening there. I just have to get used to the life here. Like my English teacher would say, "learn, learn, nothing else but learn."

OLIVER GONZALES

By Sally Ianiro

Oliver Gonzales is a 17-year-old high school student who lives in San Francisco. He was born in Managua, Nicaragua, where he lived until he was 11. His family immigrated to the United States in 1985, first to the Los Angeles area, and then to San Francisco.

Oliver lives with his mother, two aunts, uncle, paternal grandmother, younger brother, and three younger male cousins. His father is in Los Angeles and has not lived with the family for the past two years. The extended family acknowledges that Oliver's father does not live with them because he is an alcoholic.

The family lives in the Mission District of San Francisco. They rent a house three blocks from Mission Street, which is the shopping, transportation, and social hub of the Inner Mission District. Mission Street has the feel of a crowded, busy, Latin American city, but it also has a distinctly American commercial flavor and is sometimes called the "Mission Miracle Mile." Oliver's mother and aunts do not speak English but are able to get most of the services, entertainment, and goods they need on Mission Street from Spanish-speaking merchants. Occasionally the family shops at the large discount stores on downtown Market Street. Here is how Oliver explains the difference: "On Mission we use both Spanish and English. But on Market we use just English."

Historically, the Mission District has been a place where new immigrant groups take root. Irish came first, followed by Mexicans. The most recent groups are Nicaraguan, El Salvadoran, Guatemalan, and Southeast Asian. There is also a growing African American population in the Inner Mission. Low rents, coffee houses, and inexpensive restaurants also draw a substantial number of college students and artists. But tensions among races, nationalities, and gangs make it a tough place to live. A public housing center four blocks from Oliver's school is plagued with drug-related crime. Like most American inner cities, the Inner Mission has a growing number of homeless people, crack dealers, drug addicts, alcoholics, and prostitutes.

When Oliver's family moved to San Francisco, he enrolled in Mission High School. He has since been transferred to one of the school district's satellite schools. Most of his friends—other Nicaraguans, Guatemalans, and El Salvadorans—attend Mission, and he still visits friends there and feels he is a part of it. "There's a lot of fighting," he says, "but we enjoy Mission."

Oliver and his friends play baseball and basketball in a neighborhood park and go to the Boys' Club a block off Mission Street a couple of times a week. There they play pool, basketball, and video games. But his main activity is "hanging out" with his friends. Their corner is 24th Street and Mission, a few blocks from his home. Asked if his friends constitute a gang, he says, "No, they're not gangsters, but I have friends from gangs."

Although Oliver was a member of a gang when he lived in the Los Angeles area and although his brother is now a member of the 11th Street Posse, Oliver has chosen not to join any of the Mission gangs and seems to coexist with them with little anxiety on his part:

> Yeah, they tell me all the time, jump in, jump in! But, nah. I don't like that 'cause that's what my mom tells me all the time, not to get in gangs and things like that. . . . I know that's not good 'cause gangsters they go to jail every day just wasting their life. Drink, do drugs, rob. That's all what they do. They fight.

Oliver is soft-spoken and well-groomed. He is well-mannered in a quiet way and makes little eye contact when he speaks with adults. He wears his hair in a short pony tail. He appears to be at ease with his peers and has made several friends at his new school. Although a quick learner in computer class, he is reluctant to admit he has talent. "Nah," he shrugs. "I just know something."

Life and School

Managua, Nicaragua. Oliver was born in Managua, Nicaragua, in 1974, the first of two sons. His father owned a liquor store; his mother worked as a secretary. They lived five or six blocks from his father's store and only a block from a modern shopping mall.

> We had a TV. We had a stereo. My mother had a milk shaker and things like that, an iron. Yeah, we had everything . . . clocks, no video cameras but regular cameras . . . a stove, refrigerator. My

father used to have a gun for self-defense. . . . We had a typewriter but it wasn't an electric one. We didn't have a computer. We didn't have a car.

We were not rich or poor, but we had a house and everything that we needed. We were all right. We were in the middle. In this country we're about the same like Nicaragua.

Oliver sees few differences between the two countries:

Well, it looked like here in San Francisco. They got like old houses, new houses. They got malls, and they got like Mission Street. And they got stores, they got markets and restaurants, just like here. Like San Francisco.

Oliver's father had an eleventh-grade education in Nicaragua. His mother graduated from high school and attended a two-year secretarial school. While both parents read and write Spanish well, he says, "My mother do it better. She's very smart."

The Gonzales family moved to southern California, where they had relatives, when Oliver was 11 years old. Not only did his parents feel life in Nicaragua was becoming dangerous, but there was a possibility that his father would be drafted into the army. Oliver was not hesitant about the move: "I wanted to see what the U.S.A. looks like. People, other people said like in Nicaragua that here everything's beautiful."

Oliver felt little impact from the civil war in Nicaragua because fighting was confined to the mountains. Friends of the family died in the war, however, and he remembers that his parents talked about people dying and about the draft:

'Cause they got like older people, they send them to the war. They take them from their jobs and they take them to like army camps and train them. Then they send them [to war]. . . . And then sometimes they took kids, like 16, 17 year-old kids. They'd take them to the war, too.

Oliver's father did not want to serve in the Sandinista army, Oliver says, because he supported the Contras. His father supported the Contras because "the Sandinistas broke the country. The economy is down 'cause of the Sandinistas."

El Monte, California. Oliver's family lived with relatives in El Monte, near Los Angeles, for four years. Oliver says the family entered the United States as legal immigrants. Neither of his parents speaks or writes English; nevertheless, his father found a job as a security guard and his mother returned to secretarial work.

A highlight of coming to the United States was playing video games for the first time:

> They had a video game at my house with my relatives when we first came here to the United States. It was Atari 2600. They showed me how to play it. It's not that hard. All you have to do is push start and kill the space ship.
> When I was 11 I started playing on the corner stores and in video arcades.

Asked if language was a problem with video games, he says, "Nah, first you put in a quarter, then you play. There is no reading involved. There's only the name of the game on the machine."

Oliver spoke no English when, at 11, he entered sixth grade in El Monte. His teacher, who was from Puerto Rico, was bilingual, but the class was conducted in English. Only two other students in the class did not speak English. He describes his first day of school in the United States:

> That first day I went to Westmont, I didn't know what to do because everybody was speaking English and I didn't saw no one or I didn't heard no one speaking Spanish. . . . I saw a teacher, he looked to me Spanish. So I talked to him. I told him that I was looking for my classroom and he took me to my classroom and everything. He helped me a lot.

A private teacher came to his home and taught him English. He thinks the tutor was sent from the school. Later, in middle school, Oliver attended ESOL classes for two periods a day. His other classes were taught in English by bilingual teachers.

Oliver encountered few other Nicaraguans: "There's not much Nicaraguan people in L.A.—Mexican, there were some Puerto Ricans, some from other countries, El Salvador. . . . In the whole school, I just met one."

The four years the family lived in El Monte included three changes in schools for Oliver and bridged the end of elementary school through the first year of high school. Oliver says he had problems at school and at home:

> I missed a lot of school. A lot. My grades they were not that good.
> . . . I missed a lot of school because I had this problem with my dad.
> And we were having a lot of problems in the house 'cause of my

dad . . . 'cause my father, he used all kinds of stuff. He drink, he drink.

In his first year of high school Oliver joined a gang to which his brother also belonged:

And when I was in L.A., I did a mistake, too. I got in a gang . . . but in L.A. it's not the same like here. Like here, is like playing, they just fight with fists. Over there they fight with weapons. Guns, things like that. That's why I was not going to school.

After four months Oliver dropped out of the gang, but his brother stayed in. He says it was not difficult to quit, and he remained friends with members of his former gang. "I just told them I didn't want to be there no more. . . . To get in the gang, three guys got to jump you. And to get out is the same thing."

San Francisco, California. Oliver says emphatically, "This is better," when asked how life in El Monte compares with life in San Francisco. His father remained in El Monte when Oliver, his mother, and his brother moved here two years ago. He has not seen his father, who communicates little with the family, for a year. His mother is not working, but they manage with the help of the extended family. Oliver's aunt is looking for a job for him.

Oliver gets around the Bay Area easily. He does not own a bus map because, he says, "I know the city now. I can take any bus and come back." He will consult the maps at bus stops sometimes, he says. He figured out the layout of San Francisco by traveling around in cars with his friends. He learned to use Bay Area Rapid Transit, or BART, by reading the instructions:

I know that to go to Oakland, first I look at the map at the BART stop. And I know that I got to cross the bridge, so I buy a ticket to Oakland. . . . They got signs there that says how much it costs. . . . Then I just look at the BART stops.

Oliver attended Mission High School for one year and a summer.

After summer school, they sent a letter home from school. In the letter they wrote that I need like parents' counseling. And I went with my mom, and they told her that I didn't have enough credits to graduate. I used to cut a lot too at Mission. That's why I didn't earn enough credits to graduate.

He cut school, he explains, "'cause I had a lot of friends and girls that'd tell me to cut." Although he knew he would not have enough credits to graduate by age 18, he believed he could stay in school until he was 19. The school recommended he attend a satellite program run by the school district at a local community-based organization.

In September 1991, Oliver enrolled in the satellite program with 20 other 17-year-old students. The program has one teacher and one aide, both bilingual Hispanic males. Oliver attends school for four hours each morning. One hour is spent in the computer lab learning typing and playing educational games. The rest is devoted to working independently from textbooks or on an Apple computer.

Oliver's attendance has improved dramatically since he enrolled in the satellite program. Asked why he has changed, he says,

> 'Cause I'm thinking about me. 'Cause I'm thinking about the future now. . . . 'Cause I was kinda crazy you know when I was in eighth, ninth grade. It was like I didn't know what to do. I was like crazy. . . . For me it was like I wanted to be cool with everybody. You know, I wanted to cut and those things. Not no more.

Educational History. Oliver learned to read Spanish in Nicaragua when he was 6:

> First I was looking at the alphabet on a piece of paper. They told me to write, then learn them. Then they gave me this book to look at the pictures, and there was like a horse and there was CABALLO on the bottom. . . . The teacher goes, what letter is this? So that's the way I learned how to read.

His mother read children's books to him at home, and he says both parents have always been supportive of his education. "They encouraged us all the way. They wanted us to graduate and get a good job." Oliver says he learned to read quickly and helped some of his friends with reading. He now reads both Spanish and English comfortably, though his vocabulary remains limited in both:

> The Bible I read in Spanish 'cause in English there is some like words that I don't understand. It's like in Spanish there's some words that I don't understand, too. . . . Like if it's in Spanish, I ask my aunt what it means.

Language is the biggest difference Oliver has found between attending school here and in Nicaragua. Academically he was "at the same level with everybody" in his American classes. But his lack of English held him back:

> That was very difficult because I was sitting there just watching the teacher speaking but I couldn't understand what he was saying. And I remember when we was doing our test, I was doing it but I didn't know what I was doing because I didn't understood what it was all about.

Initially Oliver was discouraged by having to read in English: "Sometimes, like when I was in sixth grade, I used to say that, damn, I don't want to learn to read . . . 'cause I thought it was boring." He changed his mind, however,

> . . . 'cause I was growing up. I was older so I learned how to read well, 'cause I know reading is important now, everywhere. Like I went out when I was walking in the street and there's this sign that I wouldn't know what it says on the sign. That's how I figured it out that it was important to learn how to read.

Of sixth grade and middle school, he recalls,

> I learned a lot in those years . . . 'cause like in math I had a teacher, like when I had a D average paper, he used to get me and work on the problems that I was having with the material. That's how I learned a lot. There was a teacher and his helper. He used to work with the people that didn't know what to do. 'Cause in every classroom there's smart people and people that can't do nothing. . . . I'm in the middle.

In El Monte, Oliver was first introduced to computers:

> I didn't know what to do 'cause it was the first time I was looking at a computer. It was inside of a bus and was like 20 computers inside a bus. The teacher showed me how to do things. . . . It was cool.

When Oliver moved to San Francisco and enrolled in Mission High School, he was assigned to a three-month introductory computer class. He thought the class was easy but enjoyed it because "I learned something about computers and how to use them."

In the satellite program he now attends, he spends as much as 90 minutes of a four-hour school day on computer programs covering math, English, social studies, and typing. He describes how he learned to play "Where in the World is Carmen Sandiego?":

> You have to figure it out. I mean you learn the color of the flag of the country. . . . It took like two days for me to learn how to play. . . . I was watching [another student] 'cause he knew how to play it.

Oliver does not consider himself a good math student, but he does see the practical value of math. Asked if he used math often, he says,

> Yeah, everywhere. On the store. If I've only got $10 and I've got to buy things, first I just add the prices of the things so that I know how much I'm gonna be able to spend.

"Everybody knows how to operate a calculator," he says. Yet he does not use one himself: "It's better when you think, when you do it by yourself. You use your brain."

Oliver expresses concern about his writing ability:

> Sometimes I get worried about that 'cause when I'm doing something like here in school and I've got to write like a paragraph or something, stories, I get worried 'cause maybe I don't know what to write, you know. There's something that comes to my mind, but I don't know how to write it.
>
> Probably, to get a career you have to be able to write and read good. Probably if I want to get a business job you're gonna have to . . . they write a lot, don't they, in those kind of jobs?

When he lived in El Monte, Oliver helped out in a cosmetics store run by a friend of his family. He says, "Maybe I'm smart in business. I knew what we was selling more." He finds the idea of a business career appealing, especially "when you see a person sitting at a desk, just signing papers. There's people in the back. Just sitting there signing papers."

When Oliver turns 18 he plans to take the GED and enroll in a local adult school to earn a diploma. Eventually he hopes to get a job at a restaurant or doing janitorial work to put himself through college. The thought of college, though, is intimidating to him and his friends:

> When I think about that I get scared. . . . That's what I hear in the classroom. Everybody say the same thing: "Oh, that will be scary to go to college, to go the first day of school."

Everyday Literacy, Language, and Technology

Oliver's language skills and those of his younger brother and cousins help the family function more comfortably in American society. He explains his role in helping his uncle set up their new stereo system:

> I read the instructions for it—how to plug it in and how to connect the speakers and the radio. . . . I was reading and my uncle, he was doing the job. . . . I translate it into Spanish for him.

When asked what would happen if he weren't there to help, he responded, "I think that they wouldn't be able to plug it in 'cause nobody's reading English there except my brother and my cousins and me."

Oliver seems at ease in a bilingual environment. He is as comfortable watching sporting events and "Tom and Jerry" cartoons in English as he is watching his favorite soap opera, "El Magnate," in Spanish. He listens to cumbia or salsa on radio and tape but also likes rap music. He says all his friends like rap. "I don't understand some words, I understand most of the song. And if I don't understand the song, I play it over and over and over."

Oliver uses reading primarily for daily living, but, unlike many teens, he also seems to enjoy reading for pleasure. He reads menus, clothing tags, instructions, the family mail, and maps with ease. He spends about a half an hour a day reading the sports page of the local newspaper, the Bible, *Sports Illustrated*, or a car magazine. Approximately twice a month, his family reads stories aloud in the living room.

Oliver spends about two hours a day watching television and almost as much time playing Nintendo games. He has membership cards at two local video rental stores and rents tapes twice a week. He plays video games at the corner stores on weekends and listens to his Walkman "when I come to school, get out of school, at my house, before I go to sleep, when I'm walking in the street."

Family Literacy. As the oldest child in a household where none of the adults speak or read English fluently, it is Oliver's responsibility to act as interpreter for the family. His brother, who is 15, and his cousins, aged 13, 12, and 10, all read and write English and Spanish. Oliver speaks Spanish with the adults in his family and English or Spanish with his brother and cousins.

Because Oliver is the oldest, he accompanies other family members to medical, legal, and financial appointments. He also reads and translates the family's mail and notes sent home from school. He recently accompanied his mother to traffic court. Asked why it was necessary to go to court with his mother (and miss a day of school), he explained,

'Cause she likes to go with me. 'Cause she says she's afraid. She
don't like to go to court. She says she don't like the judge. The way
they talk and everything. She's always nervous when she goes to
court for a ticket.

Oliver describes how he spends his leisure time:

I go out with my friends in the afternoons. I go out with my girlfriend on weekends. Everything's all right. . . . We go to the movies
or walk around the city. We go to Fisherman's Wharf, Oakland, to
some other cities. We take the BART.

About twice a month, Oliver says, his mother turns off the Nintendo
game, over the protests of his brother and cousins, and reads aloud:

Sometimes they [his aunts or mother] buy books in Spanish book-
stores and we read together tales from Nicaragua. Like scary tales
. . . in our living room. My mother she reads aloud for all of us. . . .
We don't do it a lot 'cause we're busy playing Nintendo video
games.

Sometimes Oliver initiates the readings:

Oh, maybe if we're watching TV then I grab the book and start
reading so we turn off the TV and we read all together. . . . "Ichabod
Crane," it's an American story, but that story I read it to my cousins
'cause it's in English. And then when my mother reads a story for
us, she reads Spanish stories. Like that one, "The Pit and the Pendu-
lum." That's in Spanish, too.

Consumer technology used in Oliver's home includes a stereo, a com-
pact disc player, a tape recorder, three color televisions, two VCRs, Nintendo
games, a microwave oven, radios, clocks, and standard kitchen appliances.
His uncle also owns a car and a chain saw.

Oliver is very much at home with consumer electronic equipment
because "I got all that at home and I use them every day." He has learned
to operate each piece of equipment by watching or having a friend or relative demonstrate. He is a patient observer:

Looking at what other people's doing helps me a lot. . . . First when
I'm going to do something, first I like to see another person doing it
first, so like that I can see, you know, what's the error and what to do.

Sometimes it happens in games, you know, when I'm playing video games. And there's some games that I've never played before and sometimes it's hard to figure them out, how to play, what to do. 'Cause they got all kinds of figures and you don't know what to do with them. When you hit the start, you start playing, they don't tell you anything.

Probably just let the game play alone like. . . . Like if you don't know how to play something, you can just look at it for five minutes and then you know how to . . . what to do.

Sometimes I bring in my friends. They show me how to play if they know. . . . My cousin, he knows how to play all the games.

Oliver learned to read graffiti as a survival skill:

I had friends from gangs and they teach me how to read and how to write like they're writing. . . . In gangs they put their whole name, and then their name like Yogie. . . . Every time you see a tag [a set of initials] with like a number or things like that, that means the guy is in gangs . . . but it's easy to read like.

RIP—rest in peace—that means you're gonna die, I'm after you . . . and sometimes a cloud . . . and a cross. That means where you're gonna go. . . . Like sometimes they write like this [draws a circle with lightning bolts next to it]. . . . It means gunshots, we're going after you guys with guns. . . . If they put like that they're gonna kill you, you don't get worried about that, 'cause they mean that they're gonna beat you up.

Although Oliver is generally upbeat and positive about his life, he is worried about his brother's involvement in a gang:

I told him to get out, but he said, "No, I ain't like that." . . . I asked him, "What do you like about it?" He says, "I just like it." . . . Probably [he's in it] 'cause he only wants to hang around with these dudes, and these dudes are from gangs. And they got pretty girls too in the gang. . . . You know, but he never tells me what he like about the gang. There's nothing funny in that thing. It's all just fighting, that's all.

While Oliver is quiet and nonaggressive in school, he is proud of holding his own on the streets. Throughout five interviews, he was never more forthcoming than when explaining the reason for having missed one session:

It was like around 11:30 [A.M.] and I was walking on 16th and Mission. I just got out of the bus. By the corner of 16th, there was three black boys. So the bigger one he walked up to me and he told me that he liked my jacket. So I told him, "Thank you." And he goes, "I like that jacket and it's gotta be mine." And so I told him, "Take it if you can." Then the other one, that he was around 16, he punched me right in the back of my head.

The incident ended when the police intervened:

They called my parents and told them what happened, so the cops told me that it was all right for me because I had witnesses, that I didn't start anything. They were trying to jump me because of my jacket. So they let me go.

Oliver was grateful he was not put in jail:

I just went there to talk. They didn't put the handcuffs on me. They didn't do nothing. . . . I think it was a bad experience. Police have chased me because of fighting or things like that, but this is the first time they catch me. But this time wasn't my fault. . . . That's about it. I've still got my jacket.

Summary

Oliver has learned how to live in San Francisco, seems to have settled into life here, and has plans to stay and make a life for himself. He uses reading and speaking in both English and Spanish to move through his world: school, home, and the streets.

❧ 5 ❧

Learning from the California Profiles

DIVERSE IN BACKGROUND and contemporary lives, these immigrant Americans share common experiences. They came to California from many parts of the world, and they differ not only from mainstream Americans, but also from each other. Four came as immigrants, while two (Sokhhoeun and Nura Tola) were refugees. Immigrants generally plan their migration—its timing, its purpose, and its destination—while refugees usually have little choice and little knowledge of where they will ultimately land. The extreme adversity and violence that Sokhhoeun and Nura faced adds clarity to the distinctive nature of the refugee experience.

All but one of the people we profiled have worked in this country in low-paid, entry-level positions in the service economy: food-preparation worker, teacher's aide, bookkeeper, house cleaner, and fish-seller. All have studied English, and four of the six have participated in job training, although they are not always working in the job for which they trained.

EVERYDAY USES OF LITERACY

There is considerable variety in how the people profiled on the West Coast use language, what they speak and listen to, what they read, what they write, and which language—their native language or English—they use for which purposes. Table 5.1 provides a summary of their main uses of first and second languages for speaking/listening and for reading/writing.

Speaking and Listening: First Language

Everyone profiled uses their native language at home and in their local community. Most either live in a cultural community of their own native-language speakers or relate primarily to other immigrants. In most of their workplaces, use of the native language predominates, with limited use

Table 5.1. Uses of First and Second Languages

	Alicia Lopez	David Wong	Michela Stone	Sokhoeun	Nura Tola	Oliver Gonzales
Speaking/ listening	Native Language Spanish	Native Language Cantonese Chinese	Native Language Russian	Native Language Cambodian	Native Language Oromo	Native Language Spanish
L1	· Spanish TV · Spanish radio · At home · School · Public services · Shopping	· Family · Friends · Most customers · TV · Radio · Banking	· Father · Friends · Some clients · Some coworkers	· Family · Community group · Helping refugees · Videotapes	· Oromo videos · Audiotaped letters home · Husband · Translator	· In Mission district · Spanish TV · Spanish radio, audio tapes
L2	· English tapes · Medical services · ESL classes	· Some TV · Some customers · ESL class · Shopping · Audiotape for citizenship	· Some coworkers · TV news, soaps, game shows · Shopping	· At work · TV · With youngest child	· ESL class · TV news · Some shopping	· Downtown · Market St. · English TV · Radio, audio tapes · Interprets for family
Reading/ writing						
L1	· Recipes at work · School · Public Services · Credit applications	· Newspapers · Writing novel · Work information · Letters	· Russian literature · Russian newspapers	· Letters to relatives · Cambodian newspaper		· Family reads stories aloud · Bilingual instruction in middle school
L2	· Recipes at work · ESL books · Newspapers · Appliance instructions · Dictionary · Copies new words	· Bills, bank statements · Want ads · Dictionary · Bus routes · Price tags, labels · Job application forms · Citizenship class	· Accounting documents · Dictionary · Letters / notes at work · Accounting texts · Newspaper · Magazine · Shopping · Appliance instructions · Menus · Personal note	· Medical dictionary · ESL class (teaches) · Personal notes · Application forms · Newspaper headlines	· ESL class · Detergent labels · Phone numbers · Bus route numbers · Hard to recognize coin value	· Family reads stories aloud · High school · Public transportation · Menus · Clothing labels · Instructions · Maps · Sports pages · Bible · Magazines · Graffiti

of English. However, English is also spoken in some of the homes. Oliver speaks both English and Spanish with his younger siblings at home. Sokhhoeun's youngest child, age 9, speaks English at home, although Sokhhoeun speaks to him in Cambodian. This is a common pattern of interaction in immigrant homes between immigrant parents and American-raised and -schooled children.

Almost all of the people profiled here also have access to, and make use of, one or more forms of electronic media employing their native languages. There are numerous Spanish-language radio and television stations in the Bay Area, both Cantonese and Mandarin Chinese TV and radio stations, and videos available in more languages. Only Michela Stone does not seem to make much use of electronic media in her native language, although she does characterize her father as an avid watcher of the news in Russian that is broadcast nightly by one of the local cable channels.

For speakers of limited English, having access to public and private services in their native language is of paramount importance. Alicia Lopez, for example, reports that Spanish-language services are available to help her in dealing with her granddaughter's school, in meeting social needs, and in handling financial transactions. Only in health care does she need to contend with English. Nura Tola, however, appears to be almost completely reliant on her native language (Oromo), with only periodic translation available to help her negotiate the most necessary services, such as health care.

Speaking and Listening: English

None of the people we profiled speak English very much. Outside of ESOL classrooms, they have little interaction with native English speakers and encounter relatively few demands for speaking English in their communities and workplaces. For all of them, English was first and most continuously encountered in its live, interactive, and relatively natural use in the formal schooling situation of the ESOL classroom.

Some, though not all, regularly speak English when shopping. Michela Stone shops in English, although she often goes to Chinese markets, where neither she nor the merchants understand each others' English. Nura Tola finds shopping in English (her only option) a trial, so she limits herself to familiar products and much prefers her husband's assistance.

Demands for speaking and understanding English at work vary. David Wong, for example, speaks Cantonese Chinese most of the time in his work as a fish-seller, although he described how sometimes he has to handle English-speaking customers, either American-born Chinese who cannot speak Chinese or non-Chinese clients. None of the six people we profiled work in environments where only English is used. All of those who work do so in contexts where one or more languages in addition to English are in regular, not simply incidental, usage.

A significant exposure to English for almost all is in watching English-language television broadcasts. For example, Michela Stone conscientiously watches soap operas, game shows, and daytime talk shows in the hope that she will learn about American culture and perhaps extract something with which to make conversation with native speakers of English.

A final source of exposure to oral English for at least three of the people profiled is through audiotapes. Oliver Gonzales makes extensive use of his Walkman, and he includes rap music among his listening selections. Both Alicia Lopez and David Wong use audiotapes of oral English as aids to learning. Alicia goes to the local public library and checks out books with audiotapes in order to improve her English listening and reading skills. David Wong has bought a set of audiotapes that provide sample questions and answers for the U.S. citizenship exam. He listens to the tapes and drills himself for his upcoming exam when he has time. Few of these limited experiences with the English language provide the kinds of immersion in naturalistic language use that we often assume immigrants have.

Reading and Writing: First Language

Reading and writing in the first language of the people we profiled varies considerably. Nura Tola, for example, who is not literate in Oromo, does not identify any personal uses for the written form of her first language. David Wong, on the other hand, is writing a novel in Cantonese about his experiences as an immigrant.

Between these two extremes of written first-language usage fall a number of examples and a few fragmentary patterns. Sokhhoeun, Michela Stone, and David Wong, for example, all report reading newspapers in their native language. Another relatively common form of written first-language usage is the writing of letters home to relatives. Nura Tola meets the same need through the use of audiotapes. She notes that she would like to develop her first-language writing skills so that she could write to friends and family as well as document some of her experiences. There are other uses of written first language: Michela reads novels in Russian, Alicia reads announcements from her granddaughter's school in Spanish, Oliver Gonzales reads scary stories aloud in Spanish as well as English to his family.

Reading and Writing: English

Everyone encounters some level of demand for using written English in their daily lives—in shopping, transportation, paying bills, using appliances. All of the people profiled have had some exposure to written English in the formal schooling of ESOL instruction. Those who completed ESOL classes feel they have gained some measure of survival proficiency in reading and writing English. For others, such as Nura Tola and Alicia Lopez, learning to decode and write English text remains a daunting barrier.

All note that they need to be able to decode written English when using public transportation or when driving. Many also report that they can interpret and pay bills in English, and most have checking accounts. Shopping and eating out also present written English demands for most people. Sokhhoeun, Michela Stone, and Alicia Lopez note that their earliest and still most regular restaurant-going experiences are in Chinese restaurants. This is an interesting linguistic phenomenon, in that English becomes used as an intermediary language between immigrant merchants and immigrant consumers from different cultural groups.

Nura Tola probably encounters the greatest difficulties with everyday English texts. She has difficulty interpreting English signs or symbols when food shopping, so she generally avoids the purchase of canned or labeled foods in favor of fresh vegetables that she recognizes. She also notes that coins and their value sometimes presents her with problems, and she leaves all the bill paying to her husband.

There is some diversity in how the people profiled handle written English instructions for using technology. Michela Stone, Oliver Gonzales, and Alicia Lopez report that they have little difficulty with such instructions. Alicia uses a pragmatic trial-and-error approach while also noting the value of pictures in written instructions. On the other hand, Sokhhoeun, David Wong, and Nura Tola indicate that they have some difficulty reading and interpreting written technical instructions.

All except Nura Tola report that they read parts of English-language newspapers, at different times and for different purposes. They have some sense of the discourse functions of the different papers or sections that they read and seem able to accomplish their specific reading purposes. For example, Oliver Gonzales reads sports sections because he wants to find out how his favorite teams did, and David Wong looks through the want ads hoping to find his elusive janitorial job.

The use of the dictionary is another common pattern of English text usage. For example, Michela Stone reports that during her first two years in the United States she carried a dictionary around in her purse so that it would always be available. Now her English has become more proficient, but she still keeps a dictionary on her desk at work and consults it at some point of every day.

Finally, the people we profiled note a variety of other forms of written English text that they use or interpret in their everyday lives: popular and sports magazines, maps, the Yellow Pages, and a hybrid form of English text that is around in the community—graffiti, or "cholo writing."

EVERYDAY TECHNOLOGY USE

The people profiled here use a remarkable range of technology, particularly when we compare it with technologies they used in their home countries. An important message from this comparison seems to be that people will learn to use—and will search out and pay hard-earned money for—technologies that they believe can do something useful or important for them. But they will not necessarily use technologies—even if readily available to them—when they perceive no particular benefit in doing so.

Four of the six people profiled came originally from rural settings (mostly with relatively poor backgrounds), while two were from urban areas. The former used primarily traditional hand tools (although Sokhhoeun learned to drive a tractor). The latter had adequate though unsophisticated technologies available to them. Oliver Gonzales, from his description of home life in Nicaragua, was probably best acquainted with diverse forms of consumer technologies. This, along with his age, may account for his easy adoption of computer-based technologies in the United States, such as Nintendo and computer-based literacy instruction.

Current uses of technology in the home and in everyday life among the people we have profiled are similar. All now live in urban settings, most in apartments. All have televisions (sometimes more than one), stoves, refrigerators, radios, and telephones. Five of the six have VCRs. Most (four of six) have microwave ovens and tape recorders. However, other forms of technology that are prevalent in contemporary U.S. culture—ATMs, telephone answering machines, video games, and automobiles—are used less frequently.

Only one person (Sokhhoeun) owns and drives a car, although two others (David Wong and Michela Stone) proudly report having a driver's license. This lack of attachment to automobile ownership and use may have several explanations. One, of course, could be the costs involved. Another could be that there is relatively good public transportation available to most of the profile participants. Other explanations could be the barrier of literacy and language in the driver's license testing process or the recently lifted barrier of illegal immigration status.

Four of the six report some difficulties with learning to use certain technologies in the United States. Sokhhoeun and Michela Stone report that they had some trouble learning to use ATMs. Michela said: "When I first came, I couldn't understand the ATM machine at the bank. People from my class showed me. Now it's no problem."

There is a striking contrast between the manual, low-tech technology (such as janitorial equipment) in the worklives of Nura Tola, Alicia Lopez, David Wong, and Sokhhoeun, and the high-tech equipment (personal computer) that Oliver Gonzales and Michela Stone use in their daily work or school lives. It is possible that limited literacy and cultural knowledge on the part of the immigrants profiled here has contributed to their relatively high concentration in low-skill, entry-level employment such as janitorial work. However, we should also note the contrast between the low-tech equipment at work and the relatively high-tech equipment that they have learned to use at home, for which language limitations have not been an unassailable barrier.

The importance of video technology in the lives of all these people merits particular emphasis. Unlike the sporadic use of computers, televisions and VCRs are widely owned and used. Indeed, this is a phenomenon that can be seen throughout immigrant communities on the West Coast. With the earliest emergence of viable and affordable home VCR technology in the early 1980s, there was rapid growth and acceptance of its use in immigrant communities. ESOL teachers often found that the VCR, a technology that was quite new to them, was already well-known to their immigrant students.

Three reasons may explain the wide acceptance of televisions and VCRs. The first is simply the attraction and entertainment value of the medium. As countless studies of American television viewers claim, television is a magnetic, intrinsically fascinating medium, sometimes despite its content. The medium's powerful use of images and sound means that all of the people profiled watch and are entertained by English-language TV broadcasts, even though their understanding of the language may be limited.

A second reason relates to the maintenance of cultural identity. The drive to maintain and reinforce one's own cultural identity is a powerful human urge. Surrounding oneself with familiar images, symbols, sounds, and tastes of one's own culture is a common response to the anxieties of culture shock often felt when encountering a new culture over an extended period of time. VCR technology and native-language videotapes can provide a powerful means of cultural reassurance and reinforcement.

A third reason is that they value television as an information source. They use it to find out about American culture, as a news source, and as a way to improve their English by encountering—albeit electronically—actual native speakers of English, something that most cannot accomplish in their everyday real lives. David Wong, who watches whatever English-language programs his children have selected, describes how he watches TV: "I can't understand all of the dialogue. I can probably understand 30 to 40% of the programs my children watch."

Video technology, then, appears to be a form of technology that is uniquely accepted and valued among the immigrants profiled here. They and the members of their communities have proven willing to devote time and money to its acquisition and application, and they identify important resulting uses and benefits of the technology for them. Some of these uses have direct implications for language and literacy acquisition.

Two main attitudes seem to predominate among the people we profiled about both literacy and technology. The first is a sense of confidence that they can master them (although no doubt most find mastering the technology easier than mastering the English language). The second is that their most successful adoption of technology and acquisition of literacy is in contexts where there is an immediate and identifiable use for them. This is most easily shown in the contrast between computer-based technology and video-based technology: The former are hardly used, while the latter are used by almost everyone.

LITERACY DEMANDS AND ECONOMIC REALITIES

There seems to be a gap for the people we profiled between their current jobs and those of which they are capable. There may also be a gap between their aspirations for future work and what is likely to be available to them. Literacy and language play a role in these variances, but only as one factor among others. The six immigrants we have profiled—with the exception of Oliver Gonzales, who is still in high school—are working or have worked in low-paying, entry-level jobs in the local service economy. Alicia Lopez, now in training for facility maintenance work, has almost 10 years' experience in quantity food production and packing; Sokhhoeun, now a teacher's aide, was a warehouse worker and forklift operator; Michela Stone formerly did janitorial work and now works as a bookkeeper; Nura Tola does janitorial work; and David Wong worked first as a meat-seller and now a fish-seller in San Francisco's Chinatown. These are some rather sobering examples of underemployment. David Wong could put his skills in agricultural engineering to work in the rapidly developing biotechnology industries of the San Francisco Bay Area. Michela Stone could work in a far more financially rewarding and productive accounting job than her current position in a community-based organization.

The people we profiled believe their limited language proficiency, literacy, and education contribute to their lack of opportunity to do work that is more financially and intrinsically rewarding. David Wong finds the English language such an insurmountable barrier that he will pursue janitorial work instead of work in his field of expertise. The reasons for his "plateau" in learning English were not fully explained (or even understood) by him, but they probably include his difficulty in learning well in the evenings after a long working day or even in being able to attend class regularly. Additional factors may include the overcrowded conditions in many community college ESOL classes—often 50 to 60 adult learners in one classroom. Even after lowering his sights to pursue janitorial work, however, his continued lack of success in finding this sort of employment still seems to him to be due to his lack of English-language proficiency.

In addition to the barriers to better employment that their limited English proficiency present, two other important factors seem to be operating for the people we profiled. First, they often lack cultural information about the labor market. Second, the reality of the Californian economy is that immigrants are routinely slotted into low-wage, low-skill jobs, regardless of their qualifications and skills.

Lack of Cultural Information About the Labor Market

Immigrants appear to get information about jobs and the labor market through culturally influenced channels. It is quite common for the people profiled here—as well as for many other immigrants—to get information about job opportunities from friends or relatives rather than from want ads, job announcements, or employment counselors.

It is only natural to trust job information that is provided in the native language and couched in familiar cultural terms. Unfortunately, in some cases, the information is simply inaccurate due to cultural misunderstandings or miscues. Michela Stone, for example, notes how she received inaccurate information about job prospects from other immigrant friends when she was a new arrival.

The cultural job information grapevine can also raise expectations unrealistically, creating false images or hopes of job availability. Sokhhoeun, for example, mentions getting a teaching credential or becoming a medical translator. He may have seen or heard that teaching jobs are available, but he has no apparent knowledge of the BA degree and testing requirements that could stand as barriers to his achieving this goal.

A Local Economy Dependent on Immigrant Workers

The people we have profiled view their limited English-language proficiency as a key causal factor in their confinement to low-wage, low-skill jobs. However, additional analysis suggests that a more complex, symbiotic labor market relationship may be involved. It may be argued, in fact, that the local economy depends precisely on these types of workers to fill exactly these kinds of jobs.

Almost without exception, the people profiled here report that in their workplaces they are surrounded by other immigrants. Staffers of one workplace literacy program encountered the same phenomenon recently when conducting a "literacy audit" at several service industry work sites in San Francisco to prepare for workplace ESOL literacy training. When they asked about interactions the immigrant workers had with co-workers who were native speakers of English, they in turn were asked, "*What* native speakers of English?" There were simply none to be found in these jobs. It became apparent that in many service industry workplaces in the San Francisco area, entry-level jobs are filled almost exclusively by immigrants.

What is generally found at these job sites is one of two strategies for "managing the multicultural workforce." Either all the workers are recruited from the same language background (for example, Spanish speakers or Chinese speakers) for ease of supervision and native-language communication, or there are a series of clusters of workers from different language backgrounds who work together, often supervised by someone who is bilingual.

There are at least two important implications here. The first is that the immigrant workers we profile "blame themselves" and their lack of language proficiency, without realizing that there may be broader, structural economic factors at work that require their services in the work they now do. The second is that communication in English among immigrants from different cultural backgrounds is an important skill that needs to be taught in ESOL programs. For most of the workplaces reported in this study, communication with other non-native speakers of English is at least as important for job success as communication with native speakers of English.

Use of Public Services

It is important to consider the uses made of public services, as well as the contributions made toward supporting those services. It is often observed in studies of populations with limited literacy that they make relatively limited use of the entire range of public services that may be available to them. Despite this, it has recently been claimed by California state officials that immigrants represent a disproportionate drain on the funds that are available to support public services.

Overall, the people we profiled do make rather sparse use of public services, except for transportation and education. Only three have been the recipients of cash support from government sources: Alicia got unemployment benefits (paid by her former employers, not by taxpayers); and both refugees, Nura Tola and Sokhhoeun, received federally supported Refugee Cash Assistance when they first arrived in the United States as well as publicly supported medical care. On the other hand, all but Oliver Gonzales, who is still in school, were working and paying the taxes that support such forms of public assistance.

Educational programs are important public services for everyone: All have been or are in ESOL classes. Alicia Lopez is in a job training and ESOL program funded in part by government funds. David Wong is taking citizenship classes in a local community college. Others have children in school or public university. The only other public service that is extensively used is public transit.

We must conclude that these particular immigrants at least are not a substantial drain on state government resources. Rather they are hardworking contributors to government revenues.

BARRIERS AND INCENTIVES TO LEARNING

Each of the people we profiled has a complex set of expectations and aspirations for their lives in the United States. Many of them relate to issues of literacy and learning. For example, Michela Stone's hopes for the future have a direct connection to language and literacy. She wants to improve her English so that she can pass the TOEFL (Test of English for Foreign Learners—a standardized test for enrollment in U.S. colleges), enroll in college, and ultimately get a job teaching accounting.

Alicia Lopez's primary aspiration is to be able to adopt her grandchildren. In order to do so, she needs a good-paying, steady job and, therefore, more fluency in English. Oliver Gonzales's aspirations include getting his GED, working to put himself through college, and eventually embarking on a career in business. He believes that improving his writing skills will be an important adjunct to success in the business world, and he expresses some concerns about this.

Perhaps the strongest attitude commonly held by those we profiled is a strong sense of self-reliance and independence. While this is not directly a literacy-related attitude, it does have significant implications for the role of literacy and language proficiency in their lives. These six people are all strong-willed, self-reliant, and determined. They all have demonstrated considerable drive for independence, and they have acted quite dramatically and emphatically to achieve their goals by overcoming extreme forms of adversity in coming to a new country to make a better life for themselves. They all display a strong will to survive and a pragmatic outlook that focuses on the possible. These individuals are aware of the ways in which language and literacy limitations inhibit their independence and self-reliance, and they are attempting to acquire more skills in order to reach their aspirations.

In order to understand barriers and incentives to learning, we need to understand their prior educational experiences and their experiences with adversity. Both have an impact on their aspirations and expectations of education.

Educational Experiences

The people profiled have had a remarkable diversity of educational experiences. They range from the traditional oral transmission of skills through songs and games reported by Nura Tola to the postbaccalaureate-level training in accountancy teaching that Michela Stone received.

All report that they had at least one parent who was literate. All their parents, too, are said to have placed value on education. Only one person (Sokhhoeun) indicates that neither of his parents had any formal education. He reports, however, that his father could read Buddhist texts in the Khmer language, although he doesn't know how his father learned.

Formal education in the United States for all the people profiled has included ESOL instruction. Beyond this, four of the six have received some form of job training: Alicia Lopez is enrolled in facility maintenance training; Sokhhoeun was in an electronics assembly training program; Michela studied accounting in English; and David Wong has taken two janitorial courses. Oliver Gonzales is the only one of the six who has studied in a computer-based literacy setting.

Nonformal learning experiences in the United States for all six have been rich and include: using video games, reading graffiti, performing food-production processes, driving a car, operating a forklift, using a phone answering machine, operating a washing machine, and using a VCR, an ATM, or a personal computer.

Their diverse experiences of education, in formal and nonformal settings, and especially in their home countries, have given the people we profiled some confidence in their ability to learn. Their ESOL class experiences may have shaken that confidence somewhat. Nevertheless, prior educational experiences have not been the kind of barrier for these immigrants that they have been for the people of the Appalachian profiles.

The Experience of Adversity

Each of the people profiled has been faced with considerable adversity. These experiences have shaped their attitudes toward education and create both an incentive and a barrier to further learning. These experiences of adversity, both on their way to the United States and as a part of their lives at the margins of existence in the United States, have had a significant impact on them and on their abilities to live their new lives in the United States.

Undoubtedly the most wrenching and violent forms of political adversity occurred for Sokhhoeun and Nura Tola, both of whom were forced to flee their countries to escape violence and likely death because of wars in Cambodia and Ethiopia. However, all faced social adversity simply through the major decision they made to emigrate to the United States—to leave behind all that is familiar and to try to survive and support their families in a new culture. All express difficulty in making the social and cultural adjustments necessary to life in a new country.

Personal and family adversity have a heavy impact on some of these people. Oliver Gonzales, for example, was briefly a member of a youth gang when he lived in the Los Angeles area, before realizing that it offered him little other than negative prospects. Alicia Lopez was widowed at the age of 26 and never remarried. Her biggest concern now is the fate of her grandchildren who are in foster care, the children of her own daughter Maria, who has had a continuing substance-abuse problem.

These experiences of adversity have affected the lives of all of the people we profile. Such experiences are not at all unique among the immigrant and refugee populations seeking to structure new lives in the United States. In some sense they are an incentive to further education: Developing greater literacy proficiency may be seen as the avenue to greater stability in their lives, to better jobs. However, such experiences may also be a barrier to further education when continuing adversity consumes available time, energy, and resources.

For almost everyone we interviewed, survival is the central and dominant force in their lives. They may have little time and energy for further education. Five of the six people work hard for their families' economic survival, and they have little leisure time. Persistent health problems place an added burden: Nura Tola has chronic health problems and Sokhhoeun's wife had to stop working when she fell ill. Factors such as these create barriers to education.

When they do look beyond the economic survival issues, most focus on their families. Few, even upon probing by the interviewers, identify much time in their lives for leisure, personal growth, aesthetic pursuits, hobbies, or relaxation. These are serious people struggling to survive in difficult economic situations. They are living at the economic margins of existence, and consequently they have time for little else beyond economic and family survival.

LITERACY IN SOCIAL AND COMMUNITY RELATIONSHIPS

In the lives of the people we profile, literacy supports both the maintaining and the expanding of community in a variety of ways. Their uses of literacy and technology both to learn the dominant culture and to maintain their cultural community are not always what we might expect.

Isolation and Multiculturalism: A Paradox

An important theme in the everyday lives and work of the people we profile is their isolation from "Anglo" Americans—except by watching them on television. Their experience of the United States has placed them in contact with members of their own cultural groups and, in most cases, with members of many other immigrant cultural groups in the workplace or their neighborhoods. But few report extended contact—and none report friendships—with "Anglos." They express puzzlement at the fact that they could be living in the United States and yet have so few regular interactions with what they believe, and the media tells them, are Americans.

Their work, and the communities in which they congregate, place them in a kind of hypermulticultural environment that does not include members of the dominant culture. Their ESOL teachers tell them to practice English with native speakers, but they never meet any except their teachers. As Nura Tola notes, "My teacher says that we should be in contact with Americans to practice our English, but I hardly come in contact with Americans. There aren't any in my neighborhood. The only time I see them is when I watch television or go to the store."

Three important common themes emerge. The first is that the immigrants profiled rely on television for an inordinate amount of information about the dominant culture of the United States, almost as a surrogate for interactions with native speakers of English. Most desire such interactions with actual humans but must settle for them in a passive, electronic incarnation.

A second theme is that ESOL teachers play a powerful role as spokespersons and representatives of the dominant U.S. culture. In many cases the interaction with the ESOL teacher is the only sustained relationship the people we profiled have had—or are likely to have—with a native speaker of English. This places considerable pressure on the instructor and the curriculum to deliver high-quality, accurate information.

A third theme is that we are now seeing the emergence of a dominant use of English as a means of intercultural communication among different immigrant groups—none of whom are native speakers. Important and powerful language changes having to do with nuance, cultural background, language evolution, social relationships, power, and other linguistic factors could ultimately emerge from this new and highly fluid language use.

Support and Maintenance of Linguistic and Cultural Communities

An important social use of literacy among the six people profiled is in maintenance of a sense of cultural community. All report multiple forms of native-language literacy use with the clear intent of maintaining a sense of community and connection to their cultural background. The forms they employ for this function are diverse, but the purposes are similar.

Michela Stone, for example, reports that the Russian immigrant community in San Francisco is close, its members very supportive of one another. Indeed, the community center where she works has deliberately tried to become an integral part of that community. Sokhhoeun has a similar example of community cultural maintenance. He is a leader in the Cambodian community organization in Oakland and works in a refugee service agency, so he is surrounded by cultural reinforcement on a daily basis. Nura Tola, too, has developed diverse forms of cultural maintenance and community reinforcement, although the Oromo community in San Jose where she lives is relatively small.

The people we have profiled display diverse and ingenious ways of maintaining their cultural identity and sense of community while they are living and surviving in a sometimes bewildering new country. The value they place on their own language and culture is reflected, too, in their determination that their children will be proficient in and value their parent's culture and language. Alicia speaks for many when she explains her views on the importance of bilingualism for her granddaughter, Carmina. "I want Carmina to speak two languages. I don't want her to lose her roots, her customs. I want her to love Mexico."

⊰ 6 ⊱

Synthesis

THESE PROFILES DEPICT a remarkably diverse group of people, from many parts of the world, with life experiences that range from the most local to the most international. Many would seem exotic and different to one another. That diversity is an important element in understanding everyday uses of literacy. Adults with limited literacy skills do not fit common patterns and stereotypes. They have immensely diverse backgrounds, experiences, skills, and lives.

Among the Appalachian profiles, two are rural and white—Tom Addington and Marcy Osborne. They share a similar context of rural life and work in the informal sector, but their literacy skills differ. Les Willard is also white, a skilled electrician who cannot get a license because of his literacy limitations, and so is caught in a cycle of long working hours for low pay. Yuvette Evans and Lisa Bogan are both urban African American women and single parents, but with very different backgrounds in upbringing, values, life experiences, and literacy skills. María Reyes, a Texas-born Mexican American, does not read Spanish, her first language. She wants to leave her life in the migrant worker stream and settle in a small town with a better job, but finds it hard to do.

Among the California profiles, there is a wide range of literacy, language, culture, and life experience. Two are refugees—Nura Tola from Ethiopia and Sokhhoeun from Cambodia—who have experienced brutal terrors and years of disruption before arrival in the United States. The others reflect the complexity of the immigrant stream now transforming California. Oliver Gonzales from Nicaragua, Alicia Lopez from Mexico, David Wong from China, and Michela Stone from Byelorussia all came seeking a better life. Their cultural backgrounds led them naturally into immigrant communities in the Bay Area that are almost as diverse as their homelands. Their literacy and language skills vary greatly, but all experience problems not only in understanding and using the new language but also in acquiring and employing cultural and economic knowledge.

There are striking patterns of commonality and difference across these lives. Without losing individual richness and variety, we identify these patterns as well as their implications for adult basic education.

Several common themes emerge. There are shared patterns in the literacy practices of everyone we profiled. All have experienced hard times and are characterized by self-reliance and determination to be independent. They seem to live at the cultural and economic margins of society. Nevertheless, everyone shares hopes and aspirations for what enhanced literacy skills could add to their lives.

In focusing on commonalities, we do not overlook the differences that exist among the individuals and groups. Those differences are real, and they have significant implications for instructional programs. We see three key themes of difference between native and non-native English-speaking groups. First, the two groups use technology in different ways. Second, first-language usage has important impacts on the lives of the non-native English speakers, and there are different impacts on family relationships. Finally, the clarity and strength of cultural identity of the recent immigrants contrasts with the European American and African American Appalachians.

In the last section of the synthesis we focus on the implications of our findings for literacy education. These implications range from the theoretical to the practical. We examine the learning strategies people use in their everyday lives and their implications for literacy education practices. We recognize that when and what people learn may lead to a potential for mismatch between learner needs and literacy curricula. We find implications for technology uses in education and reaffirm the need for social support in literacy learning. Our findings also demand that we reexamine the concept of "functional literacy." In discussing each of these, we offer some recommendations for literacy and ESOL teachers and programmers.

COMMON THEMES

In this section we address themes that the people we profile have in common. Their lives have been difficult, but they all have used literacy and see literacy as a factor for change in their lives.

Everyday Literacy Practices

Literacy practices are mediated in part by social context: where people live, what their jobs are, what is happening in their communities. They are also influenced by personal factors: how people grew up, what their expectations are, what their family's expectations of them are. We can contrast

Oliver's family, where there is Spanish literacy, regular reading aloud, and the expectation of a certain level of education and literacy, with Yuvette, who did not grow up with books or reading, has no books in her home now, and for whom literacy is simply not a relevant part of her life. Furthermore, although there is undoubtedly some association between literacy skills and literacy practices, it is certainly not a perfect correlation. Yuvette, for example, has higher-level skills but is essentially a-literate, while Lisa, with a much lower skill level, has many more uses for literacy in her life.

On the whole, the literacy demands on the people we profile are quite low both at home and at work. Minimal levels are needed to "get by" (figure out bills, use the bus, fix things, drive around, apply for work). In this section we look across the profiles for patterns in literacy practices of the two groups. Table 6.1 summarizes the data from the profiles (for the California group combining both native and non-native language uses) using categories devised by Taylor and Dorsey-Gaines (1988), based on those established by Heath (1983). They identified six main categories of reading uses:

- Instrumental—to gain practical information (including labels, directions, maps and street signs)
- Social-interactional—for social relations (including letters and notes from family and friends, church newsletters, and other communications)
- News-related—whether national, local, work- or family-related
- Recreational—reading for pleasure, reading to pursue other recreational pursuits (including sports scores, weather reports for fishing enthusiasts)
- Confirmational—to check or confirm facts (may include looking up a word in a dictionary to check spelling; looking up a phone number in the directory; checking appliance instructions, warranties, and so on)
- Critical/educational (including materials in formal education but also others read with the purpose of acquiring new knowledge and insights, bedtime stories for children)

There are also five major categories of uses of writing:

- Substitute for oral messages (phone messages, notes to a child or teacher)
- Social-interactional (letters, greeting cards)
- Memory aids (shopping lists, notes on calendars, other notes to oneself)

Table 6.1. Literacy Practices

	Tom	Marcy	Yuvette	Les	Lisa	María	Alicia	David	Michela	Sokhhoeun	Nura	Oliver
USES OF READING												
Instrumental	•	•	•	•	•	•	•	•	•	•	•	•
Social-interactional	•	•			•		•	•	•	•		•
News	•	•			•			•	•	•		
Recreational	•	•	•	•	•				•			
Confirmation	•	•			•	•	•	•	•	•		•
Critical/educational	•	•	•		•	•	•	•	•	•	•	•
USES OF WRITING												
Substitute for oral		•				•	•	•	•	•		
Social-interactional		•					•		•	•		
Memory aid		•	•	•			•	•	•	•		
Financial		•	•		•	•	•		•	•		
Public writing								•				•

- Financial (writing checks, money orders, forms, tax returns)
- Public writing (for a church bulletin, newsletter, as well as more formal publications)

Taken together, the people we profile use reading and writing in all the ways suggested by the foregoing categories. Many individuals have quite diverse literacy practices, especially in reading, even though their literacy skills may not be especially high.

There are interesting differences between the Appalachian and California groups in their uses of writing. None of the Appalachian people do any public writing, while two of the California group do some, mainly in their native languages (Oliver's graffiti "tagging" and David Wong's novel in Cantonese). Among the Appalachian group, only Marcy does any social-interactional writing (greeting cards and notes to family), while most of the California immigrants write in their native languages to stay in touch with their widely scattered families. The exception is Nura Tola, who is not literate in her native language and uses audiotapes for this communication.

For almost everyone, the elaboration of reading and writing within each of the categories is fairly narrow. Clearly, literacy for instrumental purposes predominates. Only a few read for pleasure (Michela reads Pushkin in Russian and love stories in English; Marcy reads *Reader's Digest* and *True Story*; Les reads comics) or for some noninstrumental, aesthetic purpose.

Reading numbers and using basic math are not as problematic for most people as reading text. Often, in fact, those who are very poor at reading are quite good at simple math. They use everyday math in their work, shopping, and recreation (as with Les's bowling scores). As long as the calculations are limited and do not require fractions or decimals, most people experience little difficulty with math in everyday life.

We might have expected adults with limited literacy skills to have quite different literacy practices from those with higher skills. We might also have expected to find different patterns between the native and non-native English speakers. Neither expectation was realized. Literacy practices among these adults with limited literacy skills look much like those described for different populations by Heath (1983) and Taylor and Dorsey-Gaines (1988), although less elaborated. The types of literacy practices do not differ significantly in terms of literacy skill level or cultural and language background, although the specifics of literacy practices do differ widely among the people we profiled: What they read and write, when and for what purpose, are tailored closely to their cultural, social, and employment contexts.

Strategies for Literacy

People with limited literacy or language skills have to find ways to live in a print-based society. All of the people we profiled experience literacy demands that exceed their skill capacity, and they have devised creative literacy strategies that enable them to meet these demands. Fingeret (1983) suggests some strategies often used: the use of social networks in which members exchange reading services for other support; memorizing text materials; and using technology, such as tape recorders, in place of literacy. The people we profile use these strategies and more. We report a rich and diverse array of strategies that people can call on to meet literacy demands in their everyday lives (see Table 6.2).

These adults use four main types of literacy strategies in their everyday lives:

- Other-oriented strategies, including using regular "readers," asking others for help or information on an ad hoc basis, using other oral information sources, and observing others
- Self-reliance strategies, including guessing, extensive use of memory, learning routines, and selective use of text (including native-language text when people are literate in their native language but not in English)
- Avoidance of difficult or potentially difficult situations
- Substitution of technology for literacy, such as television, VCRS, computers, and tape recorders

Most people use more than one of these strategies, selecting the most appropriate for the situation. Which they select depends in part on the task demand, in part on the context (home, work, or community), and in part on personal preference. We see no consistent differences in the literacy strategies used by native and non-native English speakers.

Other-Oriented Strategies. People faced with literacy demands that exceed their skill rely on others to help in several ways. They may regularly use a "reader," most often a family member, to read mail and other text for them. They may ask others for help in a more sporadic manner—asking people for directions, for help in stores, for the spelling of names and addresses. They may also draw on other oral sources of information, without a formal request, and they may observe others.

Using a "reader." Among the people we profiled, use of regular readers was limited to those with the lowest literacy and/or English-language skills: Tom, Les, María, and Nura. Marcy has fairly high literacy skills but

Table 6.2. Literacy Strategies

	Tom	Marcy	Yuvette	Les	Lisa	María	Alicia	David	Michela	Sokhhoeun	Nura	Oliver
OTHER-ORIENTED												
Reader/writer	•	•		•		•					•	
Ask	•		•	•		•	•	•	•	•		•
Listen	•		•			•	•	•	•			•
Observe	•			•		•						•
SELF-RELIANCE												
Know routines								•		•	•	
Memory	•	•		•		•					•	
Guess	•			•								
Selective use of text			•		•	•	•	•	•	•		•
AVOIDANCE	•	•	•	•		•	•					
TECHNOLOGY					•			•	•	•	•	•

uses a reader (actually a writer) in a limited way: Her sister regularly helps her with filling in forms.

The other people we profile may ask others for help with literacy or language tasks, but in a much more sporadic way. They do not have regular "readers," handling most of the literacy tasks they encounter in other ways. Oliver is himself a "reader" for other family members, despite his limited vocabulary in both English and Spanish. He translated the English instructions for setting up a new stereo system for his uncle, and he accompanied his mother to traffic court as well as going with other family members to medical, legal, and financial appointments.

Asking others. In a related strategy, many of those we profiled ask others for information or to show them how to do something. The people they turn to are not regular "readers," but people on the street, in stores, or family and friends who are consulted as needed. They may ask for directions, bus numbers, help in stores, or help in spelling names and addresses. Commonly, literacy difficulties are covered up by asking how to spell words. María, for example, finds taking phone messages difficult and asks callers to spell their names "very slowly." Both Les and Lisa use the same technique in their work when they need to write down a customer's name and address.

One way of dealing with limited literacy in shopping is to go to stores where one can talk to a salesperson, rather than a supermarket where one may need to read labels and signs. Les does this with the materials he needs in his work and for his repairs. Michela and David say they ask for what they need in stores, although David is reluctant to ask and only does so as a last resort.

For most of the non-native English speakers we interviewed, using their native language is a readily available strategy for coping with English-language limitations. Most live in communities that include speakers of their native language. Alicia, living in a Spanish-speaking community, readily asks in Spanish for directions and other advice from those around her. Oliver's strategy for dealing with an English-speaking school when first in the United States was to find a teacher in the hall who looked like he could help him in Spanish.

Listening. This strategy displays a preference for more passively acquiring general kinds of information. For example, Lisa, who is probably the only conscientious voter among those we interviewed, depends primarily, although not entirely, on oral sources—her neighbors and friends—for political guidance. Similarly, Nura, with a strong tradition of oral culture, relies on existing oral sources in Oromo for an even wider range of information about what is happening "back home."

Observing. Visual observation to gain information from others was also identified as an explicit strategy. Tom says that he decides when it is time to plant potatoes or other crops by watching when others do so. The agricultural extension agent confirmed that less literate farmers are slower at adopting new practices than others, sometimes by one or two years, presumably because they are gaining their information from observing others. Oliver, too, uses observation to get new information, especially in video games. And Sokhhoeun uses observation as part of his process for learning new skills.

Self-Reliance Strategies. Four main strategies fall within this group: memorizing the routine formats of bills and forms, using memory in other ways, making educated guesses, and selective use of text.

Memorizing routine forms. Fingeret (1983) describes memorization of routine forms as a strategy for coping with limited literacy. In our study, too, several people handle familiar texts by memorizing the format, although they have limited English literacy and difficulty with unfamiliar texts. Tom knows what his regular bills look like. Nura says she can find the amount owed on regular bills, although she does not pay them: "I do open the bills, and I know where to look for the amount."

Sokhhoeun devised a similar strategy when he first came to the United States: He photocopied all the forms he had to fill in, with the correct information entered. Soon he had a set of forms he could use as boilerplates for completing others on his own, even though he could read little.

Memorizing. Using memory as a substitute for literacy is related to the ability to understand routine forms and bills. Many adults with limited literacy skills rely on their memory instead of writing down phone numbers, directions, or lists. Marcy talks about memorizing the phone numbers she needs. Les also uses memory to get him around town, using familiar landmarks to memorize directions to jobs. María is quite explicit about using memory in learning work routines.

It is possible that the use of memory as a substitute for writing is important primarily for those who do not read and write in any language. The non-native English speakers who have high literacy skills in their native language do not seem to rely as heavily on memory or oral-language learning as do those who are not literate at all in their native language (Nura and María). Those who depend on their memories have probably developed this capacity more extensively than those who can write things down.

Guessing. Both Tom and Les talk about their use of guessing, in place of literacy, in familiar work contexts. Tom "guesses at a lot of stuff" when he plants and fertilizes. In familiar contexts, known tasks, guessing or estimating may be a very effective way of working. Les, too, uses visual estimation in his electrical work in place of measuring wire. The most startlingly successful use of guessing is recounted by Les, who passed his written, multiple-choice driver's license test by randomly marking answers.

Using text selectively. Many of the people we profiled, both native and non-native English speakers, use text selectively. The dictionary is widely used. Michela, for example, keeps a dictionary on her desk and uses it every day; for the first two years she was in the United States, she carried a dictionary with her in her purse to help with shopping and other everyday literacy demands: "Sometimes I use a dictionary to find out what's in canned foods, and for recipes." Both María and Lisa also talk about their use of a dictionary when confronted with unfamiliar words. Lisa, for example, describes a very systematic way of using the dictionary in preparing for Sunday School lessons.

There are also other ways of using text selectively when literacy and language are limited. Tom, for example, talks about skipping words he does not know, trying to get a sense of the meaning from the words he does know. Alicia uses Spanish texts to back up and reinforce her English learning: For example, she found some Spanish textbooks in the library to help her understand electricity, and she retrieves newspapers from her neighbor's recycling bin to find common English words and copy them many times. Both Oliver and Sokhhoeun write notes for themselves in English as a memory aid. David gets most of his news from Chinese television stations but with the help of a dictionary scans the want ads in his son's English-language newspaper.

Getting around, either driving or using public transportation, often involves limited use of text. Many in the study have mastered such texts, even though their general reading levels are quite low. Sokhhoeun, for example, bought a car soon after coming to the United States and learned to read signs by riding with friends and asking them about ones he could not interpret. Soon he got around on his own. David Wong made similar efforts to learn to use a map of the Bay Area so that he could move around independently as soon as possible after arrival.

Avoidance Strategies. Avoidance of difficult situations is an important literacy strategy for many, both native and non-native English speakers. Non-native English speakers may choose to interact primarily with those who share their native language. David, for example, shops in Chinatown and socializes with his family association. Native English speakers may avoid situations in which they are likely to be asked to use literacy. Tom has avoided going back to retake his driver's license test after his first embarrassing failure. Les, after graduating from high school, did not try to get jobs for which he knew he would have to fill in an application form. His limited shopping (primarily for work and repair supplies) is in building and electrical supply stores where transactions require no reading.

The avoidance strategy may also be used by those who, like Yuvette, do not regard their literacy as a limitation. For her, barriers come in the form of choices made. Her literacy skills are adequate for most situations in her daily life, but the fact that she never reads unless absolutely necessary closes a large portion of the world to her. Other than a Bible and the text on food packages and other items, Yuvette's home contains no printed materials.

Technology Strategies. One possible literacy strategy is to use technology for literacy purposes. Information may be gained from television or radio, tape recorders may be used instead of writing notes, spellers and calculators may provide backup. On the whole, the native English speakers we profiled are limited in their use of technology in place of literacy. They may watch television but do not seem to regard it as an important information source (they seldom watch the news, for example). Of all the people we profiled, the person with the most developed use of technology in place of literacy for information and communication purposes is also the one with the least experience of modern technology: Nura Tola. She uses a VCR to watch Oromo cultural shows that others in her community have taped, and she uses a tape recorder to send and receive "letters" to friends and relatives. Even though her English is very limited, she and her husband watch the television news each night.

Michela, too, uses English-language television for news as well as for other cultural information about American life. David Wong uses a VCR, tape recorder, and TV for information, but primarily in Cantonese rather than English. Sometimes he watches the English-language program that comes after the Chinese-language news, but most of the programs and the videos he watches are not in English.

Summary: Literacy Strategies. The people we profile use diverse strategies to meet literacy demands in their lives. Many strategies are similar to those used often by people with more literacy skills—most of us sometimes guess, use oral sources of information, technology for information and communication, observe, and ask others. Literacy limitations, however, make these strategies much more critical for this population.

Some strategies are more widely used among the native English speakers, some among the non-native English speakers. The self-reliance strategies, for example, including guessing and memorizing, are more common among the English speakers. Guessing, in particular, probably requires

American cultural "schemata" the immigrants have yet to acquire. By contrast, use of technology for literacy is more common among the California immigrant group. Also, those with the lowest English-literacy skills use the widest range of strategies for coping with literacy demands: Tom, Les, and María among the Appalachian profiles, and Nura and David among the California profiles. Others with higher skills experience fewer literacy demands that they cannot meet with their own literacy skills.

But on the whole, both groups use all the sets of strategies. These strategies enable people with limited literacy to function quite well in their daily lives and to cope with most of the literacy demands they experience. They enable people to lead the self-reliant, independent lives they desire.

Self-Reliance and Independence

Self-reliance and independence are a common theme in the lives of everyone we profile. All are determined to be independent, dislike having to rely on others, even family members, and do not want to live on welfare. They expect to control their lives. For some, independence means isolation, as with Yuvette, who prides herself on staying home and out of trouble. For others it means supporting extended family members, as with Les, who married his brother's ex-wife and now raises his niece/stepdaughter and his own son as well as caring for another brother, who is disabled. He is proud of his ability to "hold up." Tom speaks of needing to "try and take care of them [his family], maybe satisfy them."

Among the California immigrants, David Wong, despite his limited English, handles bills and banking, including writing checks, without asking his son, who is fluent in English, for help. He also completes his own tax returns and is working toward a more stable job as a janitor to better support his family. For him and others in the study, the drive to independence means hard work and long hours to support their families.

Alicia's drive for self-reliance was colored by life as an undocumented immigrant for many years. To avoid leaving a "paper trail," she made little use of public services, even those that would not cause her discovery, like the public library. She worked hard and long before and after her "legalization" to support her family.

Sokhhoeun, from the very beginning of his life in California, showed his determination to be independent, even from friends. He became self-sufficient in dealing with social service agencies as soon as he could, learned his way around, bought a car, which he services himself, and even devised his own method for cleaning the heads of his VCR.

For most of those we profile, the drive for self-reliance does not exclude them from family or community relationships. Sokhhoeun, for example, is a leader in his city's Cambodian mutual support network. He also helps his non-Cambodian neighbors, as well as students in the ESOL program where he works. Like most people in the study, he wants to be in relationships with others but not dependent on them.

The drive for independence is particularly important in light of the hard times in the lives of all those we profile. Survival assumes overriding significance for people who are economically at the margins. Farm laborers, food-service workers, sales clerks, caregivers: All are vital to the economy, but all are low-wage, low-skill jobs. There is little job security and high job turnover for most. Living at the margins economically means being readily replaceable in the labor market and leading a life whose stability is easily overturned by common life events, such as ill health, divorce, or job loss. Although a major medical problem can create economic chaos for most people in this country, the frail security of the people we profile is even more easily overturned. Recurring crises threaten hard-won equilibrium. Life at the margins means living on the edge of survival.

Les puts in long hours of work, does extra jobs on weekends, and fixes things around the house, all to support his extended family. He is trapped in a vicious cycle, which his own and his wife's health problems only exacerbate because they have no health insurance. Health care is an issue for others, too. Tom is still paying off bills from the hospital where his child was born two years earlier. Yuvette fears being unable to work; she recently hurt her foot but was too afraid to go to the hospital—afraid that she might hear she should miss work. When Lisa separated from her second husband, she lost her home because it was in his name and he had large debts due to alcohol problems.

The refugee experiences of Nura Tola and Sokhhoeun were terrible and grueling. For Sokhhoeun, it was six years from the time he was forced to flee his home until he came to the United States. These were years of fearful flight, forced labor, and incarceration. Survival required hard work, ingenuity, determination, and luck. Many did not live through it. Now their ongoing experience of low-income and unstable jobs means there is little room for other things in their lives—for recreation or "personal development." The absorption in getting by, the long hours worked, the focus on family—all create barriers to education. If their goals seem limited, we must recognize the considerable effort that even limited changes require for those who are marginalized.

The role of language/literacy proficiency in their economic marginalization is not definitive. There are some very clear cases of underemployment related to language/literacy proficiency. David Wong, an agricultural engineer in China, now works in a fish store and wants to become a civil service janitor. Michela, an accountant with an MA and teaching certificate in Russia, now works as a bookkeeper. Les is a skilled practical electrician tied to a low-paying job because his limited literacy skills prevent him from getting licensed.

More subtle cases of underemployment also exist. All those we profile are intelligent, hardworking, thoughtful people who are capable of much more demanding (and higher-paying) jobs. And almost all believe they could get and hold a better job if their literacy or language skills were better. But while limited literacy and language proficiencies play a role, it is not clear that these are the sole, or even main, factors holding them back. There are some important questions here. First, are there higher-skill, higher-wage jobs to which these people could reasonably aspire? Second, what would it take to get such jobs, and is literacy enough? In answering these questions, we have to pay attention to cultural as well as economic factors.

Living at the Margins

Culturally as well as economically, everyone we profile is in a marginal position in society. Living at the margins culturally means being part of a linguistic or cultural group that is distinctly different from and disempowered by the dominant cultural center. The non-native English speakers in the study are most clearly marginalized in a cultural sense. While in demographic terms California will soon be a "majority minority" state, the dominant culture in terms of economic and cultural power remains European American. None of those we profile in California interact in any significant way with native speakers of English—other than passively with TV personae or ESOL teachers; and none live in communities that afford regular contact with members of the dominant culture. However, the California immigrants live an intensely "multicultural" existence, for they often work and live among other immigrants and marginalized cultural groups.

Public media both exacerbate and alleviate the immigrants' distance from the dominant culture. There are numerous native-language TV and radio stations and print media, and these can reinforce cultural identity as well as promote cultural isolation. The main TV channels, radio stations, and newspapers are in English, and their discourse is primarily that of the dominant culture. This can both integrate and alienate, offering a "window" on the dominant culture while presenting images that remind immigrants of their distance.

María, among the Appalachian profiles, is also a linguistic minority, though Texas-born. Not only is she linguistically marginalized, but her work, community, and social interactions are all within the migrant worker stream. Her longing to settle down in a small town and become part of the dominant cultural center is constantly thwarted by economic and social pressures.

The other Appalachians are members of two other culturally distinct groups. Lisa and Yuvette, working-class African American women, are members of one of the country's most historically marginalized cultural groups. Marcy, Tom, and Les, too, as rural Appalachians, are members of a cultural minority. Their culture includes strong attachment to place; strong family ties; distinctive music, dance, and food; and nonstandard English.

Although they are different, there are important parallels among all the Appalachians in their experience of marginalization. Both cultures have survived—but been changed by—contact with the dominant culture; both have seen adversity and exploitation; and both have been simplistically reduced to economic cultural commodities and media images—whether by Motown, Nashville, "New Jack City," or "Hee-Haw." Ironically, it becomes hard even to gain access to the traditional forms of these cultures, as marginalization and exploitation change them. Yet the experience of bias and characterization of "cultural inferiority" are relived constantly in the public schools by children from the hollows or the projects. All these people live their lives at the cultural margins.

For the Appalachians as well as the Californians, these experiences can lead to worldviews and information about job prospects that limit expectations. Our profiles suggest that we need to expand our traditional conceptions of "literacy" to consider culture and discourse features; for example, to get a good job, one has to "talk right," "act right," "dress right," and "think analytically."

Becoming acculturated involves language proficiency, but also much more—and it is that "much more" which may apply as easily to native-language speakers who are part of cultures outside of the mainstream, dominant culture as to immigrants. To get a good job, for example, it is not enough simply to have literacy skills, or even necessarily to have content skills. One may also need to speak standard English, dress in a certain way, and act in a certain way. The need for these broader forms of cultural information is perhaps most clear for the non-native speakers, but it applies as well to native speakers.

Michela, for example, has quite good oral and written English skills, has the content knowledge needed for a better job in accountancy, yet remains as a bookkeeper in an emigré center. Yuvette's literacy skills are quite high, close to GED passing level, yet she holds down a series of part-time service jobs that offer no possibilities for advancement. For her to pursue her ambition to be an accountant would require a wide range of changes—not just in skill levels but also in the way she talks, interacts with others, and presents herself.

The cultural as well as economic experiences of the people we profile shape their hopes and aspirations for the future, including the role of literacy and education.

Hopes and Aspirations: Literacy and Education

The people we profile have important hopes for themselves and their children. For the most part, they want to enhance their literacy skills, see benefits in doing so, and hope the skills will help them get better jobs. They perceive that limited literacy has had a negative impact on their lives. They desire and demonstrate the ability to learn everyday skills. Although they are resourceful, "functionally competent" individuals who manage complex lives, this does not mean they do not need literacy education. In fact, they feel they need it and want it.

Some have elaborate and practical plans to reach their goals. Alicia enrolled in building maintenance training and ESOL to improve her English and get a more stable, better-paying job than she could get with no English or job skill. David Wong has a long-term, three-year strategy to get a job as a civil service janitor. Michela plans to improve her English so she can get an American business degree and a teaching position in a community college, similar to the one she had in her homeland.

Others believe that improving literacy or gaining credentials would help them, but they do not see how they can do so. Les and his electrician's license, Yuvette and her dream of a bookkeeping job and money to buy nice things, Lisa and her modeling dreams—all would like to be able to advance. They know their limited literacy and lack of school credentials deny them some options. But the process to get from where they are to their dreams is not yet clear to them.

While the people we profile are concerned with their individual skills and advancement, society also would clearly benefit by providing them appropriate literacy education. They are an untapped resource, currently largely wasted. They are competent, thoughtful, and hardworking, with strong values. They need literacy programs that recognize and build on their strengths, relate to their experiences, and support them to make changes in their lives. Such programs would enable them to move out of the margins and turn to other purposes the energy they now use for survival. We all would benefit from investing in the people we have come to know in this study, enabling them to become full citizens in the broadest sense of the word.

DIFFERENCES

We have focused so far on common themes we find within the lives of all the people we profile. But there are differences also, not just at the individual level, but between the California and Appalachian groups. Here we address themes that differentiate the two groups: their uses of technology, the impact of first-language use, the connections between ESOL literacy and family relationships, and cultural identity.

Uses of Technology

In this study we looked at three technology-related issues: how people with low literacy skills use everyday technology; how they use technologies such as television, radio, VCRS, telephones, and computers for "literacy" purposes (to gain information and communicate); and whether and in what ways limited literacy affects people's technology use generally, especially use of computers.

In terms of everyday technology use, we saw some real differences between the two groups. For the most part, the Appalachian group makes limited use of newer electronic technologies—VCRS, computers, ATMS. This is not because they do not have access: ATMS are everywhere, even in small towns; VCRS abound in people's homes. If asked, they would probably say that their lack of use is not so much because of lack of literacy as because they are poor. Nevertheless, the California group, which does not have higher incomes on the whole, makes more use of some of these technologies. In order to understand these differences, we have to examine the purposes for which both groups use technology and the items of technology they do and do not use. Table 6.3 summarizes technology access and use.

Everyone in both groups has access to and watches television. By contrast, five of the six Californians, but only one of the Appalachians (María), currently have a VCR. Videos serve the California immigrants as a medium for cultural maintenance, a way of reinforcing ties with their cultural and linguistic communities. People watch videos made in their home country, finding them at their local video store, taping them off the air from native-language television stations, or circulating them informally. In the Appalachian group, María, whose first language is Spanish, uses the VCR in the same way—to watch films in her native language—although her sons are the primary VCR users in her home.

Video and television also afford non-native English speakers a form of direct—albeit electronically mediated—contact with the dominant, English-speaking culture. As we noted, they have little other regular, meaningful contact with people they call "Americans" (European Americans as

Table 6.3. Access to and Use of Technology

	Tom	Marcy	Yuvette	Les	Lisa	María	Alicia	David	Michela	Sokhhoeun	Nura	Oliver
USED												
Computers			•						•			•
Video games				•		•						•
VCR			•		•	•	•	•		•	•	•
TV	•	•	•	•	•	•	•	•	•	•	•	•
Satellite dish		•										
Tape recorder			•				•	•	•		•	•
Microwave				•	•			•	•	•		•
ATM												
AVAILABLE/ NOT USED												
Computers				•			•	•		•		
ATM				•				•				

seen on TV) in their neighborhoods or at work. They do not understand all the language but feel the programs offer information, language practice, entertainment, and cultural insight.

Two people in each group have used a computer (for Yuvette, a computerized preregister). Three of the California group have access to computers but do not use them. Thus, while video serves a powerful function for the immigrants, they make little use of available computer technology. Only Michela, who had used computers previously in Russia, now uses one at work, and Oliver, a member of a younger generation, uses a computer in school and plays video games at home.

Other than María's use at work, among the Appalachians, only Les has access to a computer, which he does not use. This nonuse may be due to discomfort with the technology itself, and thus literacy-related. But it may also be that he, like the others of the California profiles, sees no practical application. Les does play video games with his son, a technology simpler, more graphic, and more applicable in his life. On the whole, the people we profile see limited practical benefit in computer use. If that view were to change, their use of the technology would likely change.

Automated teller machines (ATMs), too, are little used by both groups. The Appalachians live primarily in a cash-based economy, and most do not have checking accounts, so the ATM is superfluous. Of the Californians, only two use ATMs (Michela and Sokhhoeun). Until recently, Alicia lived as an illegal immigrant in a cash economy, leaving as few paper trails as possible; Oliver still lives at home; and Nura relies on her husband for all financial management.

The central difference in the patterns of technology use by the two groups is seen primarily in the use of technology by the immigrants for cultural maintenance and cross-cultural learning. While these cultural uses of television and video technologies can be seen broadly as part of literacy, the immigrants use this technology in place of face-to-face, oral interaction rather than as a substitute for text-based communication. Among those we profile, we found few examples of technology being used directly for textual literacy purposes.

We found only a few examples of people who had experienced literacy-related difficulties with technologies they encountered. Les was defeated by the ATM at his bank. Lisa avoids use of the computerized cash register at her work (although not only because of limited literacy). Almost all have mastered technologies that are perceived to have practical application, and they express confidence in their ability to master other new technologies they may need.

Impact of Literacy and Language on Families

Another area of difference between the California and Appalachian profiles is seen in the impacts of literacy and language on family relationships.
The people we profile express two main concerns about impacts on family
relationships. First there is the impact on relationships in immigrant families when children assume a brokerage role with the English-speaking
world. Second, they fear "losing" a child to the dominant culture and wish
them to value their roots.

In immigrant families children often assume the role of mediator between their parents and the dominant English-speaking culture.
According to some researchers, the role as "cultural translator" can affect power relationships within the family, may run counter to cultural
norms, and may generate issues not experienced by English-speaking
families (Auerbach, 1989). Although in some cases children act as "readers" for the Appalachian group, and parents may have some mixed feelings about it, such roles are generally more narrowly defined and have
less impact on the family.

In our immigrant profiles, Oliver reports mediating extensively for his
family with the English-speaking world, but he does not indicate that this
has been problematic in his family relationships. However, some mixed
feelings may lie behind David Wong's reluctance to ask his English-fluent
son for help with his literacy needs. David says his son is busy most of the
time and would not have time or be available to help. Among the Appalachian profiles, Les displays some of the same reluctance to have his children read for him. Nevertheless, the sense from our profiles is that the
impact of limited literacy on family relationships is more of an issue for
the immigrants than for the native English speakers, although it is not as
important an issue for these particular families as has been reported by
some researchers.

The California immigrants differ from the Appalachians, too, in their
concern about losing a child to another culture. Michela says,

> Most of my friends have kids and they ask me not to speak English
> to their children. They are frightened they will lose their Russian.
> Then parents will lose family connections and influence on their
> children.

Alicia expresses similar sentiments, but María, also a non-native English
speaker and an Appalachian, does not. Like other rural Appalachians,
wanting a better life for her children may well mean leaving her community, defined for María as the migrant stream.

In rural Appalachian communities with few good jobs, getting on usually means leaving, and education has been seen as a primary "ticket out" of poor rural areas. While there is some tension around this (people who change too much may be accused of "getting above their raising"), it is tempered by pride in children's accomplishments. There is thus less concern about the impact of language, literacy, and education on family relationships for the Appalachian group than for the California immigrants, some of whom fear the loss of their culture in following generations.

Language and Cultural Identity

The California immigrants we profile work and live in contexts in which they encounter few native English speakers. Yet at the same time—quite naturally—they display a preference for living and raising their families in cultural and linguistic contexts that are familiar to them. All of the California immigrants we profile make extensive use of their native languages in a variety of ways in their homes, communities, and workplaces as well as in their media use.

Adherence to the use of the mother tongue and culture is an important dimension of our findings about the immigrants we profile, and it must be understood as more than a simple function of isolation from English speakers. The native language and speech community provides the immigrants with a clear and unshakable identity that they neither wish nor are able to change. They are adults, fully formed and cognitively functioning in their first language. Both language and cultural identity are reinforced daily in family, community, and often workplace. The first language is a living reality, and it is entirely natural for them to use it. In fact, it seems foolish, as well as ineffective, to expect Nura and her husband to speak to each other at home in English, as recommended by their ESOL teacher.

The California profiles suggest that immigrants seek to become bilingual: to acquire as much fluency in English as possible, while maintaining their native language. They believe that becoming as fluent as possible in English will help them in many aspects of their daily lives. But they also value their native language and want their children to learn it. Alicia talks about the granddaughter she is raising. There is debate in the research literature among second-language-acquisition theorists about whether adults can become fully fluent in another language, because their cultural identity is so closely tied to their first language. Our profiles reinforce the view that language and identity are closely entangled, that adult acquisition of a second language is psychological and cultural as well as biological.

The Appalachian group also have distinct uses of language, but they speak nonstandard forms of English often characterized by the dominant culture as substandard. Their children in public schools continually hear that the language they speak at home is inferior and experience attempts to teach them to "speak it right." The cultural identity components of their language use are parallel to those of the California immigrants, but they are less clearly defined and less regularly reinforced as a source of strength. This pattern of difference between immigrant and nonimmigrant marginalized groups is supported by other research (Ogbu, 1990).

The immigrants are self-defined and defined by the dominant culture as more clearly and acceptably different, or "other," than are the Appalachians. For themselves, their bosses, and the people they meet, they are clearly defined as from somewhere else, speakers of another language, with a different culture. This can be an isolating force, but it can also be a source of strength and reinforcement of cultural identity. That identity is often reinforced through diverse and powerful media: native-language television and radio stations, newspapers and magazines, food and restaurants, video stores, and community groups. Beyond this, all exist alongside similar sources of support for other cultural groups, further highlighting and reinforcing differences.

The Appalachians we profile have access to considerably fewer sources of cultural support. For most of them, beyond the family, there are few institutions in which they participate, and there is little sense of being part of a wider community. For the Appalachians, too, the elements of their culture are much less distinct. First, there is less diversity among the cultures of their region, and so their differences are submerged rather than highlighted, as is the case with the California immigrants. Second, they are not immigrants and thus do not have official or self-designation as outsiders or the "dual frame of reference" to enable them to compare their experiences in the United States to those "back home," as immigrants may do (Ogbu, 1990). Third, the Appalachians are part of a culture that has been in contact with the dominant culture for a long time, has been changed by it and often co-opted in commercialized, stereotyped, or marginalized form. Neither national nor local TV address their cultural identity, and cable, even if they had it, would bring only more of the same. They have no newspapers in "their" language. And while country cooking and soul food restaurants do survive, they are far outnumbered everywhere by fast-food franchises.

Thus it is not surprising that the people of the Appalachian profiles do not speak much of their cultural identity: Tom does not call himself a "mountaineer," and Lisa does not talk about being African American. The only time Yuvette talks about race is in relation to her workplace, where she assures herself that racism is not the reason there are only two African American employees. Neither by themselves nor by others are the Appalachian people we profiled identified as being part of a distinctive cultural group.

IMPLICATIONS FOR EDUCATION

Literacy education traditionally focuses on the "gaps," on what people do not know and cannot do. Our profiles suggest another approach—a focus on strengths. We argue for an approach to literacy education that assumes people with limited literacy are resourceful, capable, and experienced and have already learned much in their lives. Literacy programs could do much more to value learners, capitalize on their strengths, and expand what they know.

Our profiles have a number of specific implications for how we should shape literacy education. In this section, we focus on five areas: strategies for learning; what people want to learn; the application of technology to education; the need for support; and a challenge to conventional ideas about "functional" literacy. Each of these generates some recommendations for literacy practitioners and policy makers.

Strategies for Learning

In a print-based society, it is common to assume that literacy is the skill that predates all others. This implies that adults who lack literacy skills do not learn. Yet the people we profile demonstrate a wealth of learning experiences in their lives, inside and outside of formal education. Many we profile have not learned well or easily in formal settings, have had limited access to formal education, or have faced cultural and linguistic barriers to further learning. But they have nonetheless learned many things in their lives and have developed some clear strategies for learning. Understanding these everyday learning strategies of adults with limited literacy skills, then, is important for suggesting how adult education programs can better meet their needs.

Two major types of learning strategies are employed by the people we profile, paralleling in some ways their literacy strategies: other-oriented learning strategies, including visual strategies (demonstration, observation), oral strategies (listening to explanations), and cooperative learning; and self-reliance learning strategies, including repetition and practice, selective use of text, trial and error, and a systematic, step-by-step approach to learning. (See Table 6.4.)

Other-Oriented Learning Strategies. Just as many of the people we profile look to others in various ways to help them meet literacy demands, so, too, do other people in their families and communities play an important role in their learning.

Visual learning. Demonstration, watching others, and observing may all be important learning strategies for people with limited literacy skills.

Table 6.4. Everyday Learning Strategies

	Tom	Marcy	Yuvette	Les	Lisa	María	Alicia	David	Michela	Sokhhoeun	Nura	Oliver
OTHER-ORIENTED												
Visual	•	•		•				•		•	•	
Oral						•	•			•	•	
Cooperative	•		•	•			•			•		
SELF-RELIANCE												
Repetition/practice					•	•	•	•	•	•		•
Use of text		•			•		•		•	•		•
Trial & error	•		•	•		•	•		•		•	•
Step by step					•	•	•		•	•		

Many of those we profile talk about the importance of being shown visually how to do something or watching and observing others. Tom and Les emphasize the importance of being shown in learning work skills. Observation as a learning tool is probably especially important in a primarily oral culture. Nura describes how she learned to cook, market, bargain, spin and weave cotton, and make baskets by observing the women in her family.

The broad application of the visual learning strategy is demonstrated by the parallels between Nura's use of it to learn to weave baskets and Oliver's use of it to learn to play the computer game "Where in the World is Carmen Sandiego?" From Les learning Nintendo with his son, to David Wong learning to use household appliances from his children, learning by observing is important for everyone we profile, native and non-native English speakers alike.

Oral learning. Listening to explanations, which is often linked with observation, is another important learning strategy. Oral transmission is a time-honored teaching and learning strategy throughout the world. Nura, for example, listened to stories told around the fire by the elders, the primary form of formal education she experienced growing up. Alicia pays close attention to her instructor's explanations in her facility maintenance class. Similarly, when María goes to the migrant clinic, she also asks for and relies on verbal explanations.

Sokhhoeun's limited formal schooling includes two years study in a Buddhist temple, where oral learning was the basis for literacy learning. The apprentice monks first listened to and memorized the words of Buddhist rituals, then were given books in which they were written. This form of learning is reflected in Islamic learning traditions in other cultures as well. Without formal literacy teaching, the young men gradually figured out the connections between sound and print. Sokhhoeun now applies essentially the same strategy to any learning task.

Cooperative learning. Working together can be a way of learning for some people. For his work in tobacco, Tom teamed up with someone who reads. Yuvette talks about the importance for her of working together in her Even Start family literacy class, an approach she preferred to the more formal structure of other adult education programs she had attended. One of Alicia's prime strategies for learning in her facility maintenance class is to work with other women.

Self-Reliance Learning Strategies. People have worked out a variety of ways to learn in which they do not depend on others. In these learning strategies of self-reliance, we see use of repetition and practice, selective use of text materials, trial and error, and a systematic step-by-step approach that incorporates a number of strategies in a consistent way.

Repetition and practice. Several people talk about repetition and practice as important learning strategies, especially for literacy and language. Oliver uses repetition to understand the words of a rap song. María says: "If things are explained to me clearly I learn them. I just run them over in my mind [until I learn them]." Alicia copies common English words over and over until she learns them. She also uses repetition and practice for the skills she needs to graduate from her facility maintenance class. Most people recognize the importance of repetition and practice, and they expect to repeat tasks to master a skill.

Selective use of text. Even for those with limited literacy, text can be used in a selective way to back up and extend learning experiences. Alicia uses Spanish-language texts to reinforce learning in her facility maintenance class. Lisa uses text materials aided by illustrations and a dictionary to learn how to use new products and appliances.

Sokhhoeun has developed a careful approach to learning that involves first having a new skill demonstrated and orally described to him, then writing down (or having written for him) the steps. He uses text as a way of "fixing" knowledge and information so that it can be later retrieved, which may be one of the original human motivations to create writing systems. He maintains a set of notebooks that contain these texts for "how to do things in the world."

Trial and error. Learning from experience may be a favored way of learning to use technology. Alicia finds new appliances quite easy to figure out: "It's just a matter of trying them." Michela, too, has had little difficulty with learning to use household appliances: "If I don't know, I try to just use and see how it works." In this strategy, they are like more literate people, who could read the instructions but more often try it first—then refer to the instructions if needed.

Systematic approach to learning. In contrast to the "try it and see" approach, some we profile describe very systematic, step-by-step approaches to learning. Oliver, for example, describes how he learned new video games. The first step is to try it and see if he can figure it out, or to watch someone else play. Sometimes trial and error does not work: "They got all kinds of figures and you don't know what to do with them. When you hit 'Start,' you start playing, they don't tell you anything." When that happens, the next step is to "let the game play alone . . . for five minutes, and then you know how to . . . what to do." And if that step does not work? "I bring in my friends. They show me how to play if they know. . . . My cousin, he knows how to play all the games."

Lisa describes systematic approaches to problem solving and learning, both in locating an apartment to rent and in preparing for Sunday School lessons. In both cases, she uses text in selected ways to overcome her literacy limitations. María has also worked out for herself a step-by-step approach to learning the computer at her work-experience position, and she is very clear about the sequence and the tasks involved in retrieving and entering information. Sokhhoeun's systematic approach described above—combining visual demonstration, oral explanation, and written notes on procedures—is a complex, integrated approach that seems highly functional.

A Toolbox of Strategies. The different approaches to learning that are outlined here are not mutually exclusive, nor are they always employed in the same ways by the same people. The same person may at times use trial and error, at other times observation of others, at other times selective use of text, in order to learn how to do something.

While individual learning styles may mean that some people are more comfortable with certain strategies than others, everyone in this study uses several learning strategies. Nor are there clear differences between the native and non-native speakers in terms of the types of strategies chosen. Which they choose to use first may depend partly on the setting (is there an "expert" available?), partly on the task (is this likely to be similar to other things I know how to do, so that I can use trial and error?). Alicia, for example, finds cooperative learning with other women is very effective for her facility maintenance course but much less so for her language class. This diversity of use and context for learning strategies suggests that we should remain wary of simplistic characterizations of the learning styles of individual adult learners.

The analysis of learning strategies employed by the people we profile suggests the following recommendations for teachers and program developers in ESOL and literacy instruction.

Recommendation 1. Programs should be designed not on the assumption that adults with low literacy skills are deficient and helpless, but on the assumption that they are adults who have already learned much in the course of their lives. The learning strategies they use in the rest of their everyday lives can be the basis for acquiring literacy skills, a starting point of strength rather than weakness.

Recommendation 2. Teachers should help students to identify and describe the everyday learning strategies they already employ, legitimize the strategies for use in school and work contexts, and plan how to apply them in new situations in tangible ways.

Recommendation 3. Teachers should look for and expand the selective, instrumental use of text in learning strategies. Learners in the class who already use text in some ways could demonstrate to other students how and when they use it. The use of writing for note taking, as memory aids, or to reinforce learning should be taught, but in terms of real-life uses—making grocery lists, taking phone messages, notes to teachers, and so forth.

Recommendation 4. Newspapers are quite widely used among the non-native English speakers in particular and to a more limited extent among the native English speakers. Adult education programs should expand the use of newspapers in their teaching, focusing in particular on their discourse functions (what kinds of information does one find in the different sections, in headlines, lead paragraphs, and the body of articles; how might such information be useful in everyday life?).

What People Want to Learn

Informal learning in everyday tasks contrasts with the current structure of formal education in many ways. In informal learning, the learner dictates the methods, the content, and the goals. In formal education that is seldom the case, and there is sometimes a mismatch between what adults want to learn and what educational programs want to teach them.

Our profiles shed some light on the kinds of things people want to learn. If we look at both when and what the people we profile seek to learn, we see very instrumental and tightly focused learning activity. They learn what they need to know at a particular moment in time to achieve a specific goal, and then they move on to address other pressing priorities in their lives. The goal may be to play a new video game, to perform tasks needed for a new job, to master some new equipment, or to gain enough English to get around town. Not only is learning for learning's sake not a widely practiced activity, but the learning is almost always immediate and quite specific. This finding is strongly supported by—and supports—the long-held dogma of adult education which argues that adults desire direct application of their learning. The longer-term goal of obtaining a GED or passing the TOEFL may be there for many, but the learning they actually do is mostly short-term and pragmatic. Yet in the classroom the desire to be "learner-centered" has to compete with the fact that programs are evaluated on the basis of standardized tests and GED pass rates.

The California profiles reveal some interesting mismatches between the expectations and contexts of the students, and the goals of ESOL programs and teachers. For example, programs seldom address directly the need for immigrants to communicate in English with other non-native speakers (that is, with people who have varying accents, different discourse rules, and varying cultural assumptions). Most ESOL teaching assumes that the goal is for the student to be able to interact with native English speakers. In fact, it is apparent that the people we profiled have little interaction with native English speakers. For them, a far more important role for English-language proficiency is interaction with other non-native English speakers.

Another mismatch between learner and teacher perspectives may occur at the point of deciding that a goal has been met and a skill acquired. Whether or not they use a standardized test, teachers may be looking for demonstrated mastery, using standards different from those of the student who simply wants enough to get by. David Wong, for example, was kept in the same level of ESOL class three times before he simply gave up. He decided he had sufficient English competency to meet his everyday needs, despite the fact that his ESOL program decided that he had not acquired sufficient English to move to a new level.

These findings suggest some program recommendations:

Recommendation 5. Adult education programs should start with and build on the experiences of the learners. This means giving people opportunities to share their knowledge, experience, and skills, and to learn from others.

Recommendation 6. ESOL programs should understand: (1) the inordinate power of the ESOL teacher as the learners' primary live contact with the dominant culture; (2) the fact that learners seldom can practice English with anybody outside of the ESOL class; and (3) the reality that many of the learners' primary use for English is to communicate with other non-native speakers of English, rather than native English speakers.

Recommendation 7. We need to rethink what it means for an adult literacy learner to "successfully complete" a learning experience. Leaving a program after a relatively short time should not necessarily mean failure. It is possible that the learner has met a highly focused, specific goal for immediate application in life.

We should recognize the short-term and instrumental nature of much learning and find ways for programs to meet such needs. For example, short-term courses could be offered on specific life skills—using a checking account, getting a driver's license—as well as providing longer-term classes focused on larger goals. Evaluation, funding, and retention processes currently rest on the notion that more time in a program is always better for the learner. This study suggests that the issue is more complex.

Use of Technology in Education

Differences in the ways in which the people we profile use some kinds of technology have some implications for educational uses of technology. Video technology is a widely used and accepted technology for the non-native English speakers in the study, both for maintaining links to their culture of origin and for learning about the new American culture. It could be incorporated much more extensively into educational programming. Television programs, for example, could be used as language-teaching aides, especially talk shows that feature unscripted and relatively natural English usage. (Note Michela's extensive viewing of "Donahue" and similar shows.)

Currently, computers are the favored form of technology for adult education, and we found little to suggest barriers to their use. But neither did we find evidence of their acceptance and use in everyday settings, in contrast with video technology. At the moment, it does not appear that either the native or non-native English speakers we profile have a sense of the value of computers in their everyday lives, beyond the form of computer games. Creative spirits might look to this very acceptable and widely used form of computers and devise literacy programs for adults modeled on the computer game format. These might be particularly successful for younger age groups, since the youngest person we profile (Oliver Gonzales, age 17) is also the most computer-literate.

Many of the non-native English speakers had access to computers at home or at work, as well as to video games. Software that builds literacy and language skills might well have a widespread appeal to non-native speakers if it came in an appealing format and was available in an acceptable price range. Our profiles suggest that many people, even though they have low incomes, can get access to technology that has a clear application in their lives.

Recommendation 8. We suggest that developers of technology-based educational programming pay careful attention to the ways that technology is used in people's everyday lives, to its cultural as well as pragmatic functions, and to the formats that make its use appealing. Programs could be developed using video as well as computer technology in culturally sensitive ways. New video-based curriculum development seems particularly appropriate for immigrant populations.

Recommendation 9. New forms of technology, such as multimedia, which interface between video and computers should be explored for literacy instruction. New delivery systems could be developed to make the best use of the decentralizing possibilities of the technologies to offer students multiple options to the traditional school-based learning procedures, including use in the home, workplace, and community.

Providing Support

For literacy and ESOL programs, "support" for students is often defined in terms of services such as childcare, transportation, and sometimes counseling and referrals to other agencies. These profiles suggest that programs need to be sensitive to another kind of support for their adult students: social support. When we analyze the ways in which people learn and the ways in which they live their lives, we see all of them using what we call "other-oriented" strategies for many learning needs. They watch others, ask for explanations, learn with others. They have an array of "self-reliance" strategies also, but many of them would agree with Tom when he says: "What I've pretty well learned I learned off other people."

However, there is a discrepancy between the way that people learn in everyday settings and educational methods used in formal schooling. Among the people we profiled, only a few have had experience with cooperative learning in formal education settings: Yuvette's experiences with the Even Start family literacy program, Michela's ESOL class, and Alicia's facility maintenance class. In Yuvette's JTPA class, although the students were sitting in a room together, the teacher presented some task and the students worked on it on their own. In the Even Start class, students worked together to answer questions, helped each other, and discussed their ideas. As Yuvette says, "I like Even Start better."

ESOL classes have more often provided opportunities for students to work together, learn from each other, and support each other than have traditional adult basic education classes. Michela describes her ESOL class experiences:

At first I thought I don't want to be doing this. So many different languages, you understand. I want to learn American and be in a class with Americans. But after a while I liked the other people better, and saw that they had many of the same problems I had. We talked a lot about that. We had a lot of fun laughing at everyone's mistakes.

This sense of fun, of enjoyment at being together, of the support derived from feeling part of a peer group which shares problems and is working together toward a solution, is a significant experience. The women in Alicia's informal learning group get much higher grades than the men in the class, who work independently, and she believes it is because of the cooperative learning: "It's better, working together."

Adult education programs which have a technological base probably need to pay special attention to how to enable this kind of social support to happen. No matter how effective computers may be as a learning support tool, adults often also need something else from a learning experience: to feel a valued member of a group of learners.

Recommendation 10. Adult education programs should seek ways to provide social support to learners, to build on their social orientation to learning, and to build as well on their social and cultural uses of video technology. This social support can be provided through learner-centered groups as well as through student associations and other activities.

"Functional" Literacy

As concepts of literacy changed over time and came to be seen on a continuum, rather than a simple dichotomy of literate/nonliterate, many people wanted to hang on to the idea of a goal, or a cutoff point, at which people could be said to have "enough" literacy to function in their daily lives.

The concept of functional literacy, though its meaning is debated, has been influential in educational and policy circles for many years. It places primary emphasis on the pragmatic uses of literacy—to accomplish life tasks, especially work tasks. While its proponents accept a continuum of skills from nonliterate to literate, they assume a cutoff point at which a person can be tested and declared "functionally literate." Despite a body of research and theory to the contrary, the concept of functional literacy survives and is deeply embedded in public policy, program design, and instructor assumptions.

There are many critiques of the idea of functional literacy. For example, Kazemek (1988) takes issue with the underlying assumption that literacy is a generic and definable skill that all literate adults have (and that illiterate adults should have). Here we examine two issues in particular: (1) the equation of literacy skill with ability to accomplish tasks and (2) the emphasis on literacy for purely pragmatic uses.

Proponents of the idea of functional literacy assume a direct connection between the ability to interpret text in a life-skill task (for example, reading a bus timetable) and the ability to perform that task in real life (use a public transportation system effectively). Our profiles suggest that equating literacy with competency in everyday life may be too simple. Although we are a print-based society, there are many ways of accomplishing life tasks effectively. The people we profile are very "functional." They pay taxes, hold jobs, may own homes, pay rent on time, shop, raise children, take part in their children's education, and are generally good citizens (though they seldom vote). Their literacy and learning strategies demonstrate how they function with limited literacy.

The reason for the discrepancy between their literacy skills and their ability to "function" in everyday life lies in their strategies for meeting everyday literacy demands and for learning. Even in a print-based society, there is more than one way to fulfill most everyday tasks. Competency-based assessment and its theoretical base, functional literacy, make a great leap: that if someone cannot read a bus timetable, they cannot use a public transportation system effectively; if someone cannot read a want ad, they cannot find a job; if someone cannot read appliance instructions, they cannot learn to use it effectively.

We find that this leap is not justified. Even the highly literate may use nonliterate ways of functioning in everyday life. Rather than take the time to pore over the small print of a bus timetable, we will probably ask someone standing at the bus stop when the next bus is due. We find jobs through friends, family, people we know—not only through want ads. We use trial and error to operate a new appliance. These and other strategies are also used by adults with limited literacy skills. They enable them to function quite well, despite their literacy limitations.

Our analysis of literacy strategies used by adults with limited literacy skills also suggests that literacy has many other faces, not simply the pragmatic face of "life skills" or work skills. Many of the literacy strategies we uncover are social in nature, involving cultural knowledge and cultural maintenance. We suggest that literacy is embedded in a broader social and cultural context in people's lives and that it extends well beyond the conception implied by "life skills."

To see the people we profiled as competent, resourceful, and "functional" is not to argue that they do not need or want to improve their literacy skills. For the most part they do wish for better skills, and they see specific ways in which enhanced skills would help them. They have hopes and aspirations, goals both concrete and vague. Society wastes important resources when it marginalizes people who are this resourceful, hardworking, and capable. This study offers evidence that we must lay to rest the idea that adults with limited literacy skills are incompetent and dysfunctional. Instead we must construct a literacy education that capitalizes on strengths, enabling individuals to contribute more fully to their communities.

Recommendation 11. The concept of functional literacy should be laid to rest. The concept is flawed: Its definition is arbitrary, its measurement is problematic, and the phenomenon of "functioning in life" cannot readily be equated with literacy. Adults with limited literacy skills should be credited with the skills and knowledge that they do have. Educators should start to build on and extend this knowledge and skill, based on the needs, desires, and interests of the adult learners, rather than dwelling on measuring how "functional" a learner is or needs to become, according to standardized tests.

CONCLUSIONS

In these profiles we see a strong case for the social contextual conception of literacy. Literacy is not a mechanical skill; it is not solely defined by written texts, but also by cultures. We all experience many "literacies"—at work, at home, in our communities; and in our reading for pleasure, we experience different vocabularies, different purposes, different literacy strategies—and we find different meanings. They are all part of literacy, but they can be understood only within particular contexts and purposes.

This view of literacy is much more complex than functional views and lends itself less well to P.R. campaigns and quick-fix solutions to literacy "crises." But it is a complexity with which both policies and programs need to grapple and for which educational structures must be devised and resources found—for it reflects the complex real lives of real people who seek literacy for a variety of overlapping and interwoven purposes.

These profiles of adults with limited literacy skills challenge some myths and question conventional assumptions about the lives and abilities of people who do not read well or use English well (see Table 6.5). Although we do not claim that these 12 people are representative, or typical, of the population of adults with low literacy skills, qualitative research does enable us to generalize—not to populations, but to theory. When the findings from these individuals run so consistently and strongly counter to assumptions (which themselves have little or no research backing), we must question the assumptions.

In this synthesis we have recommended conceptual and programmatic changes in our approaches to literacy education. In conclusion we should note the striking parallel between the marginal lives of the adults with limited literacy skills whom we profiled and the marginality of most literacy education. Our recommendations could not be achieved without changes in an educational context that is itself marginalized—in terms of resources, staffing, and its position in local and national educational institutions. The need for change is urgent. As immigrant populations increase, ESOL programs have long waiting lists. English literacy programs as presently constituted have difficulty reaching and keeping involved those adults who lack literacy skills. Yet our profiles indicate that a national resource is being lost—people who are hardworking, experienced, and resourceful but who remain at the margins of society. We need to find a way of capitalizing on their strengths, enabling them to further develop their skills, and opening up to them more employment opportunities. To do so, we need an adult literacy system that has the resources, the structure, and the people to meet the needs of adults with low literacy skills.

Table 6.5. Challenging Conventional Assumptions

CONVENTIONAL WISDOM HOLDS:	OUR PROFILES SHOW:
Adults with limited literacy skills	Adults with limited literacy skills who
• Don't value education	• Value education and literacy
• Cannot help children in school	• Work with their children
• Don't care about children's future	• Care about their children's future
• Don't work	• Work hard and long
• Are a drain on public resources	• Make limited use of public resources
• Don't want to learn	• Want to learn
• Don't know how to learn	• Have developed learning strategies
• Don't read in everyday life	• Read some in everyday life
• Cannot use modern technology	• Can use technology when shown
• Can't problem-solve effectively	• Have practical problem-solving skills
• Have low self esteem	• Have pride and self-respect
• Cannot set long-term goals	• Have goals and aspirations
• Are subject to social ills	• Are good citizens
In addition, immigrants	We profile immigrants who
• Interact with English speakers	• Don't interact with English speakers
• Need English to work	• Use little English at work
• Need English in their communities	• Don't use English in their communities

This study profiles 12 people who are all very different from one another yet have in common the experiences of limited literacy and language skills and of life on the margins of U.S. society. They share with all of us a desire for stability and security for themselves and their families. While they have been constrained by limited English language and literacy, they have found ways to meet demands and to learn. They have not been defeated by the adversity in their lives. From them we can not only learn better ways to do the work of adult education; we can but also learn from their creativity, determination, and spirit.

References

Auerbach, E. R. (1989). Toward a social-contextual approach to family literacy. *Harvard Educational Review, 59*(2), 165–180.

Cangampang, H.H., & Tsang, C. L. (1988). *Integrating limited English speaking workers into California's labor force.* San Francisco: Career Resources Development Center.

Center for Literacy Studies. (1992). *Life at the margins: Profiles of adults with low literacy skills* (Report to U.S. Congress, Office of Technology Assessment). Contract No. H3.5365.0, Final Report.

Chomsky, N. (1965). *Aspects of the theory of syntax.* Cambridge, MA: MIT Press.

Cook-Gumperz, J. (Ed.). (1986). *The social construction of literacy.* Cambridge, UK: Cambridge University Press.

Delgado-Gaitan, C. (1987). Mexican adult literacy: New directions for immigrants. In R. Goldman & K. Trueba (Eds.), *Becoming literate in English as a second language* (pp. 9–32). Norwood, NJ: Ablex.

Diehl, W. A. (1980). *Functional literacy as a variable construct: An examination of attitudes, behaviors, and strategies related to functional literacy. Dissertation Abstracts International, 41*, 570A.

Erickson, F. (1986). Qualitative methods in research on teaching. In M. C. Whittrock (Ed.), *Handbook of research on teaching* (3rd ed.; pp. 119–160). New York: Macmillan.

Fingeret, H. A. (1982). *The illiterate underclass: Demythologizing the American stigma. Dissertation Abstracts International, 43*, 2767B.

Fingeret, H. A. (1983). Social network: A new perspective on independence and illiterate adults. *Adult Education Quarterly, 33*(3), 133–146.

Fingeret, H. A. (1992). *Adult literacy education: Current and future directions An update* (Information Series No. 355). Columbus, OH: Ohio State University Center on Education and Training for Employment.

Freire, P., & Macedo, D. (1987). *Literacy: Reading the word and the world.* South Hadley, MA: Bergin & Garvey.

Goetz, J. P., & LeCompte, M. D. (1984). *Ethnography and qualitative design in educational research.* Orlando, FL: Academic Press.

Heath, S. B. (1983). *Ways with words: Language, life and work in communities and classrooms.* Cambridge, UK: Cambridge University Press.

Hemphill, D. (1985). *Promising programs and practices: Vocational education for limited-English proficient students*. San Francisco: Chinatown Resources Development Center.

Jupp, T. C., & Hodlin, S. (1975). *Industrial English*. Portsmouth, NH: Heinemann.

Kazemek, F. E. (1988). Necessary changes: Professional involvement in adult literacy programs. *Harvard Educational Review, 58*, 464–486.

Latkiewicz, J. (1982). *Industry's reactions to the Indochinese*. Salt Lake City, UT: Utah Technical College (ERIC Document No. ED 241 664).

Lave, J., Murtaugh, M., & de la Rocha, O. (1984). The dialectic of arithmetic in grocery shopping. In B. Rogoff & J. Lave (Eds.), *Everyday cognition: Its development in social context* (pp. 67–94). Cambridge, MA: Harvard University Press.

Lytle, S., & Wolfe, M. (1989). *Adult literacy education: Program evaluation and learner assessment*. Columbus, OH: Center on Education and Training for Employment, Ohio State University.

Marshall, C., & Rossman, G. B. (1989). *Designing qualitative research*. Newbury Park, CA: Sage.

McCracken, G. (1988). *The long interview*. Newbury Park, CA: Sage.

Mikulecky, L. (1982). Job literacy: The relationship between school preparation and workplace actuality. *Reading Research Quarterly, 17*, 400–419.

Mikulecky, L. (1984). Preparing students for workplace literacy demands. *Journal of Reading, 32*, 253–257.

Mikulecky, L. (1985, March). *Literacy task analysis: Defining and measuring occupational literacy demands*. Paper presented at the Adult Education Research Conference, Chicago, IL.

Mikulecky, L., & Ehlinger, J. (1987). *Training for job literacy demands: What research applies to practice*. University Park, PA: Institute for the Study of Adult Literacy, Pennsylvania State University.

Mrowicki, L. (1984). *Project work English. Employer needs assessment: Preliminary report*. Arlington Heights, IL: Northwest Educational Cooperative.

National Center on Education and the Economy. (1990). *America's choice: High skills or low wages* (Report of the Commission on the Skills of the American Workforce). Rochester, NY: Author.

Neilsen, L. (1989). *Literacy and living: The literate lives of three adults*. Portsmouth, NH: Heinemann.

Ogbu, J. (1990). Minority status and literacy in comparative perspectives. *Daedulus, 19* (2), 141–168.

Prewitt-Diaz, P., Trotter, R., & Rivera, V. (1990). *The effects of migration on children: An ethnographic study*. State College, PA: Centro de Estudios Sobre La Migracion, Pennsylvania State University.

Rogoff, B., & Lave, J. (Eds.). (1984). *Everyday cognition: Its development in social context*. Cambridge, MA: Harvard University Press.

Scribner, S. (1984). Studying working intelligence. In B. Rogoff & J. Lave (Eds.), *Everyday cognition: Its development in social context* (pp. 9–40). Cambridge, MA: Harvard University Press.

Scribner, S. (1986). Thinking in action: Some characteristics of practical thought. In R. J. Sternberg & R. K. Wagner (Eds.), *Practical intelligence: Nature and ori-*

gins of competence in the everyday world (pp. 13–30). Cambridge, UK: Cambridge University Press.

Spencer, S. J. (1987). *Occupational literacy as a variable construct in the mineral extraction/energy and service industries.* Unpublished doctoral dissertation, Texas A & M University, College Station.

Spradley, J. P. (1979). *The ethnographic interview.* New York: Holt, Rinehart & Winston.

Spradley, J. P. (1980). *Participant observation.* New York: Holt, Rinehart & Winston.

Sternberg, R., & Wagner, R. (1986). *Practical intelligence: Nature and origins of competence in the everyday world.* Cambridge, UK: Cambridge University Press.

Sticht, T. (1975). *Reading for working.* Alexandria, VA: Human Resources Research Organization.

Sticht, T., & McDonald, B. (1989). *Making the nation smarter: The intergenerational transfer of cognitive ability.* San Diego, CA: Applied Behavioral and Cognitive Sciences, Inc.

Sticht, T., & Mikulecky, L. (1984). *Job-related basic skills: Cases and conclusions.* Columbus, OH: ERIC Clearinghouse on Adult, Career, and Vocational Education Information, National Center for Research in Vocational Education.

Szwed, J. F. (1984). The ethnography of literacy. In B. Rogoff & J. Lave (Eds.), *Everyday cognition: Its development in social context* (pp. 13–15). Cambridge, MA: Harvard University Press.

Taylor, D., & Dorsey-Gaines, C. (1988). *Growing up literate: Learning from inner-city families.* Portsmouth, NH: Heinemann.

U.S. Congress, Office of Technology Assessment. (1993). *Adult literacy and new technologies: Tools for a lifetime* (OTA-SET-550). Washington D.C.: U.S. Government Printing Office.

Wagner, R., & Sternberg, R. (1986). Tacit knowledge and intelligence in the everyday world. In R. J. Sternberg & R. K. Wagner (Eds.), *Practical intelligence: Nature and origins of competence in the everyday world* (pp. 51–83). Cambridge, UK: Cambridge University Press.

White, L. (1988). Island effects in second language acquisition. In S. Flynn & W. O'Neill (Eds.), *Linguistic theory in second language acquisition* (pp.144–172). Dordrecht, The Netherlands: Kluwer.

Yin, R. K. (1989). *Case study research: Design and methods.* Newbury Park, CA: Sage.

Zeigahn, L. (1990). The formation of literacy perspective. In R. A. Fellenz & G. J. Conti (Eds.), *Adult learning in the community* (pp. 1–31). Bozeman, MT: Center for Adult Learning Research, Montana State University.

Index

About the Authors

JULIET MERRIFIELD is a researcher and adult educator who lives in Britain. She was the first director of the Center for Literacy Studies in Tennessee and led some of the Center's work with adult literacy practitioners and learners. She was formerly co-director of research at the Highlander Research and Education Center. She has a D.Phil. in politics from the University of Oxford as well as a B.A. and M.Phil. in anthropology from the University of London. She is now visiting fellow at the Centre for Continuing Education, University of Sussex.

MARY BETH BINGMAN is associate director of the Center for Literacy Studies at the University of Tennessee, Knoxville, where her work includes research, staff development, and curriculum design. She has wide experience as an educator in a variety of settings and has done extensive work with community organizations and advocacy groups in the Appalachian region. Her doctoral dissertation at the University of Tennessee, *Appalachian Women Learning in Community*, built on that work.

DAVID HEMPHILL is professor and director of graduate studies in the College of Education at San Francisco State University. Prior to coming to the university he worked for 10 years in adult literacy education programs for refugees and immigrants in northern California. His research interests include culture, cognition, language, and power in education. Recent research projects have focused on media literacy, family literacy, metacognition, and language acquisition in multilingual settings. He is also a jazz trombonist.

KATHLEEN P. BENNETT DEMARRAIS is associate professor at Northern Arizona University, where she teaches courses in literacy education, sociology of education, and qualitative research. She earned a doctorate in educational foundations at the University of Cincinnati, then moved to Bethel, Alaska, to serve as a University of Alaska–Fairbanks regional coordinator for a field-based teacher education program for Native Alaskan students. She spent nine years at the University of Tennessee, Knoxville. Her research and writing are concerned with equity issues in the structure and practice of schooling, particularly as related to women and diverse student populations.